(cook)

LAST CHANCE TO EAT

LAST CHANCE TO EAT

The Fate of Taste in
a Fast Food World

GINA MALLET

W. W. NORTON & COMPANY

NEW YORK   LONDON

For information about permission to reproduce selections from this
book, write to Permissions, W. W. Norton & Company, Inc.
500 Fifth Avenue, New York, NY 10110

Manufacturing by R.R. Donnelley, Harrisonburg
Book design by Lovedog Studio
Production manager: Amanda Morrison

Library of Congress Cataloging-in-Publication Data

Mallet, Gina.
Last chance to eat : the fate of taste in a fast food world / Gina Mallet.
p. cm.
Includes bibliographical references and index.
ISBN 0-393-05841-7 (hardcover)
1. Gastronomy. 2. Cookery, English. I. Title.
TX635.M35 2004
641'.01'3—dc22
2004012960

W. W. Norton & Company, Inc.
500 Fifth Avenue, New York, N.Y. 10110
www.wwnorton.com

W. W. Norton & Company Ltd.
Castle House, 75/76 Wells Street, London W1T 3QT

1 2 3 4 5 6 7 8 9 0

To Lynn,
Patrick, Mowbray,
and Larissa

Contents

LAST CHANCE TO EAT

. . . . . .

THE
FIRST ENCHANTMENT

I was reviewing restaurants for a Toronto newspaper, in the midst of a veal chop, in fact, when I stopped eating. I was bored with food. I had so looked forward to dining out at someone else's expense, but how quickly it palled. This was in the late 1990s, when restaurants were matching the giddy excess of the stock market, and fresh foie gras was de rigueur on the menus of even modest establishments. It wasn't that the food and cooking were bad. No, there was something missing, something I couldn't put my finger on.

Not until I went backstage at another restaurant—and as a former theater critic, a restaurant was always theater to me—did I realize what it was. It wasn't the no-frills French restaurant itself but the chef, a tight-lipped Breton, who I knew right away had sorcerer genes. His food wasn't generic the way so many restaurants' food was, menus put together by opinion polls, or consultants. It was just the food he personally knew: fish soup, pan-fried red snapper laid on a bed of saffron fennel, a little apple tart that sprang to life in the oven and melted in the mouth.

This wasn't critics' food; it wasn't trying to make a splash; it wasn't imaginative or exotic, as so much restaurant food was; but it tasted so good that it touched the emotions. It was in its way soul food. As I left the restaurant, I looked through the glass storefront at the few customers left with their wine in the candlelight. I wondered what they were talking about because I realized that that, too, had been missing from my usual restaurant experience. Conversation. Then came the first prick of memory. Around my parents' dinner table, talking about food was at the top of the menu. And the talk wasn't so much about how a dish had been cooked, or the food itself; rather, it came out of the experience of enjoying food with others, a sense of companionship that prompted confidences. I must have been about twelve when Piper, my father's bibulous cousin, advised me gravely that the way to a man's heart was through his stomach, "not, as so often thought, through sex."

As I walked home, I felt exhilarated by the memory. But the problem of restaurants remained. They all served the same food. The menus were short and always included a veal chop, a steak, rack of lamb, pasta. But why did that matter? It doesn't matter that all over France, bistros still serve steak frites, escargots, onion soup, skate and black butter sauce, lemon tart. It doesn't matter that a sushi bar serves tuna and yellowtail over and over again. In fact, it's reassuring to keep running into old friends.

I thought at first the difference lay in the cooks' commitment. In North America, and also in some of the most praised and expensive restaurants in France and Britain, the cooking may be good, but it is presented in a summary way. That's that. When I read about Escoffier, the chef who made the Edwardian age a pinnacle of over-the-top food, I felt so hungry. Eating out at the turn of the century had been an unabashed binge: Escoffier's à la carte menus could include as many as a hundred dishes. The customer had to be wooed and won. Perhaps the *froideur* of the modern restaurant arises because no restaurant can afford to be prodigal on the Escoffier scale, or because cooking is not so much a vocation as a career choice for the middle class, and this leads to a certain detachment from the consumer.

Then the real answer came into focus. The art of cooking is dying. Once, it was the heart of home and evoked a dense web of feeling. But now the communal family meal has dissolved into individual eating units. More and more, cooking has been marginalized as an add-on to home decoration, a branch of fashion. As I traced my eating life through the sixties in Los Angeles, the seventies in New York, the eighties in Connecticut, and the nineties in Toronto, I realized how ineluctable the march to fast food and solitary eating has been. And it isn't just Big Macs, but high-end takeaway, and the cold and cured delights of the Mediterranean. Noncooking has reached the stage where there are now self-styled "rawvolutionaries" who believe that all cooked food is dangerous: forty thousand years of perfecting grilling and baking tossed overboard.

Paradoxically, although cooking seems doomed, it is being promoted today in an unprecedented way—more cookbooks, more columnists, more star chefs, the Food Network on TV, the slow food movement—but woven into the bright chatter is a baleful leitmotif: food as death. Food is shaping up as the single greatest threat to life. The first assault on food as pleasure came from food science, which parsed ingredients for nutrition, reducing food to fuel. Further scientific discoveries were more sinister. The old saying, a little learning is a dangerous thing, turned out to be true—even for biochemists.

The first big scare was the dear little egg, an esteemed natural food for centuries. Eggs, it was alleged by food scientists, were bad for your heart. That turned out not to be true, but the scare dented the public's confidence in food safety. A second, unsubstantiated scare about an inorganic chemical sprayed on apples virtually destroyed the American apple industry. Just this year, the public, which was gobbling up farmed salmon, tasty, cheap, and full of the valuable Omega-3 fatty acid, was advised to cut its consumption to a few ounces once a month. A single small study had found that the farmed fish had higher levels of potential poisons in it than did the wild salmon. The levels, however, are well under the safety limits set by the U.S. Food and Drug

Administration. Beef, a food of symbolic grandeur, has been brought to its knees by mad cow disease, caused by the traditional practice of cattle cannibalism—even though the chances of getting the disease are about as remote as the average person getting to the moon. Each day another food is declared suspect. We are now in the throes of a food fear frenzy.

This has opened up a profound rift with the past. A century ago, happiness meant enough food to eat. Good cooking was an unalloyed pleasure. While I was researching the fate of food, I came across Agnes Jekyll's *Kitchen Essays* (1922), a collection of columns first written for *The Times* of London. I probably wouldn't have read the book if my English grandmother hadn't known the author and no doubt tried, as all her friends did, to model her household after Aggie's oasis of comfort and beauty. The recipes are interesting, but their meaning much more so because they represent stability and continuity in an uncertain world. As the author wrote in her introduction:

> When homes dissolve or reform, or the main prop of a household is withdrawn [as of course had been the case in the recent Great War], it is often found that a good tradition or a valued formula, painstakingly acquired, has vanished beyond recovery, and that the pleasant things we enjoyed in youth, the unfamiliar foods which added interest to our travels abroad, or the specialité of some clever long-lost cook, have all been swept irrevocably down Time's rolling stream.

Now I understood why I remember so acutely the food, or lack of it, when I was growing up after World War II: food is a potent bond to the past. I understood why the rituals of meals continued as if there had been no war at all. Food was not simply to be eaten, it was as well a living memory bank. I remembered how my father still put on a smoking jacket for dinner even if dinner was bread and cheese. He ate a beaten wheat biscuit with a glass of hock at eleven in the morning at the weekends, an eighteenth-century custom that seemed too good to forget. He insisted on spicy Cumberland sausage with mustard for Saturday lunch and he complained that my mother never made a salmis of pheasant as his mother's cook had done. In her turn, my mother would describe the food of her youth, the softshell crabs of the Chesapeake Bay—how exotic that sounded to us children—and shad roe, and a New England specialty, bacon and kale.

So it was that the first enchantment of my life was cast by the last carefree generation of eaters. My parents couldn't have conceived of food as death. They were greedy not so much for the food itself as for what the food represented, their own piecemeal memories. To us, their children, they passed down their tastes, just the way they left us their books and Chinese ancestor portraits, a few poignant letters charged with complicated emotions, and the funny stories about grandparents and assorted eccentric relations. When I thought of food, I automatically thought of the food they ate in the sunset years of Escoffier's cuisine. I swear I could taste *oeufs en cocotte*, cheese soufflé, English macaroons, a raw milk Brie with soul, Thames Mud or the original chocolate mousse, *Tournedos Rossini* with Béarnaise sauce, broad beans in their jackets, apple fritters, the crunchiest roast potatoes, *Sole Véronique*. Where now could I find those tastes? When I went to find out, I stepped through the looking glass and discovered the world of food had been turned upside down. To understand how and why is what made me write this book.

. . . .

CHAPTER ONE

THE IMPERILED EGG

The egg that lay in my mother's palm was small by today's standards, small and pale brown. But in 1947 it represented the greatest luxury, one beyond price. England, during postwar rationing, was often eggless. Our young Scottish cook, Christine, looked at the egg and said doubtfully, "What's that?" After all, she had never seen a whole egg before, having been raised on dried egg, the war staple. Just as with all memories, my first ones of food are the sharpest and most lingering. We lacked beef, pork, lamb, fish, butter, and jam. But the lack of the egg is the deprivation etched in my memory.

My parents, fully industrialized, that is to say, divorced from the wherewithal of the food they ate, could not believe there were no eggs. But then they, like almost everyone else, had never known the true state of food in Britain. When the war started, the British larder was as bare as it had been when the Great War began twenty-five years earlier. Even before the war, Britain had not produced enough food for its people, and eggs had to be imported from faraway places like China and Poland. How old they must have been when they arrived on the English breakfast plate! Was this why the British actually *liked* dried eggs? Dried eggs were part of the American Lend-Lease pact (which gave food, among other supplies, to countries whose defense was considered vital to the defense of the United States) and hungry Britons fell on them. The government even introduced a cookbook on how to cook successfully with powdered eggs. Many liked the flavor that the dried egg powder gave to a Yorkshire pudding, and egg powder done properly made passable scrambled eggs, at least to some palates. So they felt abandoned when, once the war was over, Lend-Lease was stopped overnight. With the dried egg withdrawn, the country relapsed into virtual egglessness.

My parents couldn't imagine life without the egg. Between the wars, they had enjoyed an idyll of good food, in which eggs played an important part. They were cosmopolitans, a suspect word in English society, one that suggested a pleasure in foreign countries that went quite against the spirit of England, a country that had spent centuries fighting with its neighbors—the Welsh, the Scots, the Irish, and of course beyond. Only the superrich had French chefs as a matter of course; most English people considered French food a foreign plot. There was thus no incentive for English cooks to learn the superior French techniques. Moreover, cooking was low on the household agenda. My childhood friend,

Charlotte, recalls that her mother-in-law could cook well, far better than her actual cook, "but she felt she couldn't cook and at the same time maintain her upper-middle-class household properly."

Across the Channel it was all quite different. Food, not propriety, had priority. Compared to the French country-man, the average English person had little access to land because more and more people lived in cities. Food had been comprehensively industrialized, and canned and processed food was cheap. "It is unfortunate that the English working class—the English nation generally, for that matter—are exceptionally ignorant about and wasteful of food," wrote George Orwell in *The Road to Wigan Pier*, a curdling account of working-class food in the 1930s (dirty bread, canned steak pudding, stale cake), and he pointed out "how civilized is a French navvy's [roadworker's] meal compared with an Englishman's."

War made food worse, and rationing completed the bru-talization of the English palate. But there was something else: guilt. For the first time, most people were eating prop-erly because the available food was shared by rationing, and this brought home powerfully just how unfair the prewar society had been. Moreover, as few people had eaten nutri-tious and tasty food before the war, the British didn't feel nearly as deprived as they would today, British food having improved immeasurably in the last twenty years. The emphasis on fairness and on nutrition overcame any objec-tions to the lack of taste. Even Winston Churchill went along. Churchill, who might have had the phrase *bon vivant* coined just for him, and who had a palate so discerning he once refused a dessert served at the Savoy with the words, "Take away this pudding, it has no theme," reneged on his promise to end rationing when reelected in the early 1950s. He did so after being told that the British public had never been so healthy before. To many people, this was the moment to be self-righteous and to eat indiscriminately for the sake of the new Britain—one in which everybody would be allotted the same amount of nutritious food, regardless of how it tasted. To consider food in terms of cooking and imaginative presentation came to signify uncaring frivolity.

This attitude infuriated my mother, who was a confirmed Democrat in America and had expected to feel solidarity with the British socialists in the late 1940s. But she was soon fed up with the general attitude of un-American downward mobility: "They don't think up but always look down." Subversion was definitely in order. Somehow, more and better food must be found. My parents took advice from similarly inclined neighbors and committed themselves to hens.

Of course it would be quite simple, opined my father, who knew absolutely nothing about nature and preferred it that way. My father may have been the only Englishman who wasn't enchanted by Beatrix Potter and thought that Peter Rabbit would be best shot and processed into one of Mrs. McGregor's pies. Not that my father was immune to the beauty of nature. When he and my mother were married in the late 1930s, they celebrated their love affair by buying a folly: an imposing house that stood high on the banks of a double bend in the Thames as the river slumbered along from Oxford to Henley. The house, which was called rather grandiosely Shillingford Court after the humble hamlet around it—a straggle of thatched cottages and a farm—was an unashamed Edwardian extravagance. It had been built by one of Edward VII's tailors. Any man who dressed the King, my father told us children, had to be enormously rich, because the King changed his clothes at least five times a day and expected those around him to do likewise. If they didn't, they became the butt of royal sarcasm. When the prime minister wore a suit to a royal audience, rather than the required knee breeches, the King acidly inquired if he was in the train of the American ambassador, who dressed sometimes as indifferently as a *sans-culotte*. The result was that Savile Row tailors were so well off they became gentry themselves, with their own country properties.

Mr. Haggie, as our tailor was called, built royally, as if summoning up past ages of glory. The Court was a mishmash of styles—a tower with battlements, some half-timbering, lead-paned windows, stone walls a couple of feet thick—and it was wrapped around a big flagged terrace with wide steps that led down to the riverbank. Seen from the river, the house was screened by trees, giving it an air of Gothic mystery. The rooms were huge: the library was thirty feet long and light poured in from the windows at either end. Even the halls were wide and long, upstairs and down, and lined with windows so the walls and ceiling rippled with the reflected light of the sun, however watery, that shone on the river.

The L of the house was the largest room of all, the size of a football field and two stories high. The river room, as we called it, stretched out over the boathouse; it had a bank of windows facing south, a range of skylights, and a minstrel's gallery approached by two winding staircases, as well as a balcony over the river itself. Mr. Haggie had built this room especially for his wife, who was a miniaturist. My father was tickled pink by the incongruity. He envisaged Mrs. Haggie—he pictured her small and frail—standing in the middle of this vast room working with tiny pincers on a Chippendale miniature so intricate it could only be seen with a magnifying glass, and he roared with laughter.

But it was the view that enchanted my parents. The view stretched out wide and seemingly infinite, rising and falling over water meadows, straggling cattle, and woods all the way to the Berkshire Downs. There wasn't a house in sight. On a misty day—and there were many, many misty days in the Thames Valley (one of the dampest places in the whole British Isles)—two little clumps of trees would float out of a sky of cotton wool; they beckoned like Shangri-La. They were the Wittenham Clumps, two peaks of the Downs that grew in mystery the closer you got to them. A Roman burial ground had been found in the foothills of one of them; there was evidence of Druid ceremonies on the peaks; and every midsummer night's eve, there was bacchanalian revelry, or would be once the country revived from the shock of war.

Nobody was in the least surprised when it was revealed that a suicide pact had taken place on the Clumps. An Oxford don had shot his girlfriend and then himself. Mr. Kent, our local bobby and taxi driver, told us on the quiet, as he put it, just how it all happened. The professor had hidden a gun in a book from which the pages had been cut out in the shape of a gun. What book? *The Oxford Dictionary of Quotations*, a doorstop of a book, the book my parents relied on to solve *The Times* crossword puzzle. Why? Even we children wondered. My mother, an avid mystery story reader, said it was ridiculous. Why should he bother to go to such lengths to hide a revolver that could have been slipped into his pocket without anyone being the wiser? This wasn't the streets of New York, where cops searched citizens without warning.

My mother, who had grown up when New York was as wild as the West, remembered how the police warned against entering Chinatown as you might never come out. She recalled one particular gun battle of the 1920s, how the police had loosed volley after volley of shots at an apartment building, causing a lot of collateral damage. And then how the mayor, Jimmy Walker, had gone on the radio to say: "Fun's fun, fellas, but shooting women and children is going too far . . ." She sometimes told this story just to see the English jaws drop.

She couldn't imagine Mr. Kent, a comfortable, mustached man in a rather shabby raincoat who looked like H. G. Wells, patting down the pockets of a negligible Oxford don; we never knew what his subject was. Perhaps *The Oxford Dictio-*

nary of Quotations was a cipher. "He was a spy!" said a neighbor triumphantly. Nobody contradicted him because spymania was in the air, after the revelation that Klaus Fuchs, a scientist at Harwell—"the atomic," as the nuclear research station only a matter of miles away was called— had stolen secrets for the Russians.

The Court flouted all the class rules about country houses. If you had not inherited a pile, the desired house was preferably Queen Anne or Georgian, mellow brick and surrounded by manicured gardens and/or parkland. Shillingford Court was by those terms parvenu. That, too, was why my parents liked it. It was a metaphor for their own brandnew lives, a thumbing of the nose at tradition. My mother had divorced her first husband, Seaton, to marry my father. As she had been married in New York, she had no trouble getting an American divorce. She simply went to Reno and lived on a dude ranch for six months. Then she and my father were married in Paris by the mayor and came happily home to London, only to learn that the Reno divorce was not recognized in Britain, and that Seaton had to divorce her all over again.

A British divorce was nothing like a Reno divorce. There was no smart lawyer waiting for her at the station with a spray of orchids, no dashing cowboys to take her riding. A British divorce was punitive. Shame was the goal. The Establishment—the upper-middle-class network which ran the country with a dense web of rules and regulations, sometimes camouflaged by ancient mumbo jumbo all designed to keep people in their place—frowned on divorce. Woe betide those who threatened the status quo, even the Empire, by showing that the rules could be broken. Adultery was the only excuse, and my mother, now pregnant, was clearly the guilty party. Even worse, while waiting out the six months required for the divorce to be made final, an official called the King's Proctor kept tabs on the would-be divorcés. If they were caught seeing each other, they were accused of manipulating the legal system, and the divorce was off—forever.

My parents lived in Paris, and when they came to London, Seaton, who was friends to them both, would visit them in disguise. He wore dark glasses and a beard and announced himself as "Mr. Smith," reckoning, he said, that the King's Proctor would think the charade too obvious to be taken seriously. Divorce was not publicly celebrated, of course, so when it finally came through, they celebrated in their own way. My parents had moved into my father's house in London, inherited the year before from his mother. On a pretty May day, my father wore a bow tie with a morning coat and my mother had on her Chanel moonstones. As they stood sipping Champagne on the balcony of their house in Eccleston Square, two open cars filled with flowers drew up. Seaton was in the second one, wearing a batik shirt and dark glasses, and sporting a lighted cigarette in a tortoise-shell cigarette holder.

The romance of Shillingford barely lasted the war. A decade later, my parents were imprisoned in it because their

London house had been let. It was wonderful in the summer, but in the winter it was freezing cold, a cold cruelly enhanced by damp. The house had no central heating, and when the catacombs of the cellars filled with water as the river rose, as it so often did, the damp rose through the house, defying all efforts to expel it. The fireplaces were useless, and experiments with oil heaters proved ineffective. On top of that, fuel was rationed. My mother, huddled in an American bomber jacket, would stand shivering in the study, the smallest room in the house and the only one ever properly defrosted. She would gaze out at the beautiful view, and she cried out, an edge of desperation in her voice, that when they bought Shillingford, they never *imagined* they would ever have to live in it.

The Unpredictable Hen

Once the commitment was made to hens, my father was obliged to acknowledge that he was stumped by the egg. As a Victorian, he had been raised on the rolling cadences of the King James's Bible, and he would always manage to find an allusion from it for any contemporary problem. But King David never cracked an egg: the Bible is an eggless book. Undaunted, my father, still the Victorian, turned to experts—or rather, the local farmer. My father was further encouraged by the revelation that Beatrix Potter had never iconized the hen in a sweetly pretty drawing;

children, in other words, would have no sentiment about the hen.

My mother, who was ignorant of agriculture and in fact feared it, was discouraging. She gave him *The Egg and I*, by her compatriot Betty MacDonald. Years later, this remains a wonderfully funny book about an innocent thrust into poultry farming. Then, it was fresh as paint, and naturally my father, who liked nothing better than to be able to laugh, laughed a lot. Never having had anything to do with chickens, he took Mrs. MacDonald's description of malevolent chicks as a tremendous joke. "The horrid little things pick out each other's eyes and peck each other's feet until they are bloody stumps. . . . Their favorite form of warfare is ripping out each other's intestines." This description of chicks' behavior confirmed my father's distaste for nature. "How perfectly beastly. But after all, I'm not going to know these hens personally."

The hens would be housed in the old tennis court, which had gone to seed in a mass of brambles and weeds, but was hedged by tall evergreens, a natural barrier enhanced by chickenwire. Nature was meant to do the rest. After all, hens had strutted at will for centuries, and given some rudimentary protection from marauding foxes and hawks, laid eggs without any supervision at all. Because my parents knew nothing of the history of the hens, they dismissed the idea of a hen as having a mind of its own. Focusing on *The Egg and I*, they failed to consult a far more insightful folktale, *The Little Red Hen*.

The Little Red Hen was in the farmyard with her chickens, when she found a grain of wheat.

"Who will plant this wheat?" she said.

"Not I," said the Goose.

"Not I," said the Duck.

"I will, then," said the Little Red Hen, and she planted the grain of wheat.

Eventually, after the animals have refused to help her get the wheat milled and the bread baked, the Hen asks: "Who will eat this bread?" The Duck and the Goose both say, "I will," and the Hen says, "No you won't. I shall eat it myself." The hen, in other words, is stubbornly independent, not to be pushed around by larger animals.

The Romans were the first to study the hen, and they observed her with fascination. The cock was relatively straightforward. He was a useful sort of clock, heralding dawn with noisy cries, and he appeared to be delightfully macho, strutting about the farmyard and chasing the hens. But the hen was a mystery. No other animal spends so much time and energy on procreation: laying an egg is a process that takes a day and consumes one eighth of a hen's body weight, far more than a mammal. A young and hearty hen can theoretically lay an egg a day at her peak, say in her second year of laying. Of course, she doesn't lay all year round; she takes a few months off in the winter to gather her resources so she can start laying again in the spring.

The egg is the nucleus of the hen's longed-for family, and

she guards it fiercely—as anyone who's tried to remove an egg from a sitting hen knows. The hen blows herself up into a large feathery missile directed at the poacher, wielding her claws like machetes. It isn't until she has a nestful of eggs that she goes broody, taking up to three weeks to hatch the chicks. The incubation of the eggs was the subject of endless speculation to the Romans, the Empress Livia going so far as to hatch an egg between her breasts to appreciate the experience. But what really astonished the worldly Romans was the motherliness of the hen once her chicks were hatched. In his essay "On Affection for Offspring," Plutarch marveled, "We have before our eyes every day the manner in which hens care for their brood, drooping their wings for some to creep under, and receiving with joyous and affectionate clucks others that mount upon their backs or run up to them from every direction; . . . if their fight is for their children, they stand their ground and fight it out beyond their strength."

Even so, the Romans wanted to eat eggs as well, and hens did not take kindly to being told by humans where to lay their eggs. Hens naturally try to find places to nest out of people's way. In the old days, before the hen was incarcerated in prison camps and forced to lay on cue, this created a problem for those searching for the fresh egg. The Romans made nests for hens, but the hens often ignored them.

Some seventeen hundred years later, in the 1740s, Louis XV of France did a better job of tracking eggs by keeping hens in the attics of the Palace of Versailles, outside Paris. The hen and its egg had been relegated to the sidelines during the Dark Ages. Not until the Renaissance did scientific inquiry into the chicken resume, and even more significant, eggs began to be taken seriously as a food. In the seventeenth century, the first meringue was made from beaten egg whites, a harbinger of its future role in classic French cuisine. Louis XIV, the food king, loved meringues and ate plates of them. Louis XV was more discriminating. He liked a good fresh-boiled egg. He made sure he was never without a fresh egg, and the best layers traveled with the court. In a pretty domestic scene, he and Madame de Pompadour went egg-gathering together. When the mood took him, Louis would crack a handful of his own eggs and whip up *Oeufs à la fanatique* (which I think are deviled eggs, fried with vinegar and black butter) for his beloved.

Louis was an egg salesman as well. He wanted his subjects to share his delight in eggs. When he was at Versailles, he summoned his people to see him eat an egg. On Sunday, the King would appear along with his egg, a courtier would cry: "The King is about to eat his egg," and Louis would knock the top off the sharp end of a boiled egg and eat it with a spoon. For the moment, he settled the argument about which part of the egg should be opened. Jews opened eggs at the round end, Italians opened the sharp end, and Germans opened them on the side. Today, Americans prefer to crack a soft-boiled egg into a bowl and eat it, while the British still like a soft-boiled egg in its shell, with pieces of buttered white bread or toast called "soldiers" dipped into the yolk.

Parisians were quite taken with the King's exhibition, and Réaumur, the inventor of the thermometer, created an incubator that produced what the modern French historian Maguelonne Toussaint-Samat rather enigmatically calls artistically designed soft-boiled eggs. It's a shame she doesn't elaborate. The history of food is full of such omissions—it's as if nobody ever thought it important to get a food story right. Surely the egg itself could not have been radically reshaped? No; somebody would have noticed.

It took several more decades for eggs to achieve such cachet in England. Chickens were valued mostly for cockfighting, a popular sport. Few recognizable domestic breeds were raised for food. They included the Dorking, which may have been brought to Britain by the Romans. The Dorking was a clumsy, five-toed chicken that fell over onto its chicks—still it survives today. The Dominique was a handsome black-and-white striper that accompanied the Pilgrims to New England, where it was renamed the Plymouth Rock. But as opposition to cockfighting rose (it was outlawed in Britain in 1849), chicken breeding became an amateur avocation. In 1846, enthusiasts got together a handful of breeds for a chicken show at Richmond, in Surrey, and in 1849, chickens got a boost with the publication of *The Treatise of the History and Management of the Ornamental and Domestic Fowl.*

The author was a clergyman, the Reverend Edmund Dixon, a hen-hugger. Hens were as dear to him as his family. They deserved love, respect, and a henhouse almost as comfortable as a suburban villa. Not only must the house be large but above all so clean "as to afford a lady, without offending her sense of decent propriety, a respectable shelter on a showery day." Laying hens should be cosseted and fed corn, wrote the Reverend Dixon. Perhaps most significantly today, when hens are raised in battery cages, the Reverend Dixon said the hen must be free to roam. Hens needed the warmth of the sun on their feathers and, of course, their favorite dustbaths.

The Reverend Dixon might have nurtured his hens to produce tastier eggs, but he never thought of making money off them. The idea would have appalled him. He knew his hens so well that he could tell which of them had laid the egg he was eating—that's how close he was to them. Across the Channel, he found a soulmate in Alexandre Dumas, who wrote in his *Dictionary of Cuisine*: "To some people an egg is an egg. This is an error. Two eggs laid at the same moment, one by a hen that runs loose in the garden, the other by one that feeds in the henyard, can be utterly different in flavor." A serious egg eater today would say the same thing about the difference among organic eggs, free-range eggs, and battery-laid eggs.

The Reverend Dixon's book couldn't have been more timely. It came out in the same year, 1849, that the Great Birmingham Exhibition, in the English Midlands, introduced the Cochin-China chicken—an animal that turned the poultry world on its head. A trader who had managed to sneak into Canton during a lull in the Opium Wars returned with three Cochin chickens. He presented them to Queen Victoria, who graciously allowed them to be exhibited.

The Cochins were a sensation—they were showgirls. Twice the size of English and European chickens, the Cochins were an explosion of feathers that covered them from head to toe, in waves and rolls, so their combs and eyes were practically invisible. They were the old English sheepdog of chickens. Tens of thousands of people flocked to see the Cochins in Birmingham, and overnight the public went mad about chickens. According to S. H. Lewer, an esteemed Victorian authority on chickens, "Every visitor went home to tell of the new and wonderful fowls which were as big as ostriches and roared like lions, while gentle as lambs." They were excellent layers, too, and in no time, poultry mania swept the land just as it was sweeping the eastern seaboard of the United States. Cochins were shipped back and forth across the Atlantic for breeding, because Americans also were besotted with them; soon there were Cochin crosses, ever finer, larger, more beautiful birds.

By the end of the century, the English countryside bloomed iridescent with the plumage of hundreds of breeds of exotic fowl. Chickens looked like players in a medieval pageant: they were striped and spotted, banded and laced, their feathers tipped in contrasting colors. A Houdan cock had a head of feathers that made him look like a helmeted warrior. The sinister Sumatra was indigo head-to-toe. The little Silky had feathers as fine as hair and turquoise earlobes—earlobes were much fancied on an ornamental chicken. The crested Crèvecoeur from France looked frankly like a two-legged poodle. Others looked like chimpanzees. There were queenly Black Minorcas, nightshade with rosy combs—even the hen had a comb, but a small floppy one, and the spangled Hamburg with black lacing was quite as elegant as the Princess of Wales.

Poultry mania reached its apogee in 1901, when in London alone there were twenty poultry shows a week. But these magnificent creatures had only a moment to strut in the sun, because by this time some people thought to mine the gold beneath the bright plumage: food for the masses. The population was increasing at an alarming rate. The chicken meant food. Now the hen was selected for frequency of laying, and the size of its eggs. The plain little Leghorn from Italy, which laid lots of eggs and was so meek and mild (in other words, so suited to industrialization), took precedence over the exquisitely spangled Hamburg, a temperamental layer. Still, the problem of where the eggs were laid remained, the hens just wandering off to lay where they wanted to.

So it was with our hens. But before the hens could even start laying anywhere, there was a great deal of paperwork to be done, because keeping hens for food for one's own consumption threw a wrench in the government's stringent rationing rules. My parents would have to give half their eggs to the government, which was a nuisance—and the egg commissar who supervised the accounting of eggs would become a considerable nuisance. But these were trying times for every gourmand.

There were about one hundred hens in the old tennis court where Ben, the part-time gardener had put together some rudimentary chickenhouses protected by a fence of chickenwire, a strategic material only recently released by the government for domestic purposes. But the chickens had no trouble scratching aside or wriggling under the wire and strolling off where they pleased. Foxes had a field day. "Might as well just hand 'em over," huffed my father, poking broken shells with his shooting stick. But the real problem was the lack of whole eggs. Where were they? This was bothersome to my parents, who had pails of waterglass (a preservative) ready to keep the eggs for those months when the pre-industrial hens stopped laying.

It was more than bothersome to the egg commissar, who asked suspiciously: "How can there be so few eggs with so many hens?" His frustration was compounded by my mother's behavior. My mother revealed to him that she was almost blind, which was true, and thus she really couldn't tell an egg from an omelette. She was more likely to step on an egg than see it. She was terribly sorry, she said firmly. The egg commissar could do nothing but get back on his bicycle and retreat to the Kremlin, as my father said with satisfaction.

My father, having directed the egg program, then took off for London, where he spent the week in his club fed whisky by ancient servants, returning to the country only at weekends, which was when the commissar was off duty. He knew my mother would see off trouble. When they had first bought Shillingford, people came to call, as was the country way. The very first neighbor was such a nice man, my mother remembered. He told her he had just come from beagling. My mother had no idea what he was talking about, but she wanted to be friendly, so she said, "Did you shoot any?" He left shortly afterwards, went home, and died immediately. Of shock, of course, said my father, and wasn't it lucky he didn't have time to tell anyone else because then nobody else would have dared to call.

My mother coped. She was the first to admit she was far from a countrywoman. She was a New Yorker. Her idea of happiness was a centrally heated apartment. Her idea of country was the pale bone beach at Le Lavandou, where before the war, my parents had had a little vine-covered villa. Now here she was in the wilds of the Thames Valley, counting eggs. She came up with an egg hunt. The entire household was sent egg-hunting through orchard and the paddocks, the gully and the copse, the long chestnut-tree-lined drive. My brother Ian, home from Cranwell where he was learning to fly, was enlisted. So was my sister Lynn, the cook Christine, our daily maid Madge, even old Fred, who came in to polish the floors.

The glitter of hens' plumage was glimpsed in the stable block, down the river, in the old vegetable garden; the property was quite extensive, full of nooks and crannies. For all anyone knew, the hens were nesting in the dank cellars where nobody wanted to go after a tramp had been discovered sleeping there.

The egg problem came to a head in 1947. Great storms

wracked England, culminating in a hurricane on a March night. The river rose ominously, breaking records for flooding, as we could tell from the historic markers on the neighboring cottages. When we awoke to a troubled dawn, all around us were fallen trees. "What is that terrible smell?" cried my mother. "I believe it's sulphur!"

Nanny creaked open the enormous front door—Mr. Haggie had taken inspiration for the studded oak door from *Ivanhoe*—and cried, "Oh Madam!" Floods had done what nothing else had succeeded in doing: they had found the eggs and washed them up on the front steps. Dozens, scores of rotting eggs bobbed on the water.

My mother later called the commissar with what she called the "good news." The eggs were found. But of course they couldn't be eaten. The egg commissar couldn't work out what to do about so many dead eggs, which column should they fall into, and I don't believe he visited us again. He washed his hands of our problem and left my parents to find the eggs where they could.

After that, the eggs started filling up the waiting pails of waterglass. "*Oeufs en cocotte*," my mother cried with happiness. Little ramekins, filled with an egg, fresh cream from the local farm, and a dash of Worcester sauce, went into a pan of hot water and thence into the oven. My mother had had no formal training in cooking, but her many visits to France had trained her how to eat. She never forgot a taste, or how a dish should taste. She cooked by ear, which was the way she played the piano.

Although she had only the most modest amount of French, my mother knew how to decode the French menu. An *Omelette Florentine* meant spinach, *Soupe de Crécy* carrots; *Duchesse* was potatoes puréed with egg yolk. *Lorraine* meant that Gruyère cheese was somewhere in the dish, and *Nantua* indicated crayfish in the sauce. Such knowledge was essential even in England, where for years after the war menus were written in French, even in provincial hotel restaurants. I grew up believing that French was the only language for food, at least good food, and it came as a nasty shock that even a menu written in French could not guarantee good cooking. In addition, my mother absorbed French standards: we children died for milk chocolate, but my mother turned up her nose at that as an opiate for the masses. The only true chocolate was dark and on the bitter side. Milk cheapened it and ruined the flavor.

The *Oeufs en cocotte* were a triumph, emerging soft and creamy, and just a little spicy due to the Worcester sauce. Too much spice would have been ruinous, numbing the tastebuds. Poached eggs on creamed spinach were another revelation, although my mother never quite got the hang of how to poach an egg. It usually emerged from the whirlpool rather ragged. Then she would sigh and say, "Mary would know how to do it," and after a few beats, the next question was always, "And where is Mary?" Mary had been her cook before the war, a vivid Irishwoman, untrained, but a natural cook who only needed the right instructions to start turning out the flakiest pastry or the lightest soufflé. Even though

Mary had her faults, one of which was having children out of wedlock, my parents said her cooking excused anything. This cut no ice with conventional neighbors, who regarded my father with suspicion.

During the war, Mary had vanished into the maelstrom, but after we returned to Shillingford, my mother got a call from her. Mary wanted to come back. My mother was thrilled. "Give me your address and we'll send the money for the bus from London," the one that stopped at the New Inn on the main London to Oxford road. Mary, my mother could hear, sounded so happy that she seemed to be near tears. For two weeks, my mother mentioned Mary every day. But she never heard from her again. For weeks she waited and then she worried. What could have happened? Finally she decided that Mary had been murdered. Mary did like to spend time in pubs and could have picked up a wrong 'un, and that could have been the only reason she had never returned.

In the 1990s, my sister, who lives in London, opened her front door to a sixty-year-old Australian who said he was Mary's son. He had been to Somerset House, where all births and deaths are registered, and discovered that he had been born at our parents' London house, before being handed over to an orphanage and then sent to Australia. Now he wondered, as we had done, where Mary had gone. But the trail was cold. She had vanished without leaving a trace in the confusion of postwar England.

My mother's favorite cookbook was *André Simon's Concise Encyclopaedia of Gastronomy*. I still find it useful because it is a reference book as much as a collection of recipes. In addition, she collected receipts, as my father insisted on calling them, in a looseleaf book. As far as I know, she never dipped into *The Cookery Book of Lady Clark of Tillypronie* on which my grandmother had relied, which was tucked away in the library. Or perhaps she simply distrusted any cookbook that belonged to my grandmother, whose food, it was generally agreed, had been among the worst in London, mainly because she wouldn't pay enough to get a good cook. Her brother-in-law, our Great-Uncle Louis, who was a diplomat known for serving only superb food, usually came up with an excuse not to dine at her house. He would call in afterwards.

My father and his older brother, Victor, had no way of avoiding their mother's cooking, so for Christmas 1909, they bought her the bestseller of the day, Lady Clark's cookery book, inscribed unctuously by Victor, who must have been about fourteen. "To Darling Mummy, from her loving and 'gourmet' sons, who always appreciate the good dinners she gives them." Lady Clark's book is far more knowledgeable about food than Mrs. Beeton's; it was aimed at the top of the market.

The book opens with a quotation that says all beauty, grandeur, spirit, and even the gift of laughter is lost if one's digestion is bad: the stomach is the seat of all happiness. It is of course a French quotation. The author is Voltaire. Lady Clark's interest in cooking had been inspired by the émigrés of the first, often called the great, French Revolution, as her editor noted, who had been friends of Lady Clark's father, a Francophile judge. The recipes were original and were gathered personally by the writer, some from rather exalted cooks like the prince de Polignac, son of the close confidante of Marie Antoinette. He contributed *Oeufs à La Polignac*, a variation on *Oeufs en cocotte*, and there are instructions for boiling fresh meat from Baron Liebig, the pioneering chemist who invented beef extract and the calorie count of food.

But it is the changes wrought by technology that stand out. Whisks had taken over as the best tool with which to beat eggs. Canned food, especially tongue, was inestimably improved. Yeast, it was reported, could now be got through the mail rather than fetched directly from a brewery. Castor sugar and icing sugar had replaced pounded loaf sugar, a time-consuming process. And a synthesized gelatin had superseded isinglass, which the cook used to have to extract personally from fish intestines.

Escape to France

The eggs had no sooner been recovered than my brother Ian was lost, a late casualty of the war, now ostensibly over.

My father was saddened by Ian's death, but saddened more by my mother's unassuageable grief. He was, however, a Stoic. He himself had served in World War I as a midshipman, and he too had been a casualty of war. When that war was over and my father was more or less whole again, he quit the Royal Navy and went to New York in the spirit of so many immigrants, to leave a dreadful past behind.

So, at this moment, he thought again of escape. France, of course. It was so lucky he happened to be a director of a chain of luxury hotels, two of which were in the South of France. The currency restrictions were such that only spivs and millionaires with offshore accounts could travel. Others had to find a loophole. My father found his in the hotel chain.

The Metropole was a sheared-off piece of wedding cake, stories high, that rose among the palms in the center of Beaulieu-sur-Mer, a charming resort town between Nice and Monte Carlo. My parents marveled that the coast looked just the same as it had before the war when they had summered close to a sensational beach, seven miles long and quite empty, at Saint-Tropez. They divided their time between the beach and the casino at Monte Carlo, stopping to drink Champagne cocktails at the Negresco, the fashionable hotel on the Boulevard-des-Anglais in Nice, where the doormen were dressed by the *Ballets Russes*.

What my sister and I noticed was how polite the French were to children. How they didn't think twice before offering us what in England was considered adult food: strong coffee, flaky croissants, the kind so difficult to find in Paris now, and little pots of cultured butter; plenty of jam, *pots de chocolat*. The dining room did not offer the local Provençal food, but the classic French cuisine. It was, as my parents said over and over again, as if the war hadn't happened. Europe may have been turned upside down, but French food remained undiminished.

This was how I came to meet Escoffier, or rather, his cooking. Auguste Escoffier was the chef who had made classic French cuisine the international gold standard for food before 1914. He was the Swiss hotelier César Ritz's star chef. Superb food was an essential component of Ritz's concept of the grand hotel as a luxurious home-from-home for the traveling rich and famous. The idea was so successful that "Ritz" eventually became the brand name for luxury throughout the world. In 1889, César Ritz was lured to London by Richard D'Oyly Carte. The showman wanted Ritz to manage his new Savoy Hotel, which had been built over the Savoy Theatre, the home of D'Oyly Carte's popular productions of Gilbert and Sullivan operettas.

Naturally, Ritz took Escoffier with him. London was the hub of Empire, its potential for Ritz was huge, and it was essential that the restaurant be nonpareil. Grand hotels had revolutionized eating out. For the first time, women felt comfortable eating in public because the grand hotel dining room was so respectable. This wasn't just a significant advance for women, it also doubled the number of restaurant patrons, and women furthered Escoffier's fame. Indeed, he claimed that he owed his career to women, who loved his delicately nuanced cooking. It was women who most appreciated the egg, for example, which Escoffier extolled as "so fruitful of variety, so universally liked, and so complete in itself. . . ."

And the egg wasn't at all fattening. Escoffier was so sensitive to this female concern that he created a low-cal toast (later to be called Melba toast in honor of the Australian diva) just for the ladies. When the great tragedienne Sarah Bernhardt was playing in London, she always lunched at the Savoy, enjoying a half bottle of Moët et Chandon, and Escoffier personally prepared for her the lightest, most delicious egg dish, the one he considered supreme—scrambled eggs.

Escoffier's supreme egg dish was my first meal in the *salle-à-manger* of the Metropole Hotel in Beaulieu-sur-Mer. If I'd only known it, the waiters had Ritz written all over them: they wore tailcoats and white ties and handed out large menus that wouldn't have been out of place at the turn of the century. It was so formal it was hard to believe we were at a seaside resort. The menu, however, was considerably shorter than the à la carte menu of more than one hundred dishes offered by Escoffier at the Carlton Hotel in London in 1910. Even so, lobster salad, *Sole walewska*, *Poussin polonaise*, *Boeuf à l' anglaise*, and a fennel soufflé were all Escoffier staples. The dishes may not have been as extravagant as they once were, the truffles not so lavishly scattered over the dishes as was once the norm, but compared to the gruel of Britain, it was amazing.

I had been happy to see the word "*oeufs*" prominently on the menu. At last something I recognized. I ordered them.

My parents were dismissive. You've come to France and you're eating eggs? But then their eyes widened. Yves, our waiter, who had black patent leather hair, brought me a lovely helping of creamy scrambled eggs with not a lump in sight, nestled in a hollowed-out brioche. A few fragrant chopped tomatoes were strewn around. I had never even thought scrambled eggs could be served so deliciously. The memory of the cold, pale dried egg scrambled for breakfast at boarding school, a special treat for Sundays, began to fade.

The next day, the scrambled eggs appeared in a little pastry shell which had first been spread with a sort of meat glaze. The great thing about good food is you don't have to know what you're eating or be an expert to know that it's delicious. The same is true of any art: it is second-rate cooking or painting that is incomprehensible. Then the eggs came neatly on the plate, dusted with crescents and diamonds and stars of puff pastry. The final surprise was a ring of scrambled eggs around a mound of mushrooms sautéed in butter. We all had that, and my mother came away thoughtful.

Classic Cuisine and the Egg

Scrambled eggs were my introduction to Escoffier's cooking, but it took several more years before I understood how vital the egg was to his cuisine. Classic cuisine is a philosophy of cooking specific to the French, based on techniques and recipes developed over the centuries. Aside from Escoffier, two names stand out. A Florentine, Catherine de' Medici, the wife of Henri II, is credited with bringing the civilizing pleasures of the table to sixteenth-century France. (She also happened to be a skilled and prolific poisoner, and I wonder what both ideas together might mean.)

Marie-Antoine Carême is the second name. Carême rose from the ashes of the French Revolution, which had destroyed the great houses, and thus the great kitchens, and released the bonded chefs to go freelance. Carême, born into poverty, was lucky to land a job in a pastry shop, and as he had no options, he poured all his energy and imagination into food, shaping it to his own infinite ambition—laying down the template of ego chef. Cooking itself was not enough: he designed food, finding his vocation in sugar— towers, minarets, noble ruins, temples rose in sugary splendor above the most extravagant, multitiered buffets. He was greater than nations. Prince Talleyrand was his patron until Napoleon fell, but Carême had no trouble cooking dazzlingly for both sides. He graciously agreed to cook for the Czar, the Prince Regent, the Baron de Rothschild—but what were they beside his own place in history? Before he died, of the accumulated fumes from charcoal rotis-series, Carême ensured his immortality as author of a shelf of books that would become the basis for the classic French cuisine.

More than a hundred years after Carême's death in 1833, I had my Carême moment. Each Christmas, an ancient pastry chef in the bowels of the soot-stained Grosvenor Hotel (rising above Victoria Station) would labor over a rock-solid pastry palace. It was then presented to my father, a director of the chain that owned the Grosvenor, who gave it to us. One year, the palace was the hotel itself. Another, Buckingham Palace, as detailed a model as Carême might have wrought. The models were first coated in marzipan icing, which I hated, then topped with royal icing that had the consistency of plaster of Paris—a cleaver was necessary to crack it. The cake itself was disappointing, an austerity product with too little fruit, too little sugar, and too little butter. My mother hated fruit cake normally, but she quite liked this dry, sour cake.

Carême created the classic cuisine as a surprise. Ingredients were often hard to identify in his most ingenious creations. A hare might be stuffed and braised, then boned and shaped into a ring. Ortolans, tiny fat birds, were stuffed with black truffles and cooked in the stomachs of partridges. One of his masterpieces was *Chevreuse de perdreaux*, roast partridges and cabbage hidden under a carapace of exquisitely arranged vegetables—carrots and green beans, peas and glazed onions, boiled potatoes. It looked like a cross-stitch sampler.

The egg was essential to this cuisine of transformation, a food to conjure with. Would the classic cuisine have existed at all without the infinitely adaptable egg? Of course not. Mayonnaise, Hollandaise, Béarnaise, *Crème anglaise* among the sauces; mousses from fish to the one and only chocolate mousse made with just eggs and chocolate. Custards and creams, meringues of course, and *Oeufs à la neige*, a food so simple as to be genius itself, foamed egg whites floating on a pool of *Crème anglaise*.

The egg could do so many things without overly asserting itself. Over-egging the pudding has real meaning. There are many dishes which benefit from the properties of eggs but shouldn't taste of them. *Crème caramel* is a good example. It should slip down smoothly, almost anonymous except for the kiss of burnt sugar. If it tastes eggy, it is off. The same is true of *Crème brûlée*, once enchanting and now a food cliché, ruined by commercialization, the urge to exploit perfection. Today, there is rosemary *Crème brûlée*, and chocolate *Crème brûlée*, both inferior to the original. The Spanish flan, similar in intent to the *Crème caramel*, is often over-egged.

The egg's effect is best invisible. You may add an egg to potato croquettes, and nobody notices the taste of egg, but its effect is nothing short of brilliant. It coats the breadcrumbed croquette to produce a frizzled crust. Eggs are the base for choux pastry. Mixed with flour and butter, they produce the crunchy puffs that can be stuffed and piled into a *Croquembouche*—a tower of cream puffs swathed in spun sugar. The spongy *Crème St. Honoré* owes its ineffable lightness to beaten eggs. Beaten whites make cakes rise and mousses burst with bubbles. Beaten heated yolks make the exquisite sabayon that can be savory or sweet. An egg wash makes a pastry glow. Egg whites make one of the subtlest of cookies, the chewy English macaroon, which becomes a

Sarah Bernhardt when one side is stroked with dark chocolate. The classic cuisine has sometimes been dismissed as a soulless exercise in rigid technique. The result, however, is as lighthearted as summer laughter.

. . . .

ENGLISH MACAROONS

Makes 12 macaroons

Not to be confused with the French *macaron*, a meringuelike sandwich that comes in many flavors. The English macaroon is 3–4 inches in diameter, with a chewy almond center and a toasty crust that is pocked like orange peel.

¾ cup finely ground blanched almonds
1½ cups confectioner's sugar
4 large egg whites
2 tsp almond extract
12 whole blanched almonds

Preheat oven to 350°F.

As macaroons are sticky, the rimless tin baking sheet must be covered, preferably with wafer paper (edible ricepaper), available in cake supply stores or online at BakingShop.com. Failing that, use inedible parchment paper.

Mix the almonds and sugar well. Beat two of the egg whites until frothy. Using a wooden spoon, stir the frothed whites into remaining egg whites, almond mixture, and almond extract.

Either pipe the mixture onto the baking sheet or use a large soup/cooking spoon to shape it into 3-inch rounds, leaving at least 1 inch between macaroons—mixture spreads as it heats.

Bake for 20 minutes until the macaroons are a pale copper color. Then remove them to a rack and lightly press an almond into the center of each cookie. Leave to "ripen" for an hour. Macaroons naturally stick to the ricepaper so use scissors to cut away the paper around each cookie.

If you bake the macaroons on parchment paper, give them another 10 minutes at 300°F so they can be removed easily. Peel them from the paper and stroke the bottom of each one with melted semi-sweet chocolate to make a Sarah Bernhardt.

. . . .

The soufflé was the Mont Blanc of this insouciant cuisine. Auguste Escoffier, Carême's successor and the last, greatest exponent of the classic cuisine, said there was "the same mysterious gap between a musical scale and a Debussy prelude as between an egg and a soufflé." The basic recipe is deceptively simple: butter and flour, separated eggs, and flavoring of choice. Success lies in the precise execution of the instructions. A spell in the oven, and the result is magical: a bronzed, puffed, and wholly insubstantial mouthful of flavor. A properly risen soufflé was as festive a moment as *Crêpes Suzettes* flambéed tableside.

But time and again a chef was mortified to find out that when he opened the oven, the soufflé had collapsed, and his moment in the limelight was lost. The fallen soufflé covered a chef with ignominy. Carême worked obsessively on this problem. He did not invent the soufflé, but he perfected it. The soufflé appears to have evolved from a custardy mixture recorded by Apicius, a famous first-century Roman gourmet. The cookbook named for Apicius never mentions foaming egg whites. Their arrival is undated. The first experiments mixed beaten egg whites with cream, and it didn't work at all because egg whites cannot foam properly with so much as a smidgeon of fat in them. An egg white tainted with just a smear of yolk (which has fat in it) should be rejected, else it will impede the foaming of the other whites. Before the French devised the wire whisk, a bunch of twigs probably sufficed. Obviously the twigs would have to be clean, otherwise the white might have traces of bark in it. The receptacle for beating must have been a bowl. I don't know if Carême used a copper bowl, but gradually cooks learned that egg whites foam more voluminously in a copper bowl, and that they also stay stiff. Only in the 1950s was it discovered why: copper bonds with the protein in the albumen to hold together the foam.

Carême finally worked out that opening the oven door prematurely, which lets in a blast of cold air, causes a soufflé to flop. A minimum time was set for the soufflé to set, and the final measurement was in place. After that, there was really no problem.

I say this with authority. For several years, I ate a soufflé regularly at the house of a friend and never once did it fall. Lina, the cook, was French, and when she brought in the cheese soufflé, she wore a black sateen dress and a lace apron, and she was always totally assured—even beaming. Lina's soufflé rose a couple of inches above the soufflé dish, and burst out a little bit from the bronze crust. When Lina passed you the dish, the soufflé seemed to tremble with anticipation; and when you sank the spoon in, the soufflé yielded voluptuously. The interior was creamy, not runny and certainly not dry, dryness being the death of the soufflé. My father always made the same toe-curling joke: A cousin of his called Susan had once left the spoon in a soufflé and her dinner partner had shouted at her what seemed incomprehensible insults until she realized he had a lisp. What he was saying, she worked out finally, was: "Thuthan, Thuthan, don't leave the thpoon in the thoufflé."

. . . .

LINA'S SOUFFLÉ AU FROMAGE

Serves 4

This is the recipe I use to make a cheese soufflé. It is from *The Constance Spry Cookbook*. Constance Spry was a British version of Martha Stewart in the first half of the twentieth century.

1 Tbs unsalted butter to oil dish
2 Tbs unsalted butter
3 tsp all-purpose flour
½ cup milk
3 large egg yolks
¼ tsp salt
3 large egg whites
⅓ cup each grated Parmesan and Gruyère cheese
1 tsp grated Parmesan cheese
¼ tsp paprika
⅛ tsp cayenne pepper

Preheat oven to 425°F.

Take an ovenproof dish about 4 inches deep and 6 inches across and oil it thoroughly with 1 Tbs of unsalted butter. Cut a 3-inch-wide piece of parchment paper to make a collar that is tied around the dish and rises 2 inches above it.

Melt 2 Tbs butter in a 1-quart pan, blend in the flour, add the milk (I recommend warmed milk), and stir over heat until close to boiling. You now have a Béchamel sauce, one of the classic cuisine's mother sauces, from which many other sauces are derived.

Remove the sauce from the heat and allow to cool for 5 minutes. Then beat in the egg yolks, adding salt and a little cayenne pepper.

In the meantime, beat the egg whites with an electric beater until they stand in solid peaks. If you are using a copper bowl, the whites will be reliably firm; otherwise a stainless-steel bowl is recommended.

Stir the Parmesan and Gruyerè and one spoonful of the egg whites into the Béchamel, then fold in the remainder. Turn the mixture into a prepared ovenproof dish, turn down the oven to 375°F, and bake for about 20 minutes. *Never, never open the oven door before then.*

The soufflé is done when it has risen and browned a little and the top is cracking. Remove paper and serve at once, sprinkled with the reserved grated cheese and paprika.

. . . . .

THATCHED HOUSE PUDDING

Serves 6

The most popular cold soufflé used to be lemon. Actually, a cold soufflé is a mousse, the egg whites stabilized with gelatin. But hot lemon soufflé, an old country house favorite, is even more delicious and less stressful to make. It also comes with its own sauce.

3 large lemons
8 Tbs (1 stick) unsalted butter
¾ cup white sugar
4 large eggs, separated
6 Tbs all-purpose flour

2 cups whole milk

1 Tbs almonds, toasted

Preheat oven to 350°F.

Butter a 2-quart round ovenproof dish.

Take out a roasting pan, and start heating water in a kettle.

Using a zester, scratch off the zest of 2 lemons. Then squeeze the juice from all 3 lemons.

Using an electric beater, cream butter and sugar until light. Add lemon juice and zest.

Beat in the egg yolks one at a time. When they're mixed, add the flour and milk together and beat vigorously.

With a clean whisk, beat the egg whites until they stand in stiffest peaks, then fold gently into mixture.

Pour into the buttered dish, then set the dish in the roasting pan with enough hot water to come halfway up the sides of the dish. Bake for 45–50 minutes, until the sponge has risen and set.

Remove from oven, sprinkle with toasted, slivered almonds, and pass around some heated, strained apricot jam. When served, there will be a delicious lemon custard sauce beneath the soufflé.

. . . .

Before the war, the soufflé—hot or cold, savory or sweet—was a feature at smart luncheon and dinner parties, common in French restaurants. But after the war, the dish proved too demanding for what were often servantless

households. Although housewives, if they applied themselves, could easily make a soufflé, they didn't want to. The
postwar cookbooks emphasized logistics. The housewife-cook
was urged to prepare a dinner menu that didn't require her to
keep dashing to and from the kitchen. A soufflé required much
dashing and anxiety. Today, the soufflé is an awkward
anachronism in the age of the casual stir fry. Few restaurants
serve one, and if they do, they advertise it forbiddingly: if you
insist on a soufflé, you'll have to wait anywhere from twenty to
forty minutes, a downer for today's speedeater.

Showman Chef

Carême died in 1833, but as he had planned, his cooking continued. His five-volume *L'Art de cuisine française au xixème
siècle* was the inspiration for Escoffier's *Guide Culinaire*
(1903), which became the bible of the classic cuisine. Carême
and Escoffier were complementary. Carême was the Byron
of the kitchen, while Escoffier, the son of a blacksmith, was
the Barnum. Carême delighted in dazzling the world with
special effects, while Escoffier concentrated on selling them.
As a marketing ploy, Escoffier named dishes after celebrities,
reckoning this would keep them coming back. Questions
remain. Why was *Lady Egmont* a fillet of sole with asparagus tips and minced mushrooms? Sometimes, Escoffier created a dish reflecting an event of the day. The *Jeannette* was
an American ship that foundered in the Arctic in 1912. Some

of the explorers escaped safely, but others were left on board, and as the ship was slowly, excruciatingly borne away by the icebergs, the crew was entombed alive in ice, their arms outstretched for help. Escoffier reported this tragedy in poached escalopes of chicken breast, decorated with tarragon, and laid on layers of foie gras mousse and chicken jelly encased in a block of ice. People ate it apparently without a qualm.

His greatest promotion was the *Pêche Melba*, created for Nellie Melba, the boisterous Australian soprano, who was to the Edwardians what a TV star is to the public today. She frequently stayed at the Savoy, just round the corner from the opera house at Covent Garden. Escoffier couldn't do enough for her (he even named his low-cal toast for her). He no doubt beamed with pleasure when she gave him tickets to hear her sing in *Lohengrin*, and he came home walking on air. Oh, Melba was all right, but the swan! I see him marshaling his cooks: First the swan, a large one carved of ice, with great spread wings, and between them a silver dish of vanilla ice cream on which would rise a tower of golden peaches dripping with fresh raspberry purée. This apparition would be veiled in delicately spun sugar.

Pêche Melba has entered the language even though Nellie Melba herself is largely forgotten. By 1930, her name had faded so much that the concierge at the Ritz in Paris couldn't place her when her secretary arrived to confirm the diva's reservation. The secretary was my father's cousin, Susan of the soufflés, down on her luck after her husband lost his money in the stock market crash. Susan had no practical skills to offer Melba, but that didn't matter. Melba was a terrific snob and simply wanted a titled companion.

"The suite for Madame Melba," she said to the concierge.

"Melba, Melba." He clicked his tongue, flung his head back, frowned, and studied the reservations. It all seemed to take so long. Susan said she kept praying that Melba, whose ego was fraying as her fame dwindled, would not walk in. Finally , he cried: "Ah, *Pêche Melba!*" And he smiled, a huge smile of remembered pleasure. Susan said she was surprised he didn't add when he'd last sampled it.

Pêche Melba even crossed over to the America soda fountain as peach melba. It comes in a steel dish containing two halves of a banana that flank a scoop of vanilla ice cream and a peach, usually canned; both are draped in bottled fruit sauce and topped with whipped cream, often squirted from a can. Escoffier would have had a heart attack. He permitted *no* variations to his perfect recipes. Even in his lifetime, *Pêche Melba* was violated. When he heard that strawberry jam was being substituted for fresh raspberry coulis, he complained that would alter the taste completely, and decorating the peach with whipped cream could hardly satisfy the palate of a real connoisseur. Of course, he was right.

There is no such flight of fancy in the 5,000-plus recipes in *Le Guide Culinaire*. It wasn't until I looked up a very terse recipe for a swanless version of *Pêche Melba* that I realized I was reading the gastronomic equivalent of a mechanic's manual. First the necessary tools: the principles of the cuisine, the leading sauces and the small compound sauces, the cold sauces and compound butters, followed by court bouillons, broths, and marinades. Then the recipes. Escoffier industrialized his cuisine by stamping out recipes, thousands of them, that could be replicated in any Grand Hotel. Many of them were just variations on a basic model, another industrial trait. The tyro chef had only to flip to the right page and follow instructions. This was essential because grand hotels required an assembly line of cooks who were grouped in specialties. There was the *chef de parti* and his *sous-chef* and fish chefs and assistant fish chefs, and sauce chefs and assistant sauce chefs, and so on down the line, right to the beginners who did a little of everything.

Grand hotels attracted an international clientele, and Escoffier prepared global menus, including curries and pilafs, *Bananes à la norvegienne* (bananas mixed with banana ice), and lobster American style. He even had a recipe for gumbo. But, of course, the recipes were always processed by the Escoffier methods so that their essence was rendered light and digestible. It is a canard that the classic cuisine was the quickest way to ruin your liver. Carême prided himself on the fact that one of his employers, the Prince Regent (later George IV), who was immensely greedy, said that Carême was the only chef whose cooking had been easy to digest. Escoffier, always respectful of Carême, wrote that his predecessor had grasped the essential truth that the richer the cooking is, "the more speedily do the stomach and palate tire of it." For himself, Escoffier wanted his customers to delight in the taste of his food but never to rise from the table feeling either stuffed or queasy. His aim, he wrote, was to cook "in such a way as to allow for easy digestion by the frequently disordered stomachs of the consumers." By "disordered" he implied too rich, too spicy, and poorly cooked food—food that hadn't been cooked by his acolytes. What would he have made of a Big Mac or salsa?

Le Guide Culinaire hasn't a smidgeon of charm, unlike the cookbooks of today, which so often make cooking sound as rewarding as motherhood. Nor has it a flash of humor. *Chaud-froid Félix Faures*, small round sandwiches made of foie gras and truffles stuffed between chicken breasts, was created by Escoffier to commemorate the death of the president in the arms of his mistress in 1899. It was not intended to be funny.

A sense of humor about food could be left to the English. *Tiens*, if you didn't laugh about English food, you would have to cry. The French treasured the story of a Frenchman invited to spend a few days on a great estate in the English countryside. The Frenchman was bowled over by the beauty of the house and its furnishings, the well-stocked library, the perfect service, the vintage wines. On the third day, his host took him to the highest point of the estate and showed him a ravishing landscape, perhaps even pointing out where a village had been moved to create the symmetry essential to the overall aesthetic. The Frenchman took a long, appreciative look, and then said, "Please, never, never cook it."

Eggs and More Eggs

There are 546 egg recipes in Escoffier's book. For scrambled eggs, Escoffier recommends a heavy-bottomed pan, an ounce of butter, six eggs moderately beaten together with a good pinch of salt and pepper. The pan should be placed over a moderate "fire" (Escoffier believed cooking over a woodfire was best and there was always a woodfire in his kitchens), and stirred constantly with a wooden spoon, "taking care to avoid cooking too quickly, which, by instantaneously solidifying the egg-molecules, would cause lumps to form in the mass—a thing which above all should be guarded against." Once smooth and creamy, the eggs should be removed from the heat, and one and a half ounces of butter and three tablespoons of cream stirred in.

I looked in vain for garlic. When Escoffier scrambled eggs for Sarah Bernhardt at the Savoy, he would at the last minute stir them with a fork on which he had speared a sliver of garlic. Madame Bernhardt was always asking him what he had done to make his eggs taste so good. He never told her. Garlic was taboo in grand hotel cuisine because the British and the Americans didn't like it. Garlic reeked of French peasantry—actually, all peasantry. This was ironic because it was the French peasantry that made and continues to make French food so good.

Food was, like everything else, regarded snobbishly. Even Sarah Bernhardt, French herself, was not immune. London was one of her major markets. She didn't want an English admirer to draw back from a kiss. Of course, he would be too polite to say anything but he would be thinking . . .

When I make scrambled eggs now, I skip Escoffier for my own simpler recipe. Break a couple of eggs into a bowl and beat them lightly with a fork. Add a couple of pinches of sea salt. Put a big pat of butter in a stainless-steel frying pan. Once it's melted and just starting to smoke, add the eggs and let them sit while you say, "For this may we be truly thankful." Then take the fork and begin to scrape the cooked eggs from the center of the pan and mix them with the rest. Remove from the heat before they are completely cooked as they will go on cooking, and there is nothing worse than overcooked scrambled eggs. The French insist the best accompaniment is fresh black truffles. Nowadays, truffles are hard to come by and expensive when you do find them; but if you do, put them in with the eggs you have brought home from market, so the eggs themselves are infused with the rooty fragrance. If truffles aren't available, wild mushrooms, gently sautéed, are an excellent substitute.

Scrambled eggs are an ideal fast food: they are made in a couple of minutes and go with anything—rosti potatoes are particularly good. But who, other than me, makes them any more? I don't think it's just that eggs were the subject of a (false) health scare in the past thirty years, but rather that scrambled eggs demand a level of attention that fewer and fewer people want to spend on preparing food. Scrambled eggs have the potential to disappoint. A moment's inattention and they may overcook. You can't put scrambled eggs in the microwave and take them out in perfect shape a minute later. Industrial fast food is never disappointing: it is reassuringly the same. It is the food of the pessimist. Nothing can improve it. But then, nothing can make it worse.

Escoffier was fond of another quick egg dish, *Oeufs-sur-le-plat* (Eggs on the Dish). You put a lump of butter into an ovenproof dish of any kind and when the butter is melted, add two whole eggs, lightly salt them, and spoon more butter over. Put them in the oven for a couple of minutes or until the whites have become milky. No temperature is specified because restaurant ovens were, and still are, always kept on high heat as the doors are opened and shut so frequently. When the eggs look right, remove them and serve right away. *Oeufs-sur-le-plat* could be recycled a dozen ways, garnished with minced onions as *Oeufs Omar-Paćha*, or with spinach in *Oeufs à la Florentine*. *Oeufs au Diable*, garnished with browned butter and vinegar, must be a spin on Louis XV's *Oeufs à la fanatique*.

Fresh eggs in one hand, Escoffier's bible in the other, the grand hotel chef was never bereft of ideas. Menus had to be dynamic. The eating classes expected it. They wouldn't have had anything to do with the sameness of the menus in today's restaurants, where certain generic foods—rack of lamb, steak, pork chop, fish of the day—appear routinely. They ate out frequently and demanded variety. This tradition would be continued on the steamships crisscrossing the Atlantic, floating three-star restaurants that boasted they never served a dish twice, unless it was asked for, as in, "I'll have another caviar sandwich."

The egg's stardom in the classic cuisine brought it unprecedented attention. The cuisine demanded more and more eggs, and Escoffier insisted they be "strictly fresh," an indication that this was not always the case, and in those days an old egg might well be a rotten egg. The words "fresh egg" are rarely mentioned in any modern cookbook because rotten eggs are such a rarity. Thanks to refrigeration, eggs can sit on a chilled supermarket shelf or in the home refrigerator for a month without going bad. But an old egg is still an old egg, its white runny, its taste stale.

In Escoffier's day, an egg that old was bad. Chefs would crack the egg into a bowl and sniff for sulphur before incorporating it into a dish. We did the same thing after the war with the eggs from our wandering hens. Escoffier undoubtedly had a system to ensure a steady supply of fresh eggs; perhaps he had contracts with farmers who rotated their flocks so there was always a flock laying. Even then, he could never be sure just how fresh an egg was.

Which Ended First, the Cooking or the Egg?

The lunch that lingered to teatime, the dinner that went into the early hours of the morning, the constant eating—early morning tea, breakfast, elevenses, luncheon, tea, dinner, supper, the endless flow of dishes and new dishes—all these were already coming to an end by the time the Great War broke out in 1914. Before he died in 1911, King Edward VII, who had characterized the self-indulgence of his age, had declared he would no longer sit still for more than an hour at luncheon. His motor was waiting to take him to the races. He had eaten partly out of boredom; now the car banished boredom. Escoffier was quick to sense the change and downscaled his menus, offering a *prix fixe* for the hurried eater; and like many French chefs, his eyes turned westward to the United States. Rich Americans were the most frequent patrons of grand hotels. In fact, their desire for decent bathrooms had transformed the grand hotel into a place where private spaces were as important as the great salons. The fact that the Savoy had an unheard-of sixty-nine bathrooms raised not entirely approving eyebrows. Oscar Wilde hated the decadence of running hot water. Americans not only wanted the hotels to meet their demands, they also wanted everything that rich Europeans had, and that included a trophy French chef.

The relationship between the French chef and the United States paralleled the industrialization of the egg itself. French chefs found they were not treated much better than the hens in American chicken factories. In Europe, the diners listened to the chef and more or less obeyed him; at least they took his advice. Escoffier was revered. Should he emerge from the wings of the dining room and suggest, say, *Bombe Neron*, an iced sweet he had named in honor of a verse drama called *Nero*, the patrons bowed their heads and ordered it. But Americans liked to make up their own minds, and a chef to them was basically just a cook, however much he gave himself airs. As the chicken squawked in frustration on the assembly line, so the French chef grumbled in the kitchens of the Robber Baron heirs. A chef who had been placed by Escoffier himself in a New York hotel wrote his old boss plaintively that he couldn't keep staff: Americans would not work without machines. The classic cuisine never really got a proper toehold in restaurants, and Prohibition was the final straw. It destroyed the French restaurant, which relied so heavily on wine. What few French chefs remained were stereotyped as grumpy and worse, kitchen dictators like the chef-autocrat of Billy Wilder's movie *Sabrina* (1954).

My family had their own memory of such a chef. Ulisse was a French chef marooned in the kitchen of a great news-paper family in New York, heirs to a gold rush fortune.

The Fate of Ulisse

The thread that led us to Ulisse started after the Great War, when my father left London for New York. He was tempted to do so by the visions of an exciting New York life projected by an American cousin. And almost the first person he met in New York was Mrs. Whitelaw Reid, the daughter of Darius Mills, who had made his millions from the richest strike of all, the Comstock Lode. Of course she had a French chef installed in her house on Madison Avenue, a house famous for its Stanford White interiors—and in another link between past and present that Agnes Jekyll would have appreciated, Mrs. Reid's gold ballroom is now the bar for Le Cirque 2000. Mrs. Reid's daughter-in-law, Helen Rogers Reid, was married to Ogden Reid, the publisher of the *New York Herald Tribune*. Ulisse had been hired in the 1930s after Helen tasted his exquisite celery soup at a Left Bank hotel not far from the newspaper's Paris office.

Twenty years later, when my father came back to New York, posted to the Brooklyn Navy Yard during World War II, he stayed with the Reids, and so eventually did all my family—and we too learned about grumpy French chefs.

Even a very small child couldn't ignore Ulisse's unhappiness. In Paris, he had been a chef of note, my mother said, and famous people, politicians, would swoon over his *Suprèmes de pigeonneaux à la Sainte-Clair*, the most elegant platter of squab's breasts piled on wild mushrooms and surrounded by quenelles made from the squab legs floating in a delicate velouté. But Helen Reid ate like a bird—an exquisite jeweled bird, as one *Tribune* staffer described her—and her dinner parties were about politics, not food. And so, Ulisse grew sad.

We children were in and out of the kitchen at the Reids' country house, and we knew how things were. Ulisse stumped around, an angry red-faced man with a mustache, scowling at the sight of a child, and delegating much of the cooking to the amiable pastry cook, Helvi, who made heart-shaped cookies and let us stroke melted butter for tiny sand-wiches to be served upstairs. But there was one chore Ulisse couldn't shirk. Helen Reid, an early suffragist, was very interested in women's issues; she herself had suggested that the paper hire Clementine Paddleford, the foremost writer on cooking in America, as a food columnist. Now she wanted her chef to try out the new pressure cooker, a gift for the busy housewife.

Before the microwave was invented, the pressure cooker was the speediest cooking appliance. Why, a lamb stew that took hours in the oven could be made in twelve minutes in a pressure cooker. The technology was simple: When water boils, it produces steam. The pressure cooker locks the steam into a tightly sealed pot and so the temperature rises far more than is possible under normal conditions. The superheated steam then cooks foods fast, and because the steam con-denses in the pot rather than in the air, few nutrients are lost. Naturally, nutritionists, then the gurus of food, loved pres-sure cookers.

Ulisse's frown, however, deepened when the order came down. The pressure cooker may have been invented by a Frenchman, but it hadn't yet been perfected. There were horrible stories of pressure cooker lids flying off and kitchens spattered with not-yet-instant pot roast. In fact, this was exactly what happened to Ulisse. He loaded up, locked the pressure cooker, and waited for it to start hissing. A siren screamed throughout the kitchen, the lid shot off and hit Ulisse on the head. After that, the pressure cooker was never mentioned again.

Pressure cookers, safe now, are still around—sixties' heads loved them because they cooked brown rice so fast. I've only ever seen one used—and that was to accelerate the steaming of a Christmas pudding. But I have heard that you can make a mean risotto in six minutes. Of course, my informant acknowledged, the risotto didn't have the silkiness achieved by forty minutes or so of steady stirring by a human hand, but by God it was easy, and so good for you.

Ulisse, however, left us one wonderful legacy: the recipe for the classic chocolate mousse—which has vanished from restaurants, I can't imagine why. My brother Ian called it Thames Mud. It is just eggs and dark chocolate, and much lighter than the popular mousse of today, which is cloyingly thick and stiffened with whipped cream.

· ·

IAN'S THAMES MUD

Serves 8

8 extra-large eggs, separated
8 oz bittersweet chocolate
3 Tbs black coffee
1 Tbs brandy

Separate the eggs.

Beat the egg yolks until pale yellow.

In the oven, melt the chocolate in the coffee, and before it starts to thicken, blend in the beaten egg yolks with an electric beater or balloon whisk. Add the brandy.

Beat egg whites until absolutely stiff.

Put 2 spoonfuls of beaten egg white into the chocolate mixture, then carefully fold in the rest of the egg whites.

Spoon mixture into a glass bowl or individual bowls; leave in the refrigerator for several hours.

· ·

Escoffier's Greatest Triumph

By the end of the 1950s, there was really only one classic French restaurant worthy of the name in New York, Henri Soulé's Le Pavillon. Le Pavillon's clientele was rich and famous and old—the Duchess of Windsor and Babe Paley among them. The classic cuisine was clearly terminal in America. Not so fast. In 1961, Julia Child's *Mastering the Art of French Cooking* was published and Escoffier was reborn. Julia did what no other acolyte of Escoffier had managed to do: she turned on the American middle class to classic cuisine and Escoffier became famous beyond his wildest dreams.

The French hated Julia. She was too successful, for one thing. She was also a woman, and to the French, a female chef was an oxymoron. For another she was an American, and an American chef was a further contradiction in terms. Then, she had the gall to demystify the classic cuisine. Imagine saying, as Julia did, that a child could make Hollandaise sauce, one of the mother sauces, in a blender. Imagine making Béchamel, another mother sauce, in five minutes. It did not matter that the results were pleasurable, and that there might be no mother sauce at all unless it was adapted to these rushed times. The dismaying thing was that these were not *French* results.

I think now of Julia as the Winston Churchill of classic cuisine. *Mastering the Art of French Cooking* was shamelessly, gloriously anachronistic. If Escoffier was old hat, she'd never heard about it, and so she just barged ahead in her ebullient way, and influenced people—too many to count properly, but eventually millions—to start making food that was wholly out of date. Julia was cooking without fear. People who shrank from a recipe with French words in it started making *Caneton rôti à l'alsacienne* and *Blanquette de veau* as routinely as if they were grilling hamburgers. Julia's recipe for French bread awoke eaters to the poverty of industrial bread. Julia's wielding of the sauté pan goosed the kitchen hardware industry. And she shook up television, a wasteland of bland stereotypes. The camera adored Julia's authenticity, the trills and growls as she tossed a crêpe. Julia was an icon to everyone, even those who didn't cook.

Now, her timing seems amazing luck. She had only a tiny window—a few years—to establish herself. By the time the second volume of *Mastering the Art of French Cooking* was published in 1971, freshets of rebellion were sparking a whole new idea of food in North America, and in 1970 Alice Waters had opened her all-organic restaurant, Chez Panisse, in Berkeley.

Ironically, the organic movement took root not far from Petaluma, in Sonoma County, where the first egg factories were started in the 1880s. American entrepreneurs initiated the egg assembly line. Americans had quickly grasped how much food a chicken could produce if it was properly exploited. Why should the hen waste so much time hatching the eggs she laid? Surely a machine would do the job faster and leave the hen to simply go on laying eggs? That way there would be more chicks and more eggs and an egg factory could make more money. And so the hen was reduced to an economic unit, something that would have appalled the Reverend Dixon, the old hen-hugger.

Americans had perfected the caged-hen system by the 1950s, a decade after American consumption had peaked at 405 eggs a year. The hen herself was completely denatured by this time. Up to nine birds were crammed into a cage the size of a microwave oven, so small they couldn't lie down. The cages were piled on top of each and at an angle so the eggs rolled onto the conveyor belt and were carried away. Blazing lights stimulated the hens' ovaries night and day, so they laid and laid and laid.

The old hen might lay 120 eggs a year, then lay off, or molt, for a few months before, her body restored, she started again. The new hen was stimulated to lay 220 eggs a year; one hen actually laid 330 eggs. The old hen laid splendidly for a couple of years and by her fourth year was made into soup. The new and exhausted hen goes for pet food after a mere fifteen months.

One bad idea led to another. The factory hens produced an enormous amount of excrement. What could be done about it? The answer was simple. It was excellent for gardening, and good too for nourishing other animals. When you eat an industrial steak, you are eating an animal raised on a diet that includes composted chicken manure. In 1997, the U.S. Food and Drug Administration (FDA) confirmed that chicken droppings in cattle feed were GRAS—FDA-speak for "generally recognized as safe." "Recycled animal waste, such as processed chicken manure and litter," stated a representative of the FDA's Center for Veterinary Medicine, "has been used as a feed ingredient for almost forty years. This animal waste contains . . . protein, fiber, and minerals and has been deliberately mixed into animal feed for these nutrients."

As for the hen, she was and remains miserable. At the University of Guelph in Ontario, Dr. Ian Duncan, a professor of ethnology, is developing methods of examining chickens' reactions to the conditions and procedures to which they are subjected. He hasn't yet decoded hen language, so we don't know the full range of their emotions, or how complex those emotions may be. But when I learned that the hen had tear glands, I assumed she could cry. Dr. Duncan said he has

not observed a hen crying, but rage is certainly in the picture. Deprived of their eggs, hens pace back and forth and
attack each other. We know, he said, that they feel chronic
pain from debeaking, the routine removal of a chick's beak
to stop them taking out their anger on their fellow prisoners.

The Egg Trauma

Even as hens were being martyred for food, egg eaters in
North America and Britain were oblivious to their pain.
They had another concern, on their minds: Health. By the
middle of the twentieth century, North Americans had never
been so healthy or so susceptible to health scares. Public
health had successfully routed the great plagues—killers like
typhoid, vanquished by better sanitation—but the insidious
killers, heart disease and cancer, still remained. As scientists
increasingly linked these diseases to lifestyle and food, a new
philosophy evolved: Healthism. It was based on the notion
that death could be delayed, perhaps even cheated, if a person monitored every single piece of food she ate. Thus, the
food scientist rose to power.

Not until the 1960s did the biochemists cast their baleful
eyes on the egg. The egg was a mother food and clearly too
good to be true. There must be something wrong with it.

When I look back, I remember the first sign that all was
not well with the egg. It was some time in the sixties. A
friend of my parents refused a helping of Béarnaise sauce on

the grounds that her doctor had told her that such a rich combination of butter and egg yolks was life-threatening. My father was furious. He had personally made the Béarnaise. Late in life, he had decided to learn how to cook the classic cuisine and was pleased to find how easy it was. Don't deviate: a simple principle. What was all this fuss about good cooking? Béarnaise was a snap, and delicious not only with tournedos but in a roast beef sandwich, or with grilled chicken, or to cheer up a dull fish. So many uses. My mother closed her eyes and ignored the comment. She was a Christian Scientist and did not talk about health.

In any case, the very idea of an egg endangering health was implausible. Eggs were the nutritionists' darling. The egg is packed with good things. It has the highest quality protein of all foods and is the source of eleven essential nutrients and fifteen important vitamins and minerals. They include B vitamin folate, which has been found to reduce birth defects, carotenoids (lutein and xanthophyll) that may reduce the risk of cataracts and macular degeneration, and half the required daily dose of choline required to protect memory. Of the 5 grams of fat in an egg, only 1.5 comprise saturated fat, the fat fingered as harmful to the heart, which makes eggs positively virtuous. An egg, moreover, is as slimming as a bottle of vitamins: it contains only seventy calories. An egg does lack vitamin C, but that can be added with a glass of orange juice, a staple of the American diet. Home economists, the experts of the women's magazines, were never able to praise eggs enough because eggs have always been so cheap. Irma S. Rombauer referred to them as the kitchen's "maid of all work" in her original, encyclopedic *Joy of Cooking* (1931), which has loads of egg recipes.

In the early 1970s, out of the blue, the American Heart Association declared the egg a threat to the heart. The egg contained 278 milligrams of cholesterol, and food scientists had just decreed that no one should consume more than 300 milligrams of cholesterol a day. The trauma that resulted lasted more than twenty years, almost crashed the egg industry, and turned what was then the largest egg-eating country in the world against eggs.

The attack would prove to be a classic case of food science gone awry. As scientists worked on the connections between high cholesterol and heart disease—the leading cause of death in the United States—they determined that there must be a level of cholesterol in the human body that was "safe." Scientists then believed that the cholesterol in a food had a direct impact on the level of cholesterol in humans. Thus, eating these foods should be limited.

When I learned this, I thought of course that the scientists, being scientists, had arrived at a safe level of dietary cholesterol through proof. How wrong I was. In 2002, I asked Dr. Donald J. McNamara, a biochemist and the executive director of the Egg Nutrition Center, the egg lobby in Washington, D.C., what happened to take the egg off American plates for the past thirty years.

But first, how come the safe cholesterol level? Dr. McNamara laughed. This was disconcerting. Then he said that the deed had been done in 1968, a day in infamy as far as egg producers and of course egg consumers were concerned. Dr. McNamara explained that a group of food scientists got together and hashed over the idea of setting a safe cholesterol standard. Some thought the whole idea unnecessary, but others were adamant. So the debate went back and forth, and finally a compromise was reached. The average human intake of cholesterol is 580 milligrams (per liter of blood) a day, so let's just halve that. Make it 300 milligrams. "There's not one bit of scientific evaluation in that number," Dr. McNamara added.

Subsequently, the whole idea of a total cholesterol level would be rendered meaningless by the discovery that cholesterol is far more complicated than that. Cholesterol is created by the way the body *processes* food, not by food like eggs that contain cholesterol. Moreover, the body processes some foods into "good" cholesterol, essential for health, while others become "bad" cholesterol.

So, overnight as it were, and on the basis of an arbitrary calculation, the egg was in trouble, deep trouble. My God, just one egg, and a person would have eaten up almost all their cholesterol allowance for the day. The egg was a walking time bomb. It was enough for the American Heart Association to sound the alarm.

People today are blasé about food science, because they have been frightened into changing their diets so many times, only to be told later that the scientists were wrong. For years, people believed in food science and obediently ate fiber to stave off colon cancer. Then, suddenly, they were told, fiber makes no difference. Margarine was briskly touted as an excellent, healthy substitute for butter, cheaper too; and even though margarine has a disgreeable taste and ruins any dish it is cooked with, people obediently used it, thinking they were lengthening their life span. Now, of course, margarine is ringed with red flags as a trans fat, the deadliest of fats.

Every month brings a report of some new food worry. In 2002, Swedish scientists announced they had identified a potential carcinogen in fried and baked foods. The media, which saw sensational story possibilities—food as death—in Healthism, was quick to follow up. Acrylamide is made when a naturally occurring amino acid called asparagine is heated with glucose. The result is a useful plastic, an adhesive, a water purifier, and lots of delicious food—new-risen bread, toast, roasted asparagus, French fries, potato chips, almonds, coffee, cocoa, you name it.

Some scientists doubted the way the evidence was tested. The mice used to test the chemical did not actually eat the French fries; instead, acrylamide was applied to a gene inserted in mice cells. The fact that acrylamide was found in foods that humans have been eating for thousands of years suggested it couldn't be much of a risk.

Never mind. The World Health Organization (WHO) and the United Nation's Food and Agriculture Organization (FAO) both issued grave warnings. The Swedish officials claimed, but did not substantiate, that several hundred Swedes died yearly from acrylamide.

When the Food and Drug Administration (FDA) in the United States did its own research, anomalies emerged. Even in the same foods, acrylamide levels varied, and on the whole the levels were too low to be called a threat to humans. But it was too late. The American media had adopted Healthism as a civic duty, and now editorials even in serious newspapers declared that here was further proof fried food was bad for you. Note how the media wasn't bothered by people eating plastic or glue.

Back in 1972, though, the egg alarm was taken with deadly seriousness. Nobody questioned the science, and egg sales started to tumble. The producers were panic-stricken. They weren't scientists, after all. To farm eggs was considered an entitlement in the United States, and so easy besides. Eggs were a wonderful democratic industry that was now in jeopardy. They pulled themselves together and launched a counteroffensive. The producers formed the first of their lobby groups, called the National Commission on Egg Nutrition (NCEN, not to be confused with the current Egg Nutrition Center), and hired their own scientists to challenge the studies on which the American Heart Association conclusions were based. The studies don't sound too convincing today, but then scientific studies often don't once they are brought into the open air. Usually, experiments consist of some animal being stuffed with a huge amount of the offending food, far more than a human being could eat in not just one lifetime but two; then, when the animal invariably dies, the food is condemned.

So it was with the cholesterol experiments. Rabbits were fed large amounts of cholesterol and their cholesterol levels shot up, which appeared to confirm the impact of dietary cholesterol. But a simple fact was overlooked: a rabbit is a vegetarian and, unlike the meat-eating human, has no way of processing cholesterol. Another study correlated populations with high heart attack rates with high cholesterol intake. As Dr. McNamara explained to me: "If you take the data and analyze it as you would today, you have to correct for the fact that those populations [notably in North America and Britain] eat a lot of saturated fat." But in those days, before the saturated fat in red meat and dairy products was identified as a villain, no effort was made to compare Britain and North America with Spain, France, Japan, Mexico— countries where people eat a lot of eggs but not a lot of saturated fat.

The National Commission on Egg Nutrition defended the egg with advertisements proclaiming its essential safety. The American Heart Association promptly accused the commission of spreading lies. The egg lobby then took the American Heart Association to court in 1975. The judge called the commission's advertisements false, misleading, deceptive, and unfair. The egg lobby countered by claiming that cholesterol was essential to life (which it is), but then they went too far. They said, so was dietary cholesterol. This isn't true. The body makes 80 percent of the cholesterol it needs; if you don't eat any food that is processed into cholesterol, your body will automatically manufacture the rest. The judge seized on the mistake and ridiculed the entire claim. How dare the egg producers challenge such systematic, consistent, and congruent science?

Over the next twenty-five years, as more and more facts about the nature of cholesterol and the way it occurs in the human body emerged, no study showed any connection between dietary cholesterol and heart disease. But the damage was done. The American diet was changed forever.

First to go was the breakfast of champions. Fried eggs with ham or bacon or sausages and hash browns, a couple of slices of butter-drenched toast on the side, was a great beginning to the day. To paraphrase Somerset Maugham, there were those who said, "If you wish to eat well in America, eat breakfast three times a day." Maugham was actually referring to the great English breakfast—a huge buffet that ranged from eggs to fish and was generally considered the best meal of the day. In her *Kitchen Essays*, published in 1922, Agnes Jekyll described an "old familiar" breakfast as follows: porridge, eggs, bacon, fish (fresh and salted), kedgeree (dry or moist, curried or diversified with smoked haddock, sardines, or minced anchovy), omelettes (plain or enfolding kidneys, mushrooms, tomatoes, or other savory fillings) . . . Devonshire cream or potted shrimps . . . American cereals, such as Post-Toasties, honey grains, Puffed Wheat or Puffed Rice, with or without cream and fruits, fresh in summer, cooked in winter . . . "Bacon with cubes of yesterday's potatoes tossed in bacon fat and try bananas skinned and halved across, and again lengthwise, and served frizzling from a buttered sauté pan on fried toast, with perhaps a dash of orange juice added, an excellent and wholesome food for the young." Now that's a breakfast!

Just as the egg began its nosedive, Julia Child's revival of Escoffier started to dominate food in America (and in Britain, too, for that matter). Once again, Escoffier's miraculous egg was celebrated as a chameleon that can be so many things. How suited to a nation on the run. Egg Mayonnaise—the egg hard-boiled and halved, the two halves laid downward on shredded lettuce and shrouded in homemade mayonnaise—was an excellent lunch made in less than ten minutes. "You don't really need a recipe," wrote Julia reassuringly in *Mastering the Art of French Cooking* (1961), but she gave one anyway because what might seem natural in France was still not natural in the United States.

But even though Julia devoted a couple of her popular TV programs to egg dishes, egg sales kept dropping. Try as she might, Julia could not save the egg, and so *Oeufs à la bourguignonne, Oeufs en croustade à la Béarnaise, Oeufs gêlée, Oeufs miroir* or shirred eggs, and all their kith and kin—not to mention the homely boiled egg, one of which was said to be better for you than an apple—began to slip away.

Escoffier's beloved scrambled eggs went over the side as well. You can't scramble a single egg, as the scientist Edouard de Pomiane pertinently noted in *French Cooking in Ten Minutes*, and two eggs would kill you. The only place you could be sure of finding an egg was in a defiant greasy spoon, because more and more people turned in fear to bran and yogurt.

No matter the resounding lack of proof linking the egg to heart trouble, or that food scientists increasingly focused more on saturated fat as the villain. The influential mass media remained eggphobic.

During their time in the wilderness, the egg producers never stopped trying to save the egg, and their industry. In an effort to woo customers, producers bent over backwards to reassure them that an egg could be safe. If consumers were worried about the cholesterol in the yolks, then producers would make waxed packs of egg whites, which have no cholesterol in them at all, then add cholesterol-free vegetable oil coloring and flavoring to simulate the yolk. "Not like eggs," says the voice-over in the television advertisement as a hand cracks a waxed pack against the rim of a frying pan. This mixture is pasteurized, which means that were there any egg taste to begin with, it has been erased, replaced by a faintly scorched taste. Supermarkets sold pasteurized and packaged egg whites for those who feared the color yellow. Hens were hustled into faster production, which reduced cholesterol in eggs. Today, the cholesterol level in American eggs has dropped from 275 milligrams to the low 200s, while Canadian eggs come in at a virtuous 195 milligrams. This is of course utterly meaningless.

All this time, the Egg Nutrition Center, desperate to clear the egg, could not persuade reputable investigators to conduct a specific study of the science. According to Dr. McNamara, "We were turned down by all of them because of the stigma of industry-funded research." So much for scientists' interest in the consumer.

The egg industry could not even begin to investigate the issue because any findings would be considered suspect. "How does one (a) prove yourself not guilty when (b) you cannot even carry out the studies?" asked Dr. McNamara in frustration.

Fortunately for the egg industry and for egg eaters, the Harvard School of Public Health, which had originally turned down the study, undertook to do one anyway, and the National Institutes of Health volunteered to pick up the tab. The study, called the Hu-Willett Study, gave the egg a clean bill of health, and since 1999, the officials at the American Heart Association have with great reluctance permitted egg eating. At first, they prescribed four eggs a week to be on the safe side. Now, with great trepidation and several qualifications, they have approved an egg a day, holding their breath while they wait for the sound of falling bodies.

Why was there no refutation of the original, damaging claims made about the egg? I asked Dr. McNamara. Why no public pulling of hair, tearing of clothes, and cries of *mea culpa*? After all, a great natural food had been all but destroyed by what now seemed to be the scientists' whim. Why, in a word, no accountability? Because, Dr. McNamara patiently explained, "old theories only die when their proponents do."

Humpty Dumpty
Can't Get Up

The egg producers had just got their heads above water when they were struck by another menace: *Salmonella enterides*, a pathogenic strain of the bacteria. *Salmonella E* produces a mild form of typhoid fever in humans, and most people don't notice it; but in susceptible people, it may be, and very occasionally has been, fatal. Before Healthism, people would have simply sniffed and gone on eating. Instead, after *Salmonella E* was first discovered in eggs in Europe and then in the United States in the 1980s, a major threat to life was perceived. One death is all it takes in a society scared witless about food safety to condemn a food. The idea that out there was a chicken Typhoid Mary laying infected eggs was bad enough; but the fact that nobody knew how *Salmonella E* got into the egg caused consternation.

An egg is a little fortress. Nature has provided it with a natural barrier, an inner skin that stalls any bacteria that may slip through the porous shell. You don't have to be a hen-hugger to suspect that nature was biting back with *Salmonella E*. Industrialized humans crammed together in slums with bad sanitation were prey to many diseases of close proximity, notably typhoid fever. Why shouldn't it be the same for hens? In Canada, where the industrial flocks are smaller, *Salmonella E* is practically nonexistent. The circumstances of an industrial hen's life seem guaranteed to weaken her. The hens are confined to battery cages crammed with other birds, deprived of fresh air, and forced to lay far too many eggs. Most of the calcium they need goes into the shells of the eggs, and so they develop osteoporosis. No wonder hens often break a leg. And the smell! Anyone who has had the misfortune to visit an egg factory wishes they'd taken along a gas mask. The hens themselves are made ill by the smell of their own excrement.

But the egg industry was less interested in finding the root cause of *Salmonella E* than in stopping it. In Europe, the hens were vaccinated. In North America, everything that could be cleansed was cleansed again, and warning bulletins about egg handling were broadcast widely. *Salmonella E* hasn't disappeared, but it has declined. According to the American Egg Board (AEB), the chance of anyone getting infected by an egg in America is about 1 in 20,000, and then if you're healthy, you probably won't get sick at all.

Even so, an industrial solution has to be found. In some parts of the United States, shell eggs are already being pasteurized. A computerized conveyor belt passes the eggs through successive baths of water, heated from 144°F to 162°F in order to destroy any pathogens. Pasteurization, of course, also wipes out any egg taste. The American Egg Board encourages the use of these eggs, even if they don't quite look right. The board advises: "The heating process may create cloudiness in the whites and increase the beating time for foam formation. When you separate pasteurized shell eggs for beating, allow up to about four times as much time for the full foam formation to occur, as you would in the whites of regular eggs."

The final solution is the irradiated egg. Irradiating eggs, or any food for that matter, is similar to radiation therapy. It is not likely to be good for an egg any more than a gamma ray is good for a human. But gamma rays, electrons, or X-rays that are beamed through the eggs will knock out all pathogens. The Food and Drug Administration admits that eggs lose 24 percent of their vitamin A when exposed to just one third of the approved level of radiation. The yolks of an irradiated egg are watery and dim, and the egg itself is no longer the cook's little helper. The irradiated egg is more difficult to cook, requires more time to whip, and yields angelfood cakes with half the volume.

Should you wish to order one of the old-fashioned natural eggs sunnyside up or over easy at your favorite diner—well, you may not be able to. In 2000, the U.S. Food and Drug Administration decreed that egg cartons must carry the warning that eggs should be cooked solid. An egg is only safe when cooked to 161°F. So over the side goes Caesar Salad and mayonnaise, just when the all-clear was sounded on eggs and cholesterol. Gone too is Thames Mud, Ulisse's classic chocolate mousse, made only from melted chocolate and raw eggs, and of course Carême's soufflés. I doubt whether a hot soufflé reaches more than 161°F in the middle, which must be creamy. Meringues are axed as well—egg whites and sugar, a dash of vanilla, baked overnight in a 100°F oven. The last straw was the FDA announcement that the venerable practice of the child licking the bowl and beaters used to make cake batter with raw eggs is a no-no. One of the most powerful and evocative memories of childhood has been obliterated, and a link to the past broken. Better safe than sorry, said the FDA spokesperson piously.

I stop right there. The future industrial egg is not going to be an egg at all. Those rows and rows of eggs in plastic packages in the supermarket are Andy Warhol eggs, clever facsimiles of the real thing. In the future, I see the end of the shell egg altogether; eggs will be shelled and repacked, six or twelve to a rectangular transparent plastic box. A whole variety of eggs will be packaged this way. We can have square hard-boiled eggs for instant picnics (if picnics have not been banned by the Food Police), and square scrambled eggs ready for nuking. One day not so far off, the properties of the egg will be synthesized in the lab and the real thing done away with altogether, along with the tiresome hens that lay them. So much cleaner and quicker.

But maybe not. The *Salmonella E* scare did something that the cholesterol scare had failed to do. For years, the Animal Rights movement had protested the cruel treatment of industrial hens, but the sight of grown men and women dressed as oversized Rock Island Reds accosting egg industry executives never moved the public. The idea of toxic eggs did. By the end of the nineties, public pressure forced the European Union to draw up a hen's bill of rights, including phasing out the ubiquitous battery cages. The great breakthrough came in 2000, when McDonald's, the global fast food giant, went further and declared that it would no longer buy chickens that hadn't been raised humanely. The cruel battery cages must be phased out in short order, and false molting (the practice of starving chickens to force them to come back to laying faster) and debeaking discontinued. Since McDonald's buys 1.5 billion eggs a year, the suppliers agreed. McDonald's followed this up with a ban on any hens being fed antibiotics—a common industrial practice to make the birds grow faster.

The American egg industry was rocked by the McDonald's announcement. If such stringent guidelines were adopted by the industry, mass egg production would cease. But consumers were now aroused, and supermarkets and fast food chains bowed to pressure and came up with their own voluntary guidelines. In 2002, the United Egg Producers followed suit with less stringent standards for hen welfare, which were also voluntary.

This turnaround in hens' fortunes was boosted by the growing organic movement. The industrial chicken was a limping disaster, and it cut a pathetic figure beside the hens raised on small farms and fed food uncontaminated by pesticides and antibiotics. As enthusiasm for organic food grew in the 1990s, so did the market for farm eggs, sold locally and over the Internet, which has become the gourmet's mail-order market.

Moreover, the farmers are proving canny marketers

themselves. They now market new categories of eggs designed to appeal even more to healthists—vegetarian eggs laid by hens on strict vegetarian diets; Omega-3 eggs laid by hens fed flaxseed. Omega-3 is a death defier of a fatty acid, fending off thrombosis and cancer, among other killers. The latest super-egg in America is "Cage Free," the hen-hugger's darling. Cage Free hens stroll free, and their beaks are clipped, a process farmers insist is no more painful than a human person clipping her toenails. And the supermarkets are taking notice, so that more and more designer eggs, from the big egg producers, get space on the shelves.

There's just one niggling problem. "Organic" eggs are hot sellers because a growing number of people believe that organic is the healthiest of all seals of approval. But is it? A U.S. Department of Agriculture (USDA) certified organic egg has been laid by a hen raised on blameless organic food. Wait a minute. The hen is also guaranteed to have been allowed outdoors to take a dustbath. But the outdoors is where the hen is most likely to pick up *Salmonella E*, according to the same USDA . . .

Then there's the environmental objection. It's one thing to have a flock of a hundred or so hens pecking around a yard, and quite another to loose a vast commercial flock outdoors. The battery system handles one aspect very well: it removes excrement efficiently and uses it in cattle feed and garden fertilizer. But if a hundred thousand hens lived outside, in a constrained space, the excrement would be overwhelming, sinking into the earth and poisoning the groundwater.

The Egg Comes Home

Recently back in France, counting the number of microwaves in the bars and avoiding the superhighway cafés, I found myself wondering how the French egg was faring. I interviewed a farmer for a story about foie gras: how ducks had taken over from geese—and while duck liver is good, it is not as good as goose liver, which glistens obscenely. Not only are ducks nicer than geese, but they are cheaper to feed. And they are greedier than geese, he said, which means they don't need so much force-feeding, an important point in the age of animal activism. Then we got onto the subject of chickens, and the farmer said, what will the Anglo-Saxons (he meant both American and British, and he practically spat out the words) protest next? Eggs, he suspected. And where then would fine cooking be?

I had a chance to find out a couple of days later when my sister met me in the Languedoc, as undisturbed a countryside as may be found, just the place to test natural food. We discovered a little village all by itself in the middle of nowhere, that seemed not to have changed in a hundred years. Until, that is, we got closer and found several bed and breakfasts, a farmers' market, a wine cooperative, and a loudspeaker that summoned the children to school in the morning.

One tradition, however, had remained. Madame shook her head regretfully when we mentioned food. It is Monday, she said, and the only restaurant is of course closed; her tone suggested we should have known about the French Monday closings before traveling at all. She and her husband, who stepped in from the garden, his hands maroon up to the elbows because he had been crushing grapes, were eating something cold—a statement that sent a chill down my spine, believing as I did that, in France, a hot meal was always on the table. But then she brightened slightly. There was this butcher's shop in the next village, and it might be open. She indicated by shaking her head, or rather, by trying to shake her head because her neck was supported by a neck brace—and here she went into a long explanation about a streak of pain traveling like lightning from the top of her brain to her toes that could only be mitigated by the brace— that the butcher's shop had unconventional ways.

So off we went, my sister and I, through dark, wandering country roads to another village, perched perpendicularly on a hill. Having taken the ninety-degree angle at full speed to get to the top, we found the butcher's shop closed. The whole village appeared closed. Then, as the car slid down the cobbles of a badly lit cliff face, we saw the sign. It hung above us, bathed in a yellow light.

A restaurant, on the second floor of a building that inclined along with the hill. It didn't seem very promising until we opened the door and the smell of meat grilling or roasting embraced us. The room was large, yellow, warm in temperature and in spirit. A small, red-faced woman with a bun bustled up, brandishing a handwritten menu even as she seated us. "*Désolée,*" she said briefly, and our hearts sank.

But she was referring only to the fact that the fresh-killed rabbit was finished for the night. She could cook us an omelette. If my heart didn't rise immediately, it was simply because omelettes are now seen mostly in coffee shops in North America, where they appear as baked slabs of egg. It is little better in London, I learned from a friend who had ordered one in what he thought was a good place, only to be told that the omelettes hadn't come in yet!

There was no alternative, and anyway I had wanted to eat eggs, and after Madame set down a bottle of the local red and brought a basket of fresh bread, my trust in French gastronomy revived, and an omelette began to seem a fine thing.

It was eggs, after all. There would be frites with the omelette, she said, and a salad. And for dessert, her own chestnut mousse, made from eggs and chestnut flour, because Languedoc relies on chestnuts for its flour the way other places rely on wheat. She rapped out the information with a reassuring authority. It might be late, but no one could do without food. We looked around at the dozen or so tables; several patrons were wiping up some delicious gravy from their plates, the rabbit no doubt. The air was heavy with satisfaction.

The omelettes arrived *baveuse*, just as they were ordered, the insides creamy, the outside quite smooth and lightly tanned. The frites were sizzling; the salad leaves wilted away in a light vinaigrette. Soon the combination of food and wine worked its magic and the room, the little village, the

Languedoc itself, and French tradition were bathed in a rosy glow. How simple it is to make a good omelette. You place a pat of butter in a solid pan heating on a stove, beat a couple of eggs, toss them into the sizzling butter, swirl them around, and then before they are set, you nudge them into a rolled-up pancake: and there you have it, perfection in ten minutes. Probably less. The next day, I had a local egg for breakfast, although Madame was rather bored when I asked where it had come from. She gestured vaguely down the street.

The egg had a pale yolk. I used to be so ignorant about eggs. I loved a gamboge yolk, but then I learned that industrial egg yolks were colored by a chemical now thought to be carcinogenic. The color of the yolk should reflect a hen's diet. The hen that laid this amber yolk must have been eating fall daisies. The egg white was firm, not watery, confirming that the egg was fresh. As I looked at the egg on my plate, I reflected on its turbulent history.

Like the gold in *The Ring of the Nibelungs*, eggs are a metaphor for human hubris. At first, people regarded the egg humbly as a gift from the hen. Then it was exploited to create the greatest cuisine in the world. Next, it was exploited to feed the growing masses of hungry people. Then subjugated to an industry's demands for profits. But just when the egg industry seemed on top of the world, it was brought low by a false charge and then tainted by disease. I can almost hear the final bars of *Götterdämmerung* as the waters close over Valhalla, that monument to the gods' greed and folly, and the gold returns to the depths of the Rhine, its home.

I dig into the egg. It tastes fresh—earthy. This is the way an egg retrieved from a Roman chicken must have tasted. The egg is home.

. . . .

CHAPTER TWO

THE LAST BRIE

When we lived in Shillingford after World War II, we hardly ever ate cheese, even though we lived in a hamlet dominated by a mixed farm, one with both cows and crops. But the milk got no further than cream and butter. We bought cheese from the Co-op, an early supermarket, in the nearby market town of Wallingford, and there was only one cheese on sale. It was called National Cheese and it looked like the clippings cut from yellow toenails. It was hard and scaly and melted only with tremendous reluctance into a cauliflower cheese. Its nickname was "mousetrap," but even the mice turned up their noses at it.

Once, the British Isles had boasted a range of farmhouse cheeses, real Cheddar (as opposed to international Cheddar, as the name of Britain's greatest cheese is now applied to many products made all over the world), Cheshire, Double Gloucester, Shropshire Blue and Green Fade, Lancashire, the Welsh Caerphilly made especially for miners' lunches, a Gloucester curiosity, Stinking Bishop, and the great Stilton.

But the twentieth century would be hard on them. First came the inevitable industrialization, specifically the railway, the single greatest destroyer of local delicacies and their unique taste. The farmer could earn more money by distributing his milk than by using it to make cheese. Farmhouse cheesemaking further declined when it became clear that it was more economic to make cheese in factories, and also often cheaper to import it. Artisanal cheesemaking slumped during the Great War; it never really picked up afterwards. During the Depression, the government set up milk-marketing boards throughout Britain as a way to revive cheesemaking. The boards bought milk from the farmers and sold it back to them at a reduced price if they planned to make butter and cheese. Even so, when war broke out in 1939, handmade cheeses made up only a quarter of British cheese, and the war put a stop to them.

Now there was a new Ministry of Food, and it decided that all milk would be pooled so factories could produce a single cheese: National Cheese.

Harrods

In the 1950s we left Shillingford and moved to London, and my mother found an apartment above Harrods, the famous department store. She always maintained it was the central heating, so rare in London, that had done the deal for her—and only later did she realize she may have had an ulterior motive because Harrods had the best food department in London.

Harrods' appearance, an intimidating chunk of Victorian purple Gothic, gave no hint of something so licentious, so sensual as the Food Hall—a large, tiled, high-ceilinged space smelling sweet and sour and earthy. The staff didn't give away the shop's greatest treasure, either; they maintained a grave formality. Harrods had digested the war without a hiccup and restored its prewar style, in which every customer was treated like royalty—and considering the number of Royal Warrants, quite a number must have been. The doors were manned by ex-Guardsmen, each well over six feet in height, who wore green uniforms and caps, and could summon a taxi with a snap of the fingers, and opened doors with smiling alacrity. The doormen were so charming in fact that one day my mother, who was often absent-minded, smiled as one opened the door for her and said, "Goodnight, darling." He took it as his due. That was the kind of assurance Harrods had. It was imperturbable, conveying the assurance of Empire, even if the Empire had gone.

A story, apocryphal but illustrative, has a new widow, distraught, approaching one of the poker-faced floorwalkers, who was dressed as usual in a morning coat.

"Where can I find a black dress?"

"Please accept our condolences, Madam. You will find mourning weeds on the second floor. May I ask is your bereavement recent and if so, may we help with the burial or, er . . . ?" Cremation, heavily endorsed by my grandparents, was as yet not generally accepted.

At Harrods you could buy an elephant, store your household belongings, have your cigars ripened, make travel arrangements, have the family silver mended or stamped with a new crest. It was Harrods' boast, although it was never said aloud but simply breathed in the right ears, that it could do anything for its customers. The Nizam of Hyderabad, the richest man in the world, was said to have his emeralds, the size of tigers' eyes, cleaned at Harrods.

Harrods' atmosphere was more country than city, and on Saturday mornings when the neighborhood, genteel South Kensington, came in to shop, it was like a country market where neighbors met. Everyone who shopped regularly at Harrods knew who the owner was. His name was Sir Richard Burbidge: he had inherited Harrods from his father. Sir Richard had a pleasant round face and a mustache, and he could be seen walking briskly through the store wearing a black jacket, striped trousers, and a bowler hat. He was usually smiling—a smile that said all was well with Harrods and therefore with the country.

Right in the middle of the ground floor was the Bank. The Bank had a couple of counters with little grilles in front of them where customers could cash checks or get counterchecks if they didn't have an account and had to pay cash. This was rare. Upper-class England still lived "on tick," although my mother said tradesmen were getting more and more reluctant to let bills linger on the way they had before the war, when credit was infinite.

The Bank was also a meeting place for customers, particularly those who came up from the country to shop for the day. There, on the fat leather sofas of faded bisque, they could put down their parcels and rest under the benign gaze of three generations of Burbidges, all looking like Sir Richard and each commemorated in an oil painting. Customers were generic, too: they looked like retired colonels or Agatha Christie, weathered, gray-haired, and secure. Conversation never rose above a muted hum.

If you were a teenager, you almost tiptoed through the Bank. Harrods did not recognize the existence of teenagers, an American word that had not yet been accepted by the store. Harrods barely recognized the existence of women, as anyone who ever saw Harrods' idea of women's clothes knew.

Of course Harrods wanted, no, *needed* its customers; but it wanted only serious customers, who were prepared to pay full price. My mother wistfully recalled the bargains to be found in the basements of New York department stores, but the idea of sales was anathema to Harrods. Its prime customers were those drawn to Harrods by the superior and unique qualities of its stock, which couldn't be bought anywhere else. The respected Harrods customer was not an impulse shopper, anxious to throw her money about. When she bought something, it was for keeps, and must therefore be of enduring quality. The purchase must be necessary, as it

was necessary to buy uniforms, and boys' cricket gear, thick
creamy stationery suitably engraved, and wine, of course.

Harrods respected thriftiness as well. Clothes had been
rationed for so long—even buttons were rationed—that
people had become used to recycling old clothes. The Haberdashery Department stocked incredibly useful things from
buttons to silks and reels of cotton, along with absolutely
everything essential to keeping up appearances because it
was unheard of to throw anything away. Something dam-
aged or frayed could always be mended or restored. Our
Nanny sniffed at the quality of the postwar clothes, finger-
ing with distaste the inferior materials. She made all my
clothes until I was seven. I remember her making me a coat
of emerald Harris tweed, "prewar quality," she said lovingly
as she ran her hands over it. Toys should not be bought, but
made. She recycled old stockings and pipe cleaners into little
pucks with painted faces and limbs easy to twist round the
arms and legs of chairs, knitted an assortment of animals
from leftover wool, and ran up Teddy bears from remnants
with buttons taken from my father's old uniforms.

But the store became unbuttoned the moment you sniffed
the Food Hall. There was no way to prevent whiffs of food
seeping out into the Haberdashery Department or Stationery. As you drew closer, you could hear a buzz, the
atmosphere lightening as you entered. People's voices were
definitely louder: if excitement is too strong a word, anticipation isn't. Customers looked far more alert than they
looked in Haberdashery, and considerably more cheerful.

Here, it was difficult not to impulse-shop, and the salesmen encouraged it. When you saw the raw food, it was impossible to believe British cooking could be bad. Mounds of feathered game filled marbled counters and haunches of Scottish beef were suspended on hooks. Whole lambs adorned a wall in the spring. Grouse was rushed in from the Scottish moors on the glorious twelfth (of August), the first day of the grouse-shooting season. There was a beautifully designed display of the freshest North Sea fish, caught daily: scarlet prawns, double-eyed flatfish, and the smallest of whitebait (a minnow that seems to grow unpleasantly larger each time I eat it today). From the rivers came vast salmon, which in those days nobody doubted were wild. In May, the blotchy gulls' eggs sat in baskets on the counter. Gulls' eggs, now a luxury—no one wants to climb the cliffs to collect them—were once a common snack. They had translucent whites with a blueish tint and pink yolks, and they were always eaten with Chinese salt (roasted and ground Szechuan pepper). Gulls' eggs were so popular they rated a mention in bestsellers (the seal of fashion) such as *The Forsyte Saga*, in which Val Dartie tells his mother to leave out some gulls' eggs for him when he knows he'll be out late, "Because they are so great to top up with."

The food didn't stop there. Potted shrimps in little round blue tubs; whole Scottish smoked salmon ready to be pared into translucent slices; smoked trout and smoked eel, sharing space with all hues of caviar. Harrods sold the very best sausages, their own skinny little pork sausages. The Food

Hall attracted a much more racy crowd than the rest of the store, theater people and American movie stars. The theater people came in costume: the men wore tweed caps and hacking jackets so they could blend in with the Army greatcoats then so fashionable in Kensington; the women wore sheepskin-lined jackets and headscarves to hide their fake diamonds. Once I saw heads turning and heard the name "Ava Gardner" whispered, but when I looked, I wouldn't have recognized her. Her face was a deep putty color.

I might also have seen Elizabeth David had I known then what she looked like, for she must have been there often enough, as the food guru to the eating classes and a consultant for the French butcher's counter, such extravagance, where dainty racks of lamb were displayed alongside mounds of tripe. I knew who she was because her *Book of Mediterranean Food*—a slim pink-and-brown clothbound volume, with a jolly cover sketch of fishing boats in a Mediterranean harbor—was a favorite with my parents.

At first, my father would have nothing to do with it because he hated the publisher, but then as my mother started reading to him from it, he relented. How seductive it was. Right there in the introduction, Elizabeth David broke the garlic taboo, quoting her favorite chef, Marcel Boulestin, whose eponymous restaurant was in London. "It is not really an exaggeration to say that peace and happiness begin, geographically, where garlic is used in cooking." Inspired, my parents were soon exchanging memories of their little vine-covered villa in Provence, exclaiming with delight over the recipes—stuffed mussels, little black olives, ratatouille, anchovy pizza. It really didn't matter that when *A Book of Mediterranean Food* came out in 1950, very few of the ingredients were available in Britain.

Olive oil was not sold in large bottles in a grocery store, for example, but in tiny bottles from Boots, the pharmacy. "I wonder what they imagine one does with it?" said my father. But the fact that you couldn't buy olive oil easily, if at all, only made Elizabeth David's book more alluring. It was nostalgic to those who had once eaten well, erotic, like Charles Ryder's dinner in Paris in *Brideshead Revisited*. Evelyn Waugh's description of the food made the deprived eater lust for blinis dripping with globules of butter, sour and frothy sorrel soup, the sound of duck juices being pressed from the carcass.

The Elizabeth David Meal

For Elizabeth David to patronize the Harrods Food Hall underlined its status as a temple of gourmandise. David had no time for the conventional people who shopped at Harrods. She had rebelled against upper-class conformity. She spent the war knocking about in the Middle East, picking up work where she could and marveling at the food. When she returned to England, she couldn't believe how bad the food was. The meals in her hotel were produced, she wrote (in an article for the *Spectator*), "with a kind of bleak triumph which amounted almost to a hatred of humanity and humanity's needs." She got it absolutely right. Rationing brought out the sadist in the English. At the first school I went to, inedible food was served as if children should be punished for being hungry. To this day, I cannot eat stew—even a fragrant *estouffade*—for fear I shall sink my teeth into a piece of gristle, the most revolting mouthfeel of all and a staple of school stew.

David's disgust at English food spurred her to publish the recipes she'd jotted down in the Mediterranean. *A Book of Mediterranean Food* exhorted readers to change their perception of good food. Her message was terse: get rid of the Escoffier food, which nobody could cook any more, and concentrate on the integrity of the ingredients. There was nothing puritanical about David—something worth remembering now that Healthism has endorsed Mediterranean food as ideal nutrition for the would-be immortal. A Dionysiac strain and an enticing sensuality runs through her book. If Escoffier food was white tie and tails, Mediterranean food was a bathing suit and sandals. Gone was the empty ritual of the four- or five-course dinner. You could, David urged in her delicately scolding way, make a delicious meal from sundried olives, sardines—and she named the best canned ones (no one would surpass David's advice about sources until Martha Stewart came along in the eighties), cheese of course, a sliver of cured ham, a glass of wine, and what's wrong with bread—good bread—and butter, unsalted, and honey as dessert?

I remember going off on a Provence adventure with a couple of friends in the early 1960s. We took the overnight car-train from the ferry to Avignon. When we left, the Normandy sky had been stormy. The next morning, the shades in the compartment slid up to reveal the hard blue of a southern sky with the sun already burning up the horizon. We started to drive south in the gathering heat and grew sleepy. The countryside looked so seductive, so foreign, the olive trees casting twisted shadows on the dried earth, that we had to stop. In a little village near Orange, we brought some local cheese, semi-hard, I seem to remember, a couple of baguettes smelling like cotton handkerchiefs, tiny wrinkled black olives, anchovies fished from a barrel, small, intense tomatoes. We picnicked in a field, with a bottle of local red—rough, and it came with no cork but a tin cap—and we laughed and laughed as we lay back in the hot sun and smelled silage and fresh hay, and cried, "This is an Elizabeth David meal!" None of us ever planned to cook again.

The Harrods cheese counter was catnip to my mother, who agreed with David that a good cheese made a meal. For years, she had suffered in the country where only the yellow toenail cheese, National Cheese, was available, so the sight of piles of real cheeses restored her faith in food. She soon made a good friend of the salesman who presided over the counter. He was a tall, spectral figure whom we nicknamed "Giacometti"; he knew to the moment the state of every cheese in his care.

Harrods may not have stocked as many cheeses as we see

today, but the cheeses Giacometti sold were far better than any in today's cheese shops. For one thing, with few exceptions, they were made of raw milk. Unlike the pasteurized cheese that dominates counters today, raw milk cheese is a living organism. Its taste is fiery in the mouth—alive with many flavors. In the 1950s, many of the raw milk cheeses were still made by farmers, and and their cheese reflected not only the qualities of an individual farm but—the *terroir*.

Terroir is centuries-old earth. I don't think anyone has better described just how the *terroir* affects the taste of a cheese than Patrick Rance, the cheesemonger who, almost single-handedly, encouraged the revival of British farmhouse cheeses in the 1970s. In his *Great British Cheese Book* (1982), he wrote of the unmistakable character of Cheshire cheese, attributed to the soil's mixture of clay and lime that came from local saltbeds and could never be replicated elsewhere, even if an exiled cheesemaker had taken the topsoil with him.

Once, thousands of local cheeses, some with no names, spread like a crazy quilt over Europe, their taste determined by *terroir*, as well as by the time of year a cheese was made, the food the cow ate, the breed of the cow, and last but not least, how long the cheeses were ripened.

Each breed of cow metabolized food differently and the result was reflected in the milk's qualities. It is the milk, with its large globules of fat, and a protein-to-fat ratio favoring fat, that produces the creamiest, tastiest cheese. A clear example of how different breeds produce different tastes can be seen in Swiss Gruyère and its French sister, Comte. Both cheeses come from the same *terroir*, and the cows that produce the milk for them eat the same plants; but they taste subtly different because it is the milk of the Swiss Brown that is used for Gruyère, while the marginally sweeter Comte is made from the milk of the spotted Montbéliards.

When the cheese is made—the time of year—is significant as well. Comte made from the milk of cows summering in the Alpine mountains is tastier than a cheese made from cows browsing the lowlands. Cheesemaking is full of such distinctions. Salers, for example, which has been made for more than two thousand years in the Auvergne, is a name-controlled cheese, the *Appellation d'Origine Controlée (AOC)* having set down guidelines for its production. Salers can be made only between May 1 and October 30, the period when the red Salers cows are grazing in the mountains. In Italy, the *Dominazione di Origine Controllata (DOC)* has similar instructions for the supreme Parmesan from Reggio Emilia, the Parmigiano-Reggiano with the big crystals that pop with flavor in the mouth. It can be made only between April 15 and November 11, when the cattle—producers of a quality milk called Pezzato Rosso—are grazing on fresh grass rather than eating silage.

I am sure that Harrods stocked only the best Parmesan. Giacometti would certainly not have put up with the gray and waxy Parmesan that Elizabeth David, who had gone on to become the scourge of inferior foodstuffs, found so often elsewhere. Parmesan was a brand name that covered, as brand names do today, a multitude of sins. Even now, millions of people all over the world are eating tasteless Parmesan just because it's called Parmesan.

Equally, I'm sure that all the fragrant wheels and discs, squares and ovals on Giacometti's counter were top of the line because no cheesemonger of stature could afford anything less—storekeepers still felt personally accountable to their customers. So the little boxes, the little cheeses that came in nets, like the Scarmorza, an Italian string cheese, and Provolone, a round firm cheese that, once cut, revealed a center of butter, could be bought with confidence, as could the Gruyère, Emmentaler and Parmesan, Comte and Munster, Reblochon and Camembert, and no end of Tommes from the Savoy. I liked best the Tomme de Marc de Raisin— a softer, whiter cheese than most Tommes and coated with a crunchy layer of grape seeds. Pont L'Evêque was pleasant enough, but nowhere near a Camembert, which had a tingling subtaste. Port Salut, a spongy cheese with holes, and Petits Suisses, little rounds of cream cheese, six to a box, gritty in texture and smelling like a dairy, delicious with black cherry jam. Petits Suisses are no more; they have been pasteurized and their delicacy destroyed. I can't remember that we ever had Epoisses, Napoleon's favorite cheese. Production of Epoisses had stopped during the war, and the cheese took time reappearing.

My mother asked Giacometti about Spanish cheese, but of course there was none. Spain, under Generalissimo Franco, was closed to the outside world. There was, I'm certain, no goat cheese anywhere. I surely would have noticed the lozenges and bells, the pyramids and buttons, some rolled in ash, that now fill a self-respecting cheese counter. I wonder if there would have been a market for it at that time. Goat cheese tastes barnyardy, mild enough when young, but increasingly so as the cheese ages. Ripened goat cheese is an acquired taste; you'd have to read a lot of Elizabeth David to get used to it. After goat cheese began appearing in shops, a rumor circulated that one must avoid any cheese made from the milk of a goat who had been pursued by a ram—how would you know?—because he may have sprayed her, and then of course the cheese smells and tastes of urine. This was not the kind of cheese the genteel eater of the 1950s wanted to hear about.

My mother felt quite homesick when she spotted a German Limburger. "Is that German cheese?" she asked Giacometti, who immediately produced a small rectangle covered in foil and looking squashed. It smelled raunchy. It was like a Liederkranz, an American cheese derived from Limburger. "American cheese? Are you sure there is such a thing?" asked Alister, my father's business partner, who couldn't believe that America—a country he had never visited but imagined as completely industrialized, filled with stainless steel and aluminum and open-hearth furnaces—had any food so natural as cheese.

Of course there was plenty of cheese in America, but

most of it factory-made. No sooner had European immigrants started to make their native cheeses than demand overwhelmed supply and the only answer was mass production.

The Limburger my family ate was a small rectangle of
soft cow's cheese washed in pungent brine. Once bought, it
had to be eaten at once, or the smell would never leave the
house. The Limburger's aroma was overpowering. "It's
like bringing a skunk into the house!" cried my father. We
ate it fast, on pumpernickel with sliced red onions, which
my mother assured us was the way Liederkranz was eaten
in Yorkville, the old German quarter on Manhattan's
Upper East Side. Giacometti confided eventually, losing his
salesman's impartiality, that he was not a blue cheese lover,
but he understood my mother's taste for Roquefort—"a
great cheese, of course." If Edam and Gouda were there,
we skipped them because we avoided the solid-looking
cheeses.

But the Brie—now there was a cheese. Giacometti had on
hand several Bries—big discs, three inches thick, with crusts
crisscrossed with caramel thatching. I only remember eating
Brie de Meaux, the champion Brie, although Brie de Melun,
the other major name in Brie, must have been stocked as
well. The Brie was made from raw milk and therefore alive;
once cut, it died and stopped ripening. There was no question of Giacometti producing an unripe Brie or a Brie that
had been cut too early. An unripe Brie is chalkily tasteless. A
cheesemonger in those days could assess the ripeness precisely, and because people differed on how they liked their

Brie, Giacometti would have several at different stages of ripeness. A Brie at stage three ripeness looked ready to break out of its toasty crust. The Brie with "eyes," little holes, was not quite as ripe, rather spongy in consistency. But the connoisseur's favorite was the Brie with "soul," a thin chalk line through the middle, the dry chalk a perfect complement to the sweet acid of the paste. We tried them all, and never could decide which we liked best. Giacometti would carefully cut a large wedge of the chosen type, and wrap it up in thick white waxed paper. I can still hear how the paper crackled as it was wrapped around the cheese. We would take the cheese home and unwrap it "to let it breathe"—why, I'm not sure—and eat it for lunch or dinner that night instead of dessert.

The Vrai *Brie*

I knew nothing then about Brie other than its taste. But a slice of cheese is a sliver of history: now I know that Brie is a dense plait of French culture—church, state, and countryside interwoven. The first Brie makers were the monks in the Ile-de-France, southeast of Paris, and the first ecstatic celebrity eater, the Holy Roman Emperor Charlemagne. In 774, on his way home to Aix-la-Chapelle after defeating the Lombards, the emperor stopped for a snack at the Priory of Reuil-en-Brie. The abbot had nothing to offer him but cheese. Charlemagne took one taste and cried (according to his secretary): "I've just discovered one of the most delicious of all dishes!" He then ordered a regular supply of Bries to be sent to his palace.

After that, royal patronage became the norm, since Brie was so accessible to Paris and the court of Versailles. It never lost its cachet because promotion begets promotion. The Brie de Meaux went to the Congress of Vienna in 1815, where state affairs competed with gastronomy for the delegates' attention, a strategy worked out by the French Machiavelli, Talleyrand. To represent France, Talleyrand took along the Brie de Meaux, discs and discs of it, and the King of Cheeses was acclaimed the best cheese just as France regained its great power status.

Amazing to say, the Brie—unlike so much food—actually lived up to the hype, although it is a little hard to believe that the Bries carted from the Ile-de-France to Vienna were all wonderful. But perhaps they were, because they were all handmade by cheesemakers who were proud of what they did. Once again, a sharp contrast to the food of today, which is die-stamped for anonymous global consumption. The Brie de Meaux had no trouble remaining supreme because while many villages had their own Bries, none approached the mellifluous paste of the Meaux.

Some say a Camembert, made in Normandy, is really a Brie. A Camembert is a small, round cheese, the consistency of its paste is thicker than that of a Brie, and its size is against it. The original Brie weighed a hefty seven pounds, was three feet in diameter, five inches thick, and had a far greater ratio of paste to crust than the little Camembert. This was a crucial difference in determining the consistency of the cheese, and in the case of the Brie, its complex taste. It is the very expansiveness of the big Brie de Meaux that makes it especially delicious.

Over the years many other Bries have emerged, but few are available in markets today. One of the most famous was made in a pot and ripened underground, but it is long gone. I once saw Brie de Nangis at a country market, but I have never seen a Brie à la Chiffe, which was apparently sold in the markets as recently as twenty years ago. This Brie was black, ripened in a cider wash, and aged for two years—its paste strong and tough and deep brown. Large cheeses like Parmesan and Gruyère have to be made by cooperatives from pooled milk. But a farmhouse Brie was made from the milk of a single farmer's herd, guaranteeing quality and cleanliness. The cows for Brie were two high-fat breeds, the Normande and the Flamande.

Making the cheese was quite straightforward, the steps common to all cheesemaking. Fresh raw milk was allowed to turn sour and rennet was added to coagulate the curds. A curd is quite delicious: for years, country people loved to eat junket, which is simply one large curd formed in a bowl. Before the 1920s, when rennet was synthesized, farmers had to wring the enzyme from the fourth stomach of a calf. They soaked the stomach for two days in order to render the rennet, a very time-consuming process. Cheesemaking became easier once tablets of rennet were available, and so did junket making. I remember eating it for quite a while after

World War II. It had a unique consistency, slippery without being slimy, and an acidic tinge; it was particularly good with a compôte of fruit.

. . . .

JUNKET

Serves 4

4 cups whole milk
6 Tbs white sugar
dash of salt
½ tsp vanilla essence
2 tablets unflavored rennet (available from pharmacies)
2 Tbs cold water

Warm milk in a saucepan, then add sugar, salt, and vanilla, making sure the milk is just warm enough to melt the sugar. Remove from heat. Dissolve rennet tablets in cold water and add to milk. Pour the mixture into glasses or a big bowl and allow to set.

. . . .

The curds for Brie were left uncut to ensure a junketlike suavity, then spooned into molds and left to drain and dry. After that, bacteria took over. Penicillin spores in the dairy's air started to work on the cheese, and as the bacteria began eating their way inward, the Brie developed a crust as white as lint.

Once the crust was formed, the farmer sold the cheese to a ripener, an *affineur*, who lived either in the same village or nearby. The *affineur*, who may be compared to a winemaker, shaped the cheese to his own taste, manipulating the ripening process, moving the Brie among cool, moist rooms so the bacteria could penetrate to the heart of the cheese.

Billions of bacteria work on a Brie, breaking down the curds into paste. The final cheese carried not only the *affineur*'s label but his or her own stamp. I have this mental picture of a circle of villagers eating a Brie Gras, made from the especially rich milk of high summer. "Is this from Madame Klein? I recognized it right away—see the eyes? She always makes her cheese have eyes. I'm sure I can taste the buttercups from old Pèreguay's field . . ."

Harrods didn't advertise the *affineur*'s name—Harrods' name was enough to guarantee quality. Now I suspect that the Bries from Harrods may well have been nonpareil. According to Prosper Montagné, the author of the *Larousse Gastronomique*, Brie was much improved by synthetic rennet for the simple reason that rennet could now be accurately measured. Too much rennet, and a cheese got dry; too little, and the cheese was runny. The curds should just spring back from the touch.

So, the Harrods Brie had been made in a moment of suspended history, the 1950s, before the changes set in motion by World War II accelerated the destruction of traditional ways of making food and eating it. Eventually, Brie would be one of the casualties.

The Passing of Brie

It was my friend Guy who told me how the Brie declined. He was sitting like a Buddhist monk, his shaven head gold in the flickering light of the fire. We were in his cottage in the Ile-de-France. He had his head in his hands as if in infinite contemplation. We had been talking about Brie. "It is all gone," he said. And then, "Let me show you." He stood up, his head almost hitting the ceiling of the little cottage, and took me upstairs to his bedroom. There he threw open a window. Before us lay the ravaged stretch of the Ile-de-France through which I'd driven from Paris, guided by signs for EuroDisney, today's growth industry in the area.

Guy grew up near here, a farmer's son. Yes, his father made some Bries, and he could remember how good they were, how the whole family (all six of them) could eat an entire Brie a night, and that meant seven pounds of cheese. That is why the Bries were so big—they were made for large families. He gestured again. Once, this was all lambent countryside—hedgerows, brooks, streams, the Oise, the Marne, the Seine, all watering rich pastures full of wildflowers, Queen Anne's lace, buttercups and bachelor's buttons and dandelions, and lots of different grasses, all for the delectation of cows. Patrick Rance said at least fifty plants went into the diet of a great milk cow. Guy sniffed at Rance's name: "We prefer our own Pierre Androuet," the famous French cheesemonger.

The cows were the right cows, too, Normandes and Flamandes, with the highest protein-to-fat ratio that would translate into the creamiest paste. It was just too bad that they didn't deliver a lot of milk, but the milk they produced in the high summer months was spectacularly good. And the farms too were filled with working families, the women in fact obliged to sign marriage contracts that committed them to work on the farm and to make cheese, among other things.

But now the hedgerows, housing dozens of species of wildlife, have been uprooted and replaced by monster fields of profitable crops like sugar beet. The fields themselves, Guy said, are poisoned by chemical fertilizers and pesticides. As for the cows! He raised a pair of binoculars and handed them to me. "Look, look!" I saw far away a patch of black-and-white spots. "Holsteins! Cows that are without any quality at all." Of course, he snorted, it was the British—the first industrialists—who cottoned to the Holsteins, a Dutch breed, because they were milk machines. Machines. He allowed that to sink in. The milk they produced ranked low in the protein-to-fat ratio, but that didn't matter because poor milk sold for the same price as good milk. And a good milker like a Holstein produced so much more milk than the Normandes and Flamandes. Today, the Holstein is growing even more productive because she is bred to have an extra large pituitary gland that makes her produce more milk. (In

America, dairy cattle are given growth hormones.) Soon, his arm was describing an arc falling fast, the Brie rendered inferior by cows who grazed on chemically dependent fields, and by fewer and fewer farmers, the family compact having dissolved. Wives were no longer required to sign a marriage contract that committed them to farmwork, while children like him left the farm to make money.

Guy had by this time produced a good stage three wedge of Brie, oozing slightly. He continued his threnody. "This isn't just about the death of a cheese, but about the culture that produced the Brie." He opened a bottle of Gerwurztraminer. "Spicy. Better than a red wine. A Brie is too strong for red wine."

The cheese was good, an artisanal Brie, that is to say, made from the milk of several herds. This is a step down from a farmer's Brie, made from a single herd, where the milk's quality is assured. But the distinction is today academic as there is only one farmhouse Brie de Meaux extant, and it is made in a museum. The Rothschilds have a farm near Meaux, the Domaine de 40 Arpents, where the Brie is brought to perfection and sold over the Internet.

The artisanal Brie is a big step up from factory Brie, the most common kind of Brie now available. Once the farm families stopped making cheese, Brie went into a free fall, its manufacture taken over by factories driven by the demands of supermarkets, which in France, as everywhere, were becoming the most popular way of selling food.

The Brie didn't fit the supermarket template. First of all,

there's the smell. The smell of Brie is one of its defining glories. A Brie smells of the countryside, of decay; it's the smell of wet wool on a sheep, and it tastes that way too, just the way wine tastes of grapes rotted by intense bacteria activity, rich and a little seedy. A philosopher might say that the smell of the Brie contains intimations of mortality. But philosophizing is out of place in a modern urban supermarket, even a French one. The Brie had to be changed to fit meet supermarket demands. No more generous-sized Bries going over the top and smelling up the store.

Does the size of a Brie matter? "Oh yes," Guy replied. "The taste of a smaller Brie is different, there's more rind, for one thing, and the whole ripening process is accelerated, and it's in the arduous ripening that the Brie gains its full complexity." But, he added, it is inevitable. The large farm family is no more, and smaller families cannot eat a large Brie at a single sitting. No Brie should hang around, or— Guy's voice darkened—"be put in the refrigerator." The Brie—any soft cheese—hates extremes of temperature. The refrigerator numbs, even destroys the valuable flavor molecules, which need a steady, cool atmosphere to come to their full glory.

In order to sell, the factory Brie had to be industrialized: it was reduced in size, pasteurized, and the paste often bulked up with cream to stiffen it. "Of course all cheese will be pasteurized," Guy said. "Already most cheese in France is pasteurized. It's inevitable. The Americans have decided on it."

He sniffed as he said the word "Americans." He considers

himself an expert on America, where he worked for several years. Guy's time in America taught him one thing: WASPs don't know anything about food. The day of my visit in 2000, he greeted me with a typical example of WASP philistinism. The Associated Press had reported that the American makers of processed cheese wanted the holes in American Swiss smaller because new slicing machines were tearing up the cheese. But there was a hitch. The U.S. Department of Agriculture (USDA), which sets standards for the characteristics and pricing of popular generic cheeses, stepped in. If the holes were smaller, American Swiss would no longer qualify as Grade A and that would translate to a loss of 15 to 20 cents a pound. In Switzerland's raw milk Emmentaler, holes (or eyes) occur naturally in the fermenting process, and the size of the holes affects the texture of cheese, which in turns affects the taste. But the American Swiss cheese's holes are mechanically punched, and their size makes no difference to the faint taste of the factory-made cheese. Holes are decorative, that's all. "You see," Guy was triumphant, "in America, cheese is a commodity, not a food."

To Guy, the American industrial attitude to cheese is sealing the fate of the remaining artisanal Brie and eventually the fate of all the great raw milk cheeses of Europe. That, and the American fear of bacteria, the microbes that give cheese and so many other ripened foods—salami, dry-aged beef—their taste and appearance. The holes in Emmentaler are made by bacteria having an attack of gas; the *Penicillium candidus* sprayed on the Brie's crust is the start of the bacte-

rial process that transforms a bland cream into a tangy
mélange of flavor. Bacteria have a role in wine's taste, too,
since wine is full of bacteria and their invisible feces.

Declaring War on Bacteria

Bacteria are everywhere, multiplying as humans multiply,
but far more effectively, reproducing themselves in a
microsecond. We humans move in a cloud of bacteria which
if they were to become visible would make us look like Fly-
face in the *Dick Tracy* comic strip. Bacteria are among the
many creatures capable of harm (the others include viruses,
protozeans, anthropods, worms, fleas, ticks) that have colo-
nized human beings and with whom we are, in the words of
the medical historian Roy Porter in *The Greatest Benefit of
Mankind*, "locked in evolutionary struggles for the survival
of the fittest. . . ."

Americans have taken this seriously, and are trying to
stamp bacteria out of our lives and food. In 1997, as part of
President Bill Clinton's Food Safety Initiative, USDA issued
a ruling on bacteria. From now on, all food would be
cleansed of bacteria—even helpful, cheese-ripening bacteria—and a zero-tolerance bureaucracy spread across America: agencies, offices, investigators armed with the latest
tools, such as carcass scanners and fiber-optic probes, and
charged with eliminating all bacteria.

USDA isn't entirely paranoid; bacteria *are* making gains.

The way the food industry produces and distributes food—
treating livestock like machinery—has spurred newly
emerging pathogens. Bacteria are opportunistic and infinitely adaptable: healthy bacteria never stop reproducing;
it's not unusual for a bacteria to spawn four thousand generations a year, each generation smarter than the last. Bacteria
have for eons been developing and discarding more antibiotics than we can hope to develop. In Britain in 1994, a newly
emerging toxic bacteria (*E coli* DT104) found in meat laid
low more than three thousand people, and killed ten because
antibiotics were helpless against it. Dr. Sean Altekruse, a
veterinary epidemiologist with the U.S. National Institutes
of Health, explains: "We're approaching an era when we
won't have any good antibiotics left, and we are being forced
by the microbes themselves to find new ways of looking at
infectious diseases."

So it doesn't matter that not all species and strains of bacteria are harmful, or that we need bacteria to keep us
healthy—the ubiquitous *E coli* family that lives in our intestines is our source of vitamin K and B-complex vitamins. It
doesn't matter that the overwhelming majority of people
who eat an egg tainted with *Salmonella enterides* never get
ill, or if they do, recover. Unless you belong to the vulnerable classes—the unborn, the ancient, those with very weak
immune systems, or the already terminal—you may eat
food infected with most pathogens without noticing it.
None of that, however, matters in the all-enveloping war
on bacteria.

Take the fuss over the wooden chopping block, which has forever been an emblem of real food. As the block ages, it becomes scarred and develops highs and lows, a monument to years of chopping and slicing. Wood in a kitchen is the sign of continuity; I can remember how the deal counters and draining board in our old kitchen were whitened by age and regular scrubbing. But the food scientists in their wisdom turned against wood. As a natural material, wood was suspect—full of microbes. Those butcher's blocks must contain dried blood, and think where that could lead. Home cooks were urged to throw away their dirty old butcher's blocks and replace them with hygienic plastic. Then, ten years ago, two researchers at the University of Wisconsin conducted an experiment with wood and plastic, no doubt hoping to confirm plastic as the chopping block of the future. They spread toxic bacteria on samples of wood and plastic, and left them overnight at room temperature. The next day, the pathogens had multiplied on the plastic, whereas none at all could be found on the wood. It turns out that wood has its own anti-pathogens, which chomp up threatening microbes. The food scientists did not acknowledge they were wrong, but instead steadily continued to assert how hygienic plastic was—because it could be popped into the dishwasher or cleaned with the chemical chlorine.

Unfortunately for us cheese eaters, raw milk cheese is on USDA's hit list. Raw milk is naturally riddled with bacteria, including harmless *E coli* and *Listeria* strains, and the very process of cheesemaking compounds the number of greedy bacteria.

For centuries, man and microbe made peace over cheese, man accepting the risk of the occasional rogue pathogen. No natural food is 100 percent safe, and when food was hard to get, safety took a backseat. People kept on eating rye bread even after it became clear that it was dangerous. Rye was vulnerable to ergot, an hallucinogenic fungus (and the source of LSD) that sent whole villages into dancing frenzy and villagers diving off roofs in the belief they could fly—something hard to miss. Today, it is speculated that the housewives of Salem weren't bewitched but were the victims of ergotism. The pathogens in cheese were by comparison benign, else—as has been pointed out frequently—the countryside of Europe would have been littered with corpses. On the other hand, personal cheesemaking probably discouraged opportunistic pathogens.

The Flavor of Raw Milk

As a child, I happily drank raw milk. For several years, it was considered the greatest of treats. In Shillingford, on Thursday afternoons, my sister and I used to stop at the farm on our way home from school. We would tap on the kitchen window, which was flung up by Cally, the farmer's cousin, a ringer for Glinda, the Good Witch of the North in the movie *The Wizard of Oz*, and she would beckon us into the sparkling tiled dairy, which smelled of washing. On a big wooden table lay large, shallow, stainless-steel pans of milk with cream rising slowly to the surface. The cream was the color of daffodils. The cows were the superrich Jerseys and Guernseys. Cally poured us a glass of fresh milk still warm from the cow, and it was so good. The milk smelled earthy and complex—today, I'd call it sexy—and so rich compared to the gray stuff we usually drank. Then Cally would hand us each a piece of fresh bread, spread with farm butter and homemade strawberry jam, and lay on it a layer of the heavy cream that spread like cheese. This was quite simply the best food we had all week.

Raw milk, as I told a food scientist I know, is a cocktail with as many hints of vegetables and herbs as V-8 Juice, a meal in itself. He would have none of it. "You think it's safe, but it isn't. It's packed with bacteria. We're finding more bacteria all the time. You were lucky. For some reason, you're resistant to bacteria, but others won't be. You must remember we live in a global market now and there are thousands, millions of people who will never have had raw milk, won't be able to digest it, and may die as a result."

I thought he was overreacting until I found out that his reaction was public health dogma throughout North America. Tom Szalkucki, the assistant director of the Wisconsin Center for Dairy Research at the University of Wisconsin, gave me the reasons. He skipped over the cosmic bacterial menace for more practical matters. From a public health point of view, uniformity is essential for safety, and no regulatory agency such as the Food and Drug Administration can allow the sale of any food that is not safe for everyone. A pathogen in raw milk cheese could hurt those with AIDS, those on chemotherapy, the old. The old, Szalkucki reminded me, are now the fastest-growing segment of the North American population and the fastest-growing population in all the industrial countries, a triumph of health science. I had a sudden vision of aged people keeling over from a taste of raw milk cheese.

Don't forget, too, that Americans are the most litigious people on earth, and others are busy trying to catch up. If the FDA allowed people to sell a food known to be dangerous, lawsuits would multiply. What it comes down to is, "Are you willing to bet your business/assets/etc. in a lawsuit if someone gets sick or dies?"

The Great
Grilled Cheese Sandwich

The epic struggle with bacteria was the furthest thing from my mind when I moved to America. I was entranced by the bright, shiny appearance of industrial food and by its convenience. I never noticed the lack of soft raw milk cheeses because I became addicted to the grilled cheese sandwich. My fast food fix. The grilled cheese sandwich was as ubiquitous in America as Brie was in France, and it was always available. The elements were unchangeable. The cheese had to be a couple of squares cut from one of those long loaves of processed orange Cheddar-style cheese, not too thick, either. Better still, the cheese slices came in plastic wrapped squares, the ones that I've since learned are bacteria-repellent for at least four days and may be left lounging around on the counter. After that I don't think there's much bacteria can do to improve the flavor and I don't think there's enough flavor to be improved.

The cheese's blandness is just right. The bread should be medium-grade industrial, not soggy, certainly. The cooking medium is the griddle. Like all great food, grilled cheese should be eaten out. That is to say, someone else should cook it. An expert. Because grilled cheese should not vary: the whole point of industrial food is that it is always the same and disappoints when it isn't. The expert is a short-order cook in a diner, or in the old days, a drugstore, a utilitarian place where the cast of *Our Town* might have happily con-gregated. At a diner the consumer sat on a stool before the communal counter to ensure close eye contact with the server, and see that the sandwich did not wait around before being served.

A grilled cheese sandwich is as delicate as any Escoffier recipe, and it is entirely digestible, another Escoffier virtue. The overly enthusiastic may want to add a tomato. It doesn't matter if the tomato is a plastic one because the color and juice are more important than the taste.

The greedier eater may demand that bacon be added. Yes and no. A slice of bacon from the griddle, yes, because it will still be exuding droplets of spattering fat, and bacon fat is of course the tastiest fat of all. If, however, a microwave is used, forget it. Bacon emerges from the microwave as shriveled and tasteless as bark from a sick elm. The final garnish must be a slim slice of a mild pickle, and the Americans make by far the best mild pickle.

Trendy cookbooks are now upgrading the grilled cheese sandwich, using Gruyère or Roquefort. Forget it. Just as the great diva Renee Fleming couldn't do justice to "I'm Your Venus, I'm Your Fire," a French chef like Alain Ducasse would be a flop with grilled cheese. Classical technique is no match for personality, whether singing pop or making a grilled cheese sandwich.

I must emphasize the importance of the bread being white. During the war in Britain, white bread did not exist because of the shortage of white flour. A whole-wheat National Loaf appeared; it was edible, which was more than could be said about the War Loaf of the Great War. Back then, the public had protested vociferously about the cement-crusted and "ropey" bread, which was infested with a bacillus called rope. In 1917, *The Times* reported how scientists at the Ministry of Food remonstrated that "The public must be educated to look upon bread as the staff of life, not as a dainty food with which their appetite is to be tickled."

After World War II ended, nutritionists pushed the superiority of whole-wheat bread over white, citing the wonders of bran. But this was somewhat misleading. Dublin had an epidemic of rickets during the war because Dubliners ate only whole-grain bread and the phytic acid in the bran blocked the absorption of essential calcium. Even so, in the new Socialist age, white bread signified the taste of an effete gentry. It wasn't long before processed white bread was attacked as being bad for you; although processed whole-wheat bread was just as polluted with chemicals.

Gastronomically, whole-wheat bread is a bust. The great sandwiches—the grandee cucumber that tastes of marsh grass, the peppery watercress, even the squashy tomato—demand good *white* bread that can be thinly sliced and on which a thin film of good butter can be spread. Whole-wheat bread overwhelms any filling. It is much too thick to absorb juice, so important in the making of, say, a summer pudding, which is nothing more than fresh berries packed into a pudding bowl lined with slightly stale thin slices of white bread.

Brieless in the New World

When I looked up from eating my grilled cheese sandwich, I occasionally wondered where French cheese had gone. Brie was about. It was served routinely at cocktail parties, but it was as lifeless as a corpse, no sparkle to the taste, no smell of soggy socks, and certainly no soul—the thin white line of chalk that is the connoisseur's passion. Brie was a brand name, so no one noticed how boring it was. The most popular and tasty cheese I can remember was a powerful industrial blue called Saga, which went well with gin and tonic in the hold of sailboats in the harbor, the favored drinking spot for the villagers of Stonington in Connecticut, where I lived then.

Nobody I knew complained about Brie. This was the Julia Child period, but she only mentioned Swiss, which is used in the classic cuisine. But then Escoffier never discussed cheeses, either.

If Julia, the era's charismatic cook, dismissed cheese in such an offhand way, small wonder that the American public didn't know what it was missing in a Brie.

How Raw Milk Became a Pariah

I eventually found out that soft raw milk cheeses have been banned since 1949. Up to that time, raw milk cheese was everywhere. Although pasteurized milk was widely available in North America by 1900, you could still get raw milk across the continent, and those who drank it would drink nothing else, despite the health risks that came with it. The risks were real. Before pasteurization, milk caused many illnesses because the dairies were often dirty. Raw milk is a dynamic, volatile substance that needs careful handling: the cows must be disease-free, the dairy and equipment (not to mention the workers) spotlessly clean. The safest milk came from a single herd of cows tended by a single farmer. But as more and more milk was needed, pasteurization became a quick safety fix for milk pooled from many farms, some of doubtful cleanliness. It was cheaper to pasteurize milk, moreover, than to regulate safe dairies.

Then, in the 1920s, a toxic bacteria *Listeria monocytogenes,* was discovered in raw milk cheese, and a cloud of suspicion enveloped raw milk. *Listeria M,* a superbacteria of uncharted potential for damage, is virulent and fast-spreading, and it flourishes in the conditions of cheesemaking. Its discovery gave impetus to the public health authorities' drive to pasteurize all milk products. But many doctors and nutritionists, who believed that raw milk was one of the great naturally healthy foods, resisted.

Pasteurization is a brutal way to try to ensure safe milk: it wipes out every benefit of raw milk. According to the American Association of Medical Milk Commissions, raw milk contains all twenty-two of the essential amino acids; it is also rich in enzymes, which help the body break down protein, thus making the milk easier to digest. Raw milk is an excellent source of vitamins and minerals, particularly vitamin B-12, an essential vitamin that is difficult to find in non-meat sources. Pasteurization destroys enzymes like lactoperoxidase, which inhibit and in some cases eliminate pathogens such as *Salmonella E* and *Listeria M*—naturally. Last but not least, pasteurization wipes out the flavor-bearing bacteria along with any pathogens.

Even so, public health concerns overrode nutrition, and in 1949, citing the dearth of experienced cheesemakers in the postwar period, the federal health authorities ordered that only raw milk cheese older than sixty days, the time determined necessary to kill any lurking pathogens, could be sold in the United States. The ban was then extended to imported cheeses—such as the fast-ripening Brie, Camembert, and Epoisses—as well.

The Fallacy of Food Safety

But what about the safety of pasteurized cheese? This is the question raised in a thick dossier on the safety of raw versus pasteurized milk safety that was presented to the Los Angeles Board of Supervisors in 2001. The case concerned Stueve's Natural, a dairy applying to sell unpasteurized milk.

The Stueve family had in fact been selling raw milk since 1945. California is one of the twenty-eight states to allow raw milk, and millions of people had drunk Stueve's milk without being sick. But according to Raymond Novell, the Stueves' lawyer, the public health authorities never stopped trying to ban raw milk. Most dairies had been harassed into closing down. The Stueves themselves were sued eight times—but the cases were tossed out of court. Then, in 1977, when the Stueves were selling $20 million worth of raw milk a year, the health authorities squeezed the dairy hard. They demanded that the milk, now called Grade A, be certified, which meant a new raft of rules and cost a great deal of money. By 1993, the Stueve family had had enough. They closed their dairy. But the public wanted raw milk! So the Stueves asked the L.A. Board of Supervisors to let them go back to the *old* Grade A standard, which had been perfectly safe.

The dossier compiled by Raymond Novell is eye-popping. Again and again, raw milk was blamed for sickness and deaths without any proof. Some of the stories are ridiculous. Stueve's milk was blamed for the death of a woman who actually died from drowning! An infant, it was claimed, died from raw milk when he actually died of complications from a broken femur. In 1990, the Centers for Disease Control trumpeted that seventy people became ill after drinking raw milk in Wisconsin. Wisconsin bans raw milk, so how did the people get it? It seems a bunch of picnickers ran out of milk, went into a farmer's barn, and scooped milk out of a barrel—milk intended not for humans but for horses. And this was just the local health authorities. In 1985, the FDA reported that 200,000 people were sickened by *pasteurized* milk from an Illinois dairy. But the report was only made after three outbreaks of the illness had occurred because without any evidence at all, the regulators had put the blame on raw milk.

In the same year, the largest number of food-poisoning deaths recorded in recent history was traced to *pasteurized* Mexican-style cheese (142 cases, 47 deaths) contaminated with *Listeria M*, a pathogen always said to be destroyed by pasteurization. In fact, *Listeria M*, a constantly evolving pathogen, is turning up in more and more pasteurized foods—it has been detected in whole milk, chocolate milk both whole and low-fat, ice cream, ice milk mix, and ice cream novelties, including bars, slices, drumsticks, ice rolls, and four-ounce cups of ice cream.

From these reports it seems that the whole question of how milk is treated—whether pasteurized or not—is irrelevant. It's the way milk is handled that is the problem. The more food is produced and distributed as if it were lifeless, the more opportunities the bacteria get. In 1994, another large outbreak of toxic salmonella in many states laid low 224,000 people. The reason? The tanker trucks used to transport gallons of ice cream previously had been used to carry eggs contaminated with the toxin. Nobody thought this could be dangerous. Catherine Donnelly, a microbiologist at the University of Vermont, said in an interview with a local Vermont newspaper: "It isn't that these [pathogenic] organisms have decided to magically appear. It's the way we have decided to produce food to feed the world now. It is intensive agriculture; it is huge mega-farms. From a microbiological standpoint, it's just cause and effect."

In 2002, the Stueve family won the right to sell Grade A raw milk, but, Raymond Novell says, "They'll still be coming after us." Raw milk remains suspect. In California, the container has to carry a warning label that it may be dangerous to your health—like cigarettes. In fact, no food is completely safe. The vicious *E coli* 0157:H7 is surfing beef, sickening 73,000 people a year in the United States and killing 60, according to the Centers for Disease Control and Prevention. But when the Food Research Institute asked why USDA didn't put a warning label on beef, the department's reply was that since "there are numerous sources of contamination which might contribute to the overall problem," it would be "unjustified to single out the meat industry." Particularly, it might just as well have added, as the beef industry is the country's largest agribusiness.

Where Can I Buy Real Cream?

In several states where raw milk is still legal, the health authorities are trying to have it banned. In 2003, Pennsylvania started lowering the bar by banning raw milk butter and cream, citing health concerns. The daffodil-colored cream I ate as a child was of course unpasteurized, and in the fifties Harrods carried cream—which was probably made from raw milk—so heavy you could stand a spoon up in it, and tasted, depending on the time of year, of herbs and grasses. Another great cream was clotted cream, made in Cornwall. It was at once viscous and crunchy. You can make clotted cream at home quite easily; one of the few edible foods at my boarding school was the clotted cream served with porridge on Sundays. The school cook was no cook but a Wagnerian soprano from Vienna, who couldn't live without cream.

Heavy cream wasn't available after the war, but as milk wasn't homogenized, she just skimmed the cream off the top of the bottle every day, and with a week's worth, she made clotted cream on Sundays. She poached the cream so that a crust developed, then folded the crust back into the cream. It was really very good.

· ·

CLOTTED CREAM

Traditionally, clotted cream was made by pouring fresh raw milk (but pasteurized milk may be used) into shallow pans and leaving it, undisturbed, for 24 hours, allowing the cream to rise.

1 quart of the richest cream available

Pour cream into a shallow skillet.

Heat gently, to about 180°F on a candy thermometer, and simmer at this temperature for 1 hour.

When the surface cream has developed a thick, yellow, wrinkled crust, turn off the heat and allow the pan to cool slowly.

Once cooled, skim the cream off and serve with fruit or pie.

· ·

The best milk with which to make clotted cream is the one highest in butterfat. In Britain, where cream is taken very seriously, heavy or double cream is 48 percent butterfat; but in North America, it is usually no higher than 36 percent, and the difference is huge. In the 1980s, however, butterfat was targeted as a killer food after saturated fat was linked to heart disease. This played right into the economics of the North American dairy industries. Butterfat is expensive, and by law, cream and butter must contain minimum amounts of butterfat. North American cream and butter producers hew to the minumum: U.S. whipping cream rarely has more than the required 36 percent (35 percent in Canada). The testers must use gorillas to beat it. The consumer would be better off buying an aerosol can of cream, the kind you shake and squirt. The butterfat content is the same, the cream is no different from that in the waxed pack as they both contain stabilizers, and the can has more uses—it's much in demand at sex orgies, the cream squirted at and then eaten off one's partner.

The minimum for butterfat in North American butter is 80 percent, which by European standards is low. European butters have a minimum of 82 percent butterfat, a big difference in taste and texture, and in cooking. Eighty percent butter goes watery when heated. Butter with more butterfat has the perfect melting point—it literally melts in your mouth—and this makes all the difference when you're making puff pastry that is loaded with butter. The secret of supreme flaky pastry lies in high-butterfat butter that has been cultured, the milk soured enough to produce an acid that tenderizes the dough.

But North Americans put their health ahead of flaky pastry. In Canada, I was told by the Canadian Dairy Commission that Canadians were too health-conscious to want richer butter. Of course, Canadians have never tasted anything else as the country has banned butter imports to keep the dairy industry happy.

But in 1999 all butters got a boost when researchers at the Harvard School of Public Health confirmed the links between heart disease and trans fats, hydrogenated vegetable oils that are the hidden ingredients in thousands of food products, including Crisco, Oreo cookies, and margarine. People eat more trans fat than any other kind of fat. Consumers became confused. Now there were so many fats identified, and it was hard to keep track of them, particularly as the scientists themselves often seemed divided over their safety. By comparison, butter didn't look so bad, and of course it tasted so much better than any oil.

Allison Hooper, a cheesemaker in Vermont, had been waiting twenty years for this moment. Ever since she started making cheese on her farm in Websterville, Vermont, in 1980, she had longed to make butter. But the time never seemed right. The saturated-fat scare had spooked people about butter, so she concentrated on cheese—first a much-admired goat's cheese from her own goats; then she increased her range by making cow's cheese, using milk from local herds. By the middle of the nineties, Hooper sensed change in the air. Now she thinks that television, specifically the Food Network, changed people's attitudes to butter even before the findings about trans fats.

The Food Network, started in 1993, is a twenty-four-hour pig-out dedicated to the joy of eating. In an age of admonitory nutritionists and food science scares, the Food Network wallows happily in food. The tone was set by Martha Stewart, as great an influence on American food as Julia Child and Alice Waters. Martha made cooking seem so soothing—preparing brownies was therapy. In her blonde and breezy way, she evoked the security of affluent suburban life and all its brand names—Topsiders, Saab, Weber grills, L.L.Bean sailbags, Liz Claiborne.

There was no pain in Martha's kitchen. Only pleasure reigned. Sleepless one night, I turned on the TV and watched Martha muse over the creation of a rustic plum tart (Martha is an inverted snob—she shuns fancy words like *galette*). She was just folding the pastry flaps over plums dotted with cubes of unsalted butter, then she brushed the pastry with heavy cream. She could have used an egg wash, she allowed, but heavy cream made the pastry more tender. She then lavished sugar on the tart. When it came out of the oven, it was bubbling. "Juicy," she said approvingly, not gooey, and immediately the Elmer's Glue filling of coffee-shop pie came to mind. After cutting a hefty slice, she garnished it with a dollop of crème fraiche just, as she said, to gild the lily more. And why not? Why not indeed? I thought, as I happily went back to sleep.

Martha had prepared consumers for the next step: pigging out off camera. Allison Hooper summed it up for me: "There was this period when no one ate butter, when they thought they would die if they did, but then they thought, I really miss fat, it tastes so good, it is so satisfying to eat butterfat." And so in 2000 she finally started making butter, a terrific butter, 86 percent butterfat and cultured, a six-ounce roll of golden bliss that melts on the tongue and warms the mouth with a hot, sexy, animal taste. Hooper's butter joined another American butter—Plugra, with 83 percent butterfat—in the superbutter market.

In Europe, butters run the gamut of tastes. My favorite I guess is the Queen's favorite, as it carries her warrant. St. Ivel Cornish Butter (81.75 percent) is made from Cornish cream churned in Somerset, and it is like eating a bouquet of flowers. I was sampling it with an English friend, but she said no, the champion had to be Gold Top Jersey Butter (81 percent), pale primrose and salted, and as she put it, "a full-throttle, in-your-face explosion of taste."

We both puzzled over the Occelli butter (83 percent) from Piedmont. Beppino Occelli makes his butter from raw milk collected daily, embossed with handmade blocks, and hand-wrapped in wax paper—and it tastes of ice cream! The French butter, Echiré (82 percent), the bakers' favorite, comes from Poitou-Charente and carries the *Appellation d'Origine Controlée* label. And these are just a handful of unique butters—what I would give for the Brittany butter studded with chunks of sea salt that I bought in Boulogne but haven't yet found in North America. Am I being too romantic about the taste of butter? Well, as the novelist George Meredith said, without romance, "the sky becomes a ceiling."

American Cheese
Finds Its Soul

American butter's breakaway from dairy industry norms has been matched by the growth of American artisanal cheese. When Allison Hooper made her first goat cheese in 1980, she was in the van of a renaissance of hand-cheesemaking in America. A handful of artisanal cheeses always existed: Colby has been made by the Crowley Cheese Company in Vermont since 1882, and in 1941, the Maytag Dairy Farms in Newton, Iowa (once owned by a branch of the washing machine people), started making Maytag Blue, a raw milk blue cheese that the cheesemonger Steven Jenkins calls the American intelligentsia's blue—perhaps because it was advertised in *The New Yorker*. Handmade cheeses appealed to the elite because they were local and authentic at a time when so much food wasn't.

The new cheesemakers like Hooper are either sixties' heads or influenced by them. The first generation to reject the corporate rat race was also the first generation to be able to afford to. What better way to turn the world into a peaceable kingdom than to make cheese? The cheesemakers are often as unworldly as the first dedicated cheesemakers, the monks. The earliest new cheeses were frequently the simplest, many made from goat's milk, and usually mild and fresh. Laura Chenel stands out among the pioneers. After a spell in France learning how to make chèvre, she returned to California in 1981 to produce an aged goat cheese that tasted gamey—an unfamiliar taste in American cheese, but one that soon won admirers.

At first, the models for cheeses were European varieties, and cheesemakers turned out copies of Goudas, Mozzarella, Bries, Camemberts, and endless Cheddars, the world's most popular variety. Some of these New World versions are wonderful: in Ontario, Mapledale Dairy is making a soft, crumbly white Cheddar from raw milk; and in Quebec, Pierre-Yves Chaput is producing a fiery raw milk Vacherin. In the Sonoma Valley, Bellwether Farms makes a rare sheep's milk ricotta; and in New England, there is a handmade blue cheese with a craggy crust called Berkshire Blue, made with the rich milk of Jersey cows. At a time when many of the old cheesemaking breeds are dying out in France because they are not economic, the American cheesemakers can afford to insist on the best breeds. In Vermont, John and Janine Pomfret produce a certified organic raw milk Tarentaise, a Gruyère-like cheese that is made from Jersey milk. Janine Pomfret sounds almost French as she derides Holstein milk as "skim milk."

As confidence grew, so did the number of cheesemakers, now reckoned to be around 750 and climbing fast. The cheese became more original as well. Humboldt's Fog is a five-pound wheel of soft goat's cheese with a line of ash running through it, and a runny edge under a crust of ash and mold, crunchy to the bite. One of the charms of artisanal cheese is that it has to be discovered—refreshing in a world of overpromotion. I discovered Capricious Washed Curd Cheese, a semi-hard aged goat cheese made by MyRanch in Eureka, at the San Francisco Food Market. Mild at first, then crescendoing to tangy, the cheese tasted as American as Zinfandel. The cheesemakers are Ginger Olsen and her partner, Diana Livingston. Livingston has turned the clock back. MyRanch is organic, a mixed herd of more than one hundred goats fed on sustainable land, and just enough Capricious Cheese is made to sustain the cheesemakers.

Even as American cheesemaking has developed, so have cheese imports, including imports of soft raw milk cheeses officially banned by the FDA. I started noticing a greater variety of imported cheeses in Toronto a decade ago. Ostensibly, Canada has the same laws for soft raw milk cheese as America, so why could I buy a raw milk artisanal Brie made in France and ripened by the *affineur* Pierre-Yves Chaput in his caves outside the city? Chaput's ripened Bries were advertised by word of mouth alone. They were, after all, illegal. The Toronto cheesemonger where I bought a wedge of Brie did not wink or demand secrecy, but she did suggest discretion.

Chaput himself was uncommunicative on the subject.

Once, I tried to ask him on the telephone about importing cheese; only after careful probing would he agree that he brought in cheese from France and ripened it in his caves.

How old are the cheeses?

"Young."

How long are they ripened?

"Some time."

Do the cheeses get to New York restaurants?

"I think so."

Then he broke off the conversation, saying the line was bad.

The Quebec countryside has always been full of small farms making cheese from raw milk, and Canadian efforts to crack down on the cheesemakers were further stalled by politics. The Québécois regard raw milk cheese as their birthright, even as the French do . . . our culture, our *pays*, ourselves. As Quebec blew hot and hotter on the idea of separating from the rest of Canada, tampering with cheese seemed foolhardy.

So I was able to go on buying raw milk cheese from France and Quebec. A Langres appeared, a tingling paste with a bright orange rind washed in wine. L'Ami de Bourgogne, a small, fat, soft cheese with a hint of lime, the bell-shaped Puligny St. Pierre, a pithy goat cheese, and the drily acidic Crottin. I began to look for the delicate St. Marcellin that came in a plastic dish. I've no idea how these cheeses passed the customs, but I assume as the boxes weren't dated, the importer just said they were more than sixty days old.

In 1998, the Canadian Food Inspection Agency issued a warning about St. Félicien, a juicy little raw milk morsel from Burgundy, saying that it "may" contain *Listeria M.* The agency justified its warning on the basis of information about the cheese's history. The importer Chaput withdrew the cheese, and the matter was closed. Nobody said anything about the fact that the St. Félicien was illegal in Canada.

The same laissez-faire attitude existed south of the border. The raw milk cheeses from Quebec started to appear in Manhattan. On the Web, all kinds of raw milk cheeses were being sold from France with U.S. Customs clearance assured. The *vrai* Brie as well. Every other day or so, a luscious Brie is pictured, made at the Rothschild farm, and for around $100 it can be flown to the U.S. consumer in forty-eight hours. Upscale restaurants started offering cheese plates that often included soft raw milk cheese. A couple of years ago, an exciting new cheese called Epoisses was discovered by the New York media. Surely, I thought as I read this, the cheese was contrabrand because a pasteurized Epoisses is not exciting at all.

Finally, the penny dropped. The Epoisses, like almost all the soft raw milk cheeses now being sold in North America, must have been *thermisé*—a process that slows ripening until after sixty days and thus makes it legal to bring the cheese into the United States. A *thermisé* cheese isn't as flavorful as raw milk cheese, but it's more flavorful than pasteurized cheese. The milk is heated for a long time at a low temperature, a process cheesemakers claim eliminates pathogens yet doesn't wipe out the flavor-bearing microflora. Steven Jenkins calls *thermisé* the best of all possible worlds—because it legitimizes the import of great soft raw cheeses without pasteurization's destructive effects. To my taste, this isn't so. Cheeses aren't required to be stamped "*thermisé*," so I had only my memories of the authentic taste of Epoisses to go on. More than a year ago, the affineur Berthaut changed its packaging and I could swear the Epoisses changed too. Epoisses used to be so aggressive—you had to eat it with a spoon if you let it go a day too long. The new one seemed firmer, and its taste less fierce. And yes, I found out eventually that it is *thermisé*.

I think this is the first sign that the French are allowing zero tolerance to get to them. In the 1990s, the European Union, showing a very unwelcome enthusiasm for food safety, pushed the French, who had been turning the usual blind eye to raw milk cheese, to step up their testing of cheese. Reluctantly, the French did so, and in 1999, to their horror, no less than four famous cheeses were found to be contaminated with Listeria. Although no one became ill after eating a St. Félicien, the cheese's sales plummeted. What followed was far worse: a mother and child died and their deaths were traced to a poisoned Epoisses. A raw milk Epoisses.

A tragedy, of course, but a personal one, reasoned the French government, hardly a state matter. This was the way cheese issues had always been treated, with the kind of nonchalance approved by the French cheesemakers, who feared as every dairy industry fears bad publicity that might taint all cheeses and affect sales. And after all, the bad Epoisses was not raw milk—another case of the food police overreaching in their desire to defame raw milk. It was a pasteurized cheese from a factory that was quickly closed down.

Too late! An alert media had seized on the story. French consumers, formerly so much less risk-averse than the Anglo-Saxons, were outraged, and a tide, small but steady, of death phobia began sweeping through the country. For the first time, there was a soupçon of distrust around raw milk cheese.

To Guy, my French adviser on the matter of cheese, the "listeria hysteria" of 1999, of course, was manipulated by the Americans. "It's part of their global food strategy," he told me. The Americans are using safety to scare consumers, but their real agenda is trade. "This is Brie versus Cheez Whiz. The Americans want to dominate the market with their own industrial cheese. If you don't believe me," he added, "check the Codex."

Americans Say, "Bacteria," Europeans Say, "Yummy"

I'd never heard of the Codex, and I'd like to bet the average innocent eater hasn't, either. In the 1960s, the United Nations' Food and Agricultural Organization (FAO) and the World Health Organization (WHO) laid out an ambitious plan to cobble together a set of world standards for food, called a Codex. It extends right down to how an individual cheese should be made. If I buy a Cheddar in Somerset, it will be made the same way as it would in Shanghai. Currently, however, the cheese sessions are stalled over the safety of cheese. The Americans are on their zero-tolerance crusade and they want cheese pasteurized worldwide, while the makers of the greatest cheeses in the world—the French, the Italians, and the Swiss—say no.

President Jacques Chirac of France has stated publicly that the Codex is nothing more than a political tool, and Guy agrees. "Look who's at the table. Representatives of the American cheese industry. The Codex is camouflage for American imperialism!"

Food has opened another fissure between America and Europe and the division is filled with emotion. Europeans complain routinely about the American cultural empire, but movies, pop, TV are ephemera compared to food. After years of living in North America, I am still struck by the difference in attitudes toward food between Europeans and North Americans. For Europeans, the idea of food as a communal pleasure is still alive; but in North America, food is an individual necessity.

Look at the behavior of the leaders. Even when the British and the French were at daggers drawn over Iraq, Jacques Chirac and Tony Blair could mellow out over luncheon at Le Touquet, once a swanky Edwardian seaside resort on the French Coast. After lunch, both sides emerged smiling rather fatuously, and I had a fugitive glimpse of the

Congress of Vienna where almost two hundred years ago, Brie was the emollient easing the tensions of a divided Europe.

I could imagine the Le Touquet menu. Centuries of Franco-British rivalry would have ensured that the French made clear the wonders of their cuisine. Champagne first, of course, because that is the only civilized apéritif, and local oysters—crayfish in cream? or the popular bar fish? A greeny Chablis. Local lamb from the Brittany salt marshes with a St. Emilion; a Diplomat for dessert (puff pastry, *Crème anglaise*, and whipped cream), and then a Camembert. Eau-de-Vie must have rounded out the meal.

Compare this to the food habits of North American leaders. The last two American presidents have favored fast food—Bill Clinton ate Big Macs and George W. Bush peanut butter and jelly sandwiches. This is food best eaten alone; the sandwich eater is not an attractive sight. Not too long ago I saw the Canadian prime minister grimly cutting into an Alberta steak at the behest of the beef industry during the mad cow disease scare in Canada. That's what food has come to—something that must be eaten to keep the economy going.

When American fast food giants began colonizing Europe in the 1970s, the public gobbled up Big Macs, Kentucky Fried Chicken, and Whoppers because, of course, they are addictive. There is nothing so seductive as a fast, sweet, hot industrial hit. But as fast food outlets began invading historic city centers, their gaudy presence provoked a backlash. In

1986, Carlo Petrini, an Italian food and wine journalist, saw the golden arches rising above the Piazza di Spagna in Rome and blew his stack. Petrini brooded over the desecration of the Piazza, which so powerfully evokes the past, and linked it to the American food industry's intention to alter forever the way people eat. Fast food itself was the tip of the iceberg. All over Europe, methods of growing food were being changed because cheap American seeds undercut local sources. European tastes were ineluctably becoming American tastes.

After brooding further, Petrini counterattacked, founding in 1989 the international Slow Food movement. Slow Food was dedicated to turning the clock back and to reintegrating food into the social fabric, making it a center of life and not just a pit stop for nutrition. A meal must be savored, lingered over, enjoyed. As for the food itself, bring on the bacteria, the greatest friend a food ever had! In Slow Food's mission statement, Petrini acclaimed bacteria as the creators of taste in some of the greatest foods—in salami, proscuitto, and of course cheese.

By 1995, Slow Food had started the Ark of Taste, a list of foods endangered worldwide. Their description is guaranteed to cause acute anxiety among gourmets. Do you mean to say I shall never get to eat the asparagus marittimus that grows submerged in the Venetian lagoon? Slow Food's action came none too soon because ancient food was indeed vanishing all over Europe. By the early nineties, hyper-hygiene was the order of the day. Europeans started to chafe at the endless diktats from Brussels: shopkeepers had to record refrigerator temperatures every three hours, the production of fresh ricotta cheese using well water was barred, buffalo mozzarella had to be kept so cold that consumers complained its taste couldn't be distinguished from other mozzarellas. Sandwiches for sale must be wrapped and homemade mayonnaise was outlawed. Once, the individual sandwich maker had his or her own followers. Homemade mayonnaise is inestimably better than the manufactured kind. Now, all were to be the same.

The European authorities were moving all over Europe throwing out some of the most beloved traditional foods in the name of safety, including cheeses like the ancient Fossa, ripened in underground pits. An EU rule forbidding wood to come into contact with ripening cheese has so far been ignored by the French because otherwise Vacherin du Haut-Doubs, an amazing soft cheese that uniquely tastes of edelweiss and must be eaten with a spoon, might be stripped of its flavor. The Vacherin is ringed with sprucewood, which perfumes the cheese, and then aged in a wooden box.

The Codex cheese meetings provide the battleground for clashes between the superhygienists and the countries which believe that cheese is their culture. Look who's sitting at the Codex table, said my friend Guy. An American troika of science, industry, and government. Kraft Foods is there, and as the manufacturer of the oleaginous Cheez Whiz, the most popular American cheese spread, the company is relentlessly pro-pasteurization.

The American cheese industry is on the defensive these days. Free trade, an American initiative, has boomeranged on the manufacturers, unraveling the tariffs and quotas that made the industry profitable. Any industry's unalterable goal is to crush competition, and naturally the American cheese industry sees any nonconforming producers as a threat. The industry's real target is not so much the European raw milk cheesemakers, despite the rise in imports, as its own artisanal cheesemakers.

American cheesemakers are producing more and more raw milk cheese, and the customers love it. To take just one example: Organic Valley in Wisconsin makes a raw milk Cheddar that consumers line up for, according to Theresa Marquez, the marketing director. The raw milk cheese, she adds, sells better than the pasteurized products.

This isn't what Kraft wants to hear. Supermarkets are nervous, too. They fear having to give valuable shelf space to another niche product. They've already gone through that with organic food. Organic sales account for about 5 percent of all supermarket sales in the United States, but organic food is rising fast in popularity, and supermarkets have had to stock it even though these boutique foods are not profit centers—no shelf life, and lacking the shiny self-esteem of their industrial peers.

The Attack on Parmesan—
and Vermont's Tarentaise

In 2000, as nations fought over cheese at the Codex meetings, which are held four times a year in different places, the FDA did its own bit for the American cheese industry, announcing that it was considering a ban on all raw milk cheeses because it had found evidence that pathogens survived in cheese more than sixty days old. The future loomed cheeseless—not just Camembert, Epoisses, and St. Félicien, but Gruyère, Comte, Roquefort, the Vermont Tarentaise, Ontario's Mapledale Cheddar, the newly acclaimed Spanish cheese Torta del Cásar, Manchego—the list was endless. Parmigiano-Reggiano!

The industrial cheesemakers cheered, and the American food industry lined up right behind them. It surely was no coincidence that the FDA had asked that the tests be done by the National Center for Food Safety and Technology (NCFST) in Summit, Illinois, whose membership is drawn from the same troika of government, industry, and scientists that represents the United States at the Codex meetings.

The artisanal cheesemakers were quick to object. The American Cheese Society, which represents them, joined forces with Oldways Preservation and Exchange Trust (a food think tank) to form the "Choice in Cheese Coalition" and get its message out. Oldways is best known for publishing its own healthy food pyramids based on the low-fat, high-grain vegetable diets of the Mediterranean, Asia, and the Latin American countries, which are the opposite of the U.S. Department of Agriculture's food pyramid that critics often call "the food industry's pyramid." Dun Gifford, Oldways' president and founder, is a canny politician who has avoided the extremes of food politics. Now he enlisted the help of Catherine Donnelly at the University of Vermont, one of the few microbiologists in America who doesn't condemn raw milk out of hand, and he focused his message carefully. Raw milk cheese is still an elitist taste, and the first line of defense had to be real cheese eaters, the people now asking for cheese plates at restaurants. They had to be made to feel that a precious freedom was about to be removed. For the masses, there was the image of a bowl of spaghetti—without Parmesan.

The subject of raw milk and raw milk cheese arouses atavistic emotions, so the first move had to be rational. Gifford's initial salvo in 2000 put the FDA on the defensive. He had found one of the FDA examples to be false. Fermentation kills pathogens in cheese, but the NCFST testers had poured toxic *E coli* into a Cheddar that had already fermented. The media caught on, and next thing, *Fortune* magazine revealed that a second NCFST test was wrong. The Canadian children who became ill after eating cheese had not eaten raw milk cheese but pasteurized cheese.

The FDA retreated as quickly as it had advanced. The ban was postponed on the understanding that further study was required. My friend Guy was puzzled at the ineptitude of the FDA case until he worked out that the health aspect was just a ruse, a way of testing the opposition. Had the FDA been serious about raw milk's threat to health, he argued, the evidence would have been watertight. On the other hand, is there really watertight evidence, or just years of dogma? Anyway, the FDA had to rethink its strategy and assess the strength of the Choice for Cheese Coalition, which was now busy making international links for future defense. The Slow Food movement had ignited fires of protest against industrial food all over Europe; could the coalition do the same thing in industrial North America? T. S. Eliot wrote that culture is that which makes life worth living. Saving raw milk cheese means saving cultures, different cultures. Diversity is the hot-button issue of today—why can't cheese be diverse? "Because," said Guy, "this is all about trade."

. . . . . .

CHAPTER THREE

THE OX IS GORED

Old Ben, the pensioner who did odd jobs round the garden in Shillingford, came into the kitchen, his breath blowing smoke. "There's a hoar frost today," he said, as he put his chapped red hands round a mug of tea, our kitchen always being good for tea, perhaps elevenses, and even a soup-lunch if he timed it right. My mother was a soft touch where pensioners—who didn't, as she said, get a pension at all but a pittance—were concerned. "Good day for killing the pigs." Of course, this was the day our pig was going to be killed.

Our pig had been bought by my parents as part of their homegrown food program, at the urging of Dick, the farmer. Dick assured them this was going to be much easier than the chickens. The pig could be kept at the farm and we'd never have to see it if we didn't want to. It would be fed with the farm pigs and slaughtered at the same time, and we would then have half of it as our own. The government, he sighed, would take the other half. Our bacon ration would be canceled for a year. Even so, there would a ham, and roasts, tenderloin, chops, our own bacon, plenty of wonderful pork fat, and trotters—pigs' feet—if anyone knew what to do with them any more. My father said, "I suspect the trotter is lost." We children had no idea what he was talking about.

My father went along with the pig plan, although he would have preferred a cow that could be slaughtered for beef—eventually. The perfect food animal would have been dual-purpose, a cow who provided cream—cream!—and could then be killed for steaks. But as things were, beef was out. During the war, beef had become a rare luxury food. Cattle required such high maintenance. Raising beef cattle languished because the farmhands were off fighting. Perhaps nothing so dented what remained of English culinary pride as the way roast beef, the national passion, had vanished during the war, to be replaced by bully beef from Argentina and Brazil. Even the common, much-loved sausage almost disappeared; when they did find sausages, consumers were doubtful about the contents and wondered whether they should be eaten with mustard or jam, they were so full of breadcrumbs.

It was the English who invented beef—the beef we eat now, that complex of mineral and fermented grain, whisky flavors that excite gourmands worldwide, the great beef breeds exported not only to Australia and New Zealand but South Africa, South America, Canada, and of course the United States, where British beef found its apotheosis as the food of the Anglosphere.

Beef had been branded on the English palate from the Middle Ages. Even when oxen were needed for their hides, for tallow, to pull carts, and generally to help out on the farm, the English still ate them. No celebration was complete without a roasted ox. By the eighteenth century, beef and England were synonymous in the person of John Bull—a rowdy, raucous extrovert, crude and funny, Squire Weston in *Tom Jones*. The reason for his extraordinary vitality was simple, too: he ate beef.

Beef was one food that the English knew they did better than anyone else. It was also the one food at which the French failed, or perhaps fairer to say, they lagged behind in breeding cattle for beef. In English eyes, the French had an effete attitude to beef. The French fancied veal. An English writer dismissed veal as having the consistency of minced kid gloves. The French national dish was *Pot-au-feu*, a spin on one of the mother recipes of Europe, a boiled beef dinner. *Pot-au-feu* has many regional variations, but the basic recipe calls for a meat broth to which various cooked meats and root vegetables are added. The English turned up their noses at boiled beef, and at roots, too. Eighteenth-century cartoonists delighted in showing skinny Frenchmen sucking on roots and being bowled over by robust John Bulls, big smiles on their faces and steaks in fist.

After Scotland joined the union in 1707 and its breeds proved to be among the best for beef, beef became British and ever more puissant. The Sublime Society of Beefsteaks, started in 1735, was dedicated to celebrating beef. The members met in London on Saturdays and and ate vast beefsteaks, drank port, and sang patriotic songs about beef:

Like Britain's Island lies our Steak
A sea of gravy bounds it
Shallots, profusely scattered, make
The rock-work which surrounds it.
Your isle's best emblem there behold
Remember ancient story
Be like your grandsires, rough and bold
And live and die with glory.

No question but Napoleon was defeated by diet, not (as claimed) on the playing fields of Eton. In 1813, just two years before the Battle of Waterloo, it was recorded that the thirty-yeoman guard (Beefeaters) at St. James's Palace received a ration of twenty-four pounds of beef a day, along with eighteen pounds of mutton, and sixteen pounds of veal. Other people's diets paled by comparison. The Neapolitans ate the greatly inferior *pasta' asciutta*, which was 40 percent less nutritious than meat. What was worse (according to a Neapolitan expert, no less), pasta is swallowed rather than chewed, and as chewing is essential to good digestion, pasta leads to lassitude, pessimism, nostalgic inactivity, and *neutralism*.

Furthermore, the English were supreme at cooking beef. The English, even the French agreed, cooked beef to perfection. The English actually taught the French how to grill "le bifsteak" when British troops were encamped in Paris after Waterloo.

But roast beef was even better. It wasn't roasting as we now know it. Meat cooked in the modern oven is baked, a far different process than the ancient and superior way of rotating (from which comes the word "roast") the ox on a spit before a blazing hot fire, the meat basted and stroked with all manner of condiments to create a pungently delicious crust for the tender pink flesh within. Eventually, the spit was moved indoors before a kitchen fire and driven by a weight-driven pulley (Leonardo da Vinci himself left a blueprint for such a household spit), but of course it took time and space. The next step was the roasting jack, and that opened the way for the inferior oven, a mistake that beef eaters try to rectify with charcoal grills, even indoor grills.

It was the English, moreover, who came up with the perfect accompaniments for this celestial food: hot mustard and spicy horseradish sauce. Eventually, they would add Yorkshire pudding, an airy pastry cooked in hot fat in the oven, and another English triumph, the densely crusted roast potato. The preferred cut of beef was the rump, whence came sirloin. The name probably stems from the French *sur loin*, meaning "top of the loin," but legend insists it was an English king, Henry VIII or James 1, who, in the style of Charlemagne anointing Brie as the King of Cheeses, took just one taste of a melting slice of beef and promptly dubbed it "Sir Loin."

First Beef

My mother finally did find some beef, sighting a fine piece of rump roast in the butcher's on what she called her "scavenging expedition" to Wallingford, our market town. She had shamelessly queue-jumped to buy it, using her near blindness as an excuse as she pushed past irate customers. We looked at it reverently. There was great anticipation: the first beef. The rump is a lean and tasty cut, but must be undercooked if it is to be tender. The adults couldn't stop talking about rump roast. The accouterments were prepared. Floury potatoes were boiled until their edges grew soggy in preparation for roasting in beef dripping. (And how good beef dripping was. Once congealed, it could be spread on toast or bread; it tasted of crisped meat and amalgam.) Leeks had been spotted at the market and they were to be braised. There would Brussels sprouts, as small as could be found, just lightly boiled and tossed with a scrap of butter begged from the farm; cream, too, contributed to the horseradish sauce, made from horseradish found growing wild in the old kitchen garden. The Yorkshire pudding had been mooted and then rejected; there wasn't enough fat. My father produced a bottle or two of red wine from the wine cellar in the catacombs that ran under the house.

And then, as Nanny put it, the oven "played up": it "had a mind of its own," as did so many household appliances in those pre-technological times. The beef was overcooked. A terrible sadness fell around the table. "Beef," reflected my father as he looked mournfully at a plate of gray meat, "should fall from the knife in fine, rippling pink slices." The potatoes saved the day. I have eaten roasted potatoes many times, but this recipe, refined by my sister, is the best.

. . . .

LYNN'S ROAST POTATOES

2 large baking potatoes per person
Kosher or sea salt
Lard or vegetable oil

Preheat oven to 375°F.

Peel potatoes and chop up into 2–3-inch-square pieces. Boil for about 30 minutes, until the edges are soft and crumbly. Drain, making sure to retrieve all crumbs, and dust with Kosher or sea salt.

Prepare a large baking pan with ½ inch lard or vegetable oil. Put the pan in the preheated oven until the fat is hot.

Add the potatoes: they should sizzle as they hit the fat. Check every 10 minutes to see how they're browning, and keep turning them. They should be ready to serve in under 40 minutes; if not, keep turning. Ideally, roast potatoes should be served right from the oven. Use a slotted spoon to remove them from the fat and rest them briefly on paper towels. They can then be kept in a low oven for about 10 minutes without losing their crispness.

. . . .

We went back to drooling over the steaks we saw in *Life* magazine, sent to us by our American grandparents, with its large Technicolor pictures showing midwestern families in sun-dappled backyards barbecuing steak, then spearing deep red slices of the precious food on long forks. My mother, on a flying visit to New York, returned with stories of just such a cookout, which friends had invited her to in suburban Bronxville. She was starry-eyed. It was all so simple. She could see it in her mind's eye: the whole tiresome business of preparing food without adequate help dissolving painlessly. (She always longed for perfected disposable cutlery and plates.) You just put hamburgers and steaks on the charcoal grill and served them right there in the backyard. As she spoke, my father glanced out at the rain lashing the terrace and wondered aloud whether eating out was really an option in English weather. And how exactly was a barbecue constructed? What was a charcoal grill? My mother was not put off. She was an optimist. The steak would come soon. So would the barbecue.

I think I ate my first real steak in Paris in the mid-1950s. The steak was a pan-fried minute steak and I loved it. The slim pink strip was served with a Béarnaise sauce, a bored waiter fetching frites and those tiny peas that only the French know how to can. Perhaps it was Escoffier who taught the French how to can peas. He was *chef de cuisine* to the French General Staff at Metz during the Franco-Prussian War in 1870, and had witnessed the horrors of starvation firsthand, which prompted his interest in canned food. Afterwards, he made several experiments canning vegetables.

In London, the steak was far more elegant, notably at the Berkeley Hotel, where the dining room was retro, darkly luxurious, reminiscent my parents said of Luigi's Embassy Club on Bond Street, the underground at the heart of Empire. There was no great social upheaval after the Great War the way there would be after World War II. Superficially, England seemed the same, caste and class boundaries firmly enforced, the cutout cardboard figures of King George and Queen Mary dominating the newsreels. But rebellion was brewing.

The Embassy Club was a beautifully appointed bunker, a long underground room in the heart of Mayfair, dominated by the dance floor, which was packed nightly with *tout* London, society mingling with the demimonde, flappers and coke sniffers, wide boys and vagrant divorcées. The food, my mother remembered, was first-rate, classic English fare. Scotch steak, Colchester oysters, grilled Dover sole, deep-fried whitebait (minnows), pheasants and grouse in season. And the service, well, English service was still considered the best in the world, deferential without being servile, knowledgeable but not pushy. The Embassy was intensely romantic. Although the place was jammed, you always knew, she said, when the Prince of Wales, a regular, had arrived with Mrs. Simpson because the bandleader Ambrose would launch into their song, "If I Had You . . ." The Embassy would have had no trouble with Queen Wallis.

I was taken to the Berkeley by a smart young officer in the Scots Guards who stunned my parents with his ultraorthodoxy. He appeared at the front door in mufti—as much a uniform, however, as the bearskin: striped double-breasted suit, bowler hat, old Etonian tie, and rolled umbrella. And he called my father "sir." He drove the requisite car, a British racing green MG.

The Berkeley's discreet glamour was a little intimidating. When I ordered a steak, the waiter, a sleek survivor from between the wars, asked me gravely whether I wanted it *bleu, sanglante, à point, cuit, bien cuit.* I couldn't understand what he was talking about. He then bent his head close to mine and whispered, "Rare?", and I nodded thankfully. The sirloin steak, about an inch and a half thick, weighing around six ounces, had been cut from Scotch beef and properly aged by the hotel itself. Then it had been grilled over hot coals, the only way a real steak (unlike that pan-fried scrap of steak I had eaten in Paris) should be cooked, so its surface was agreeably seared with grill marks. Accompaniments were simple: fresh watercress and a grilled half-tomato, and a mélange of French and English mustards that I mixed myself to the proper degree of heat. I knew how to do this because my father was passionate about mustards. I can't remember the vegetables that came as a side dish. They were not important.

Years later, I asked an English butcher about the difference between French and Scottish steak. He simply sniffed. "The French don't have proper beef cattle; for a decent steak, they import ours." In the eighteenth century, the French didn't feel the same pressure to breed cattle for food because their population wasn't multiplying the way the British population was. The population of London alone nearly trebled between 1550 and 1650; it continued to grow at a great pace throughout the 1700s, and even faster from the Industrial Revolution onward. Clearly, more food had to be found. What more likely source than the cattle who browsed throughout the kingdom?

Making Beef Best

Before industrialization began scarring the landscape, the British Isles were carpeted with speckled cattle. There weren't breeds as such, but indigenous regional cattle, although they were all descended from the original ox, or aurochs. The aurochs became extinct in the seventeenth century, the last one dying alone in a private park in Poland, but it can be seen depicted in cave paintings: a large, bony animal with sharp horns impaling stick humans.

The roaming British cattle were predominantly red in the south of England; red and white Shorthorned cattle browsed along the east coast. Dun-colored cattle were found in Devon, and in Wales the Black Finchbacks, a white stripe running down their backs, patrolled the Welsh border along with White-Faced Finchbacks. The tawny streaked Longhorns with white markings made the north their home. Farther north still, in Scotland, were mottled beasts— notably doddies or hornless cattle that would evolve eventually into the Aberdeen Angus, the Black Angus, and then just Angus. The doddies were said to have arrived in Scotland with the invading Vikings; they made their home in a landscape, warmed by the Gulf Stream, that stretched emptily for miles. Eighteenth-century travelers wrote of seeing a herd of multicolored doddies drifting down to the shore to eat seaweed.

Although the cattle were still work animals, they were also increasingly fattened for beef, herds of them driven to the cities for slaughter. The herds grew as cattle were purpose-bred, and they clogged the city streets as they were herded to Smithfield Market in the heart of London.

The market was held on Mondays and Fridays, so the livestock were around all week, standing in filth and bored to distraction. More and more animals would break free and startle the citizens. Once, a steer galloped down High Holborn and barged into a tearoom where, after admiring his reflection in the mirrored walls, he menaced two patrons he didn't like and then broke up the place. To control the cattle, the herders often beat them about the head and pricked their noses; once these practices became known, animal lovers, a new breed of human, were outraged.

Cattle breeding was an avocation for rich gentlemen on whose broad acres the most far-reaching experiments were taking place. Cattle needed capital and space. This was another reason for British supremacy. The French had a much more equitable distribution of land, while the English had the largest estates outside Russia and Poland, where the

Radziwill family, it was said, had such vast holdings that nobody could properly estimate them.

Robert Bakewell was a tenant farmer, not a rich gentleman farmer, and the first person to see the potential of cattle for industrial food. In the 1740s, in Leicestershire, he started experimenting with the Longhorn breed because the Longhorns were so efficient—a Longhorn ate less and yet produced more meat than other cattle. He crossed his Longhorns with other breeds, chosen for characteristics he fancied, to produce a radically reshaped ox. The old Longhorn had been a bony triangle with linebacker shoulders; the new Longhorn was a small-boned barrel of meat, most of it concentrated on the fat back where the richest cuts were, and fast-maturing so the owner could get his money back quickly. Once Bakewell had created the archetype, he broke the law against incest—which applied to animals as well as humans—and established the breed by inbreeding to fix the desirable traits, the bull being bred with its children, grandchildren, great-grandchildren.

When he finished, Bakewell believed he had created the model for cattle that could produce the old roast beef of England "forever and aye." But other breeders were soon surpassing him. The Shorthorns, even more efficient meat machines, pushed aside the Longhorn, and the competition to breed ever bigger meat producers became intense. The great landowners formed agricultural societies to promote the experiments taking place on their land. By 1803, there were more than thirty-two such societies, each with its own annual show where animals competed for cash prizes. The public was more than willing to pay to gape in shock and awe at behemoths like the Great Hereford Ox, six foot four inches high, ten feet round, with horns almost four feet in length, and weighing in at 450 stone—or 5,140 pounds. The Great Hereford was, however, upstaged by the 3,205-pound Durham Ox, the Shorthorn champ, a lighter but a more attractive package, and so admired by the public that from 1801 to 1807 he was taken on a tour of Britain in a specially built carriage. On a single day in London, the Durham Ox took in £97 at the box office.

The Shorthorns were ideal beef cattle because they packed on the fat so easily, and they were so successful that other nascent breeds with names like White Belted Galloway, Black Finchback, the Rubies of the West, the South Hams with yellow hair, were stopped in their tracks. Eventually, only a few breeds survived the competition to join the Shorthorn as the founding beef cattle of the New World: they included the pie-faced Hereford and the sooty Black Angus, the Scots contender that dominates the world today.

The Angus made the list in the new-fangled way: through marketing. By the nineteenth century, all beef cattle had been Bakewellized, and it took a showman called William McCombie of Tillyfour in Aberdeenshire to raise the Angus above its motley-colored peers. The Angus, McCombie decreed, would be bred to be all-black. Fame and fortune followed after the development of the champion Black Prince of Tillyfour, whose DNA can be found in every extant Angus ox today. In 1867, Black Prince cleaned up at the major shows and was granted an audience with Queen Victoria. She was keenly interested in livestock breeding, an enthusiasm picked up from Prince Albert, who had raised prize-winning pigs. The Queen was most impressed with Black Prince, a glossy black hunk, and was graciously pleased to accept a tranche of the slaughtered bull as a Christmas present because she shared her subjects' belief that beef was best—cold rare sirloin being her daily fancy.

Beef Emigrates to America

Since Queen Victoria's approval represented the highest attainment in Britain, the Angus then moved on to America to make serious money. Four champion bulls were loosed on the Kansas plains in the 1870s, where they joined other British champion breeds. After judicious crossbreeding, the results proved very promising. The beef tasted much better than the meat of the native Texas Longhorn, a pre-industrial breed, lean, humpbacked, and slow-maturing.

Before the British invasion, the Texas Longhorn had fed the growing taste for beef in the northeastern industrial states, and the millions of cattle driven to the railheads for shipment had prepared the way for the newcomers by wiping out the buffalo and the Plains Indians. Now, in turn, the

Texas Longhorns were to be driven almost to extinction as the Great Plains filled up with the British breeds.

Americans were even keener beef eaters than Englishmen, and if John Bull personified beef in England, the cowboy would personify beef in the United States. Teddy Roosevelt dreamed up the image in his saga *The Winning of the West* (1889–96), a paean to the pioneers who were the right kind of Americans—hard, stoic, and WASP. But it was Owen Wister's novel *The Virginian*, published in 1902 and illustrated by Frederic Remington, that made the image of the cowboy endure. The Virginian was an enigmatic vigilante who stalked the western landscape, gun at the draw. He was made for the movies. Hollywood loved him right away and branded him on the world's imagination in the person of Gary Cooper. Thereafter, a cowboy would be stone-faced and conversationless. Even when cowboys started to vanish from the screen, the cowboy himself didn't. In *Dirty Harry* (1971), Clint Eastwood plays an urban cop who is by any other name Gary Cooper. As the punk readies to shoot, Eastwood squeezes out the minimum. "Make my day." An existentialist had supplanted the carousing patriot John Bull.

The cowboys herded cattle to the railroad depots for the trip to Chicago, which by the 1890s was the largest meat market in the world. The Chicago stockyards then sent the carcasses in refrigerated cars to customers, who aged the beef themselves in their own cold lockers. Aging was critical because fresh-killed beef was featureless and tough. Beef needed to be mortified to develop taste, hung in a chilled room for three weeks or more so the microbes could impart flavor to it. Once again, man and bacteria shared a common interest. A side of beef could lose up to 15 percent of its weight as the meat shrunk, but the result was rated sublime by a growing band of beef connoisseurs.

The American beef was richer than British beef. Cattle in Britain ate a mixed diet that included some grain, but the American cattle were finished with corn, a diet that produced greater marbling—the fat capillaries that streak through the flesh—tenderizing it and enhancing the flavor. And the growing popularity of steakhouses—Chicago had no less than thirty—fed the fame of American beef.

The Student Prince
Steakhouse

I didn't learn any of this until, in the 1970s, I got to eat at a great steakhouse in New York. I had consumed a lot of steak after I moved to America. There was a clutch of little French restaurants in midtown Manhattan that served an excellent cheap lunch of grilled flank steak cut into crimson slivers and smothered in a goodish wine sauce. And there was the ubiquitous barbecue, a cliché by this time, on which slabs of sirloin were grilled and then chopped up. Good but humdrum.

So, even when I was asked to go to Peter Luger Steak House, it meant nothing to me. Particularly as Frank, who had asked me, was something of a joke. Frank himself was a

man-boy of unimpeachable decency, with first-rate teeth
and button-down shirts and tassel loafers, and he was fast-
tracking to the top of the publishing company where I
worked. As far as I knew, Frank was the only person who
didn't call the corporate floor "the blimp hangar." Each
afternoon, Frank was first out of the office, just as he had
been first in, and he would say in his pleasant breezy way as
he went out the door, "I'm going down on the subway, anyone coming?" If Waxy, the art director, heard him, he would
lift his wounded eyes—the eyes of Peter Lorre contemplat-
ing murder—and whimper, "Can I watch?"

Frank asked me out to dinner, and Waxy overheard the
date being made, as he managed to overhear everything that
went on in the office. "So," Waxy lisped to me in his soft
voice, with just a smidgeon of German accent, "you're going
to the Cherman steakhouse with the Student Prince." Waxy
laughed a little unpleasantly as he slid away. Later, he ambled
over with a sketch he'd drawn of a cow. It was unrecogniz-
able. The animal's head was a triangle, and its body another
bony triangle. "Aurochs, the original cow," whispered Waxy.
"A noble beast." The next day, he brought a drawing of a fat
dwarf of a cow. "Disgusting, isn't it? That's what you are
going to be eating, you know, a gross animal, so fat it can
hardly walk; it falls over going round corners." With a thick
black pen, he began dividing up the cow into fat sections.

"I expect you are one of those people who think beef is
wonderful, of course you are, because you are British, and
the British invented beef." I said nothing, so he went on.

"They broke the incest taboo to invent beef, you know, went against God's word. But then the British long ago abandoned God, didn't they? And they went on breeding the cattle until they had perfection." He added long horns to his fat cow. "The horns had to go, they were dangerous, and the cattle had to be made defenseless. The brains went next. A smart animal wants to fight. The beef you eat is from a cow bred to be so dumb it's hardly an animal at all. It's a *Lumpenfichen.*"

At this, Waxy let the lids of his eyes fall in desolation. Over the next week, Waxy dropped off on my desk drawings of various cattle with comments scrawled over them, and sometimes an article about what was happening to beef—nothing good, I could see, as food science was surging with confidence, attacking right and left any food that might be vulnerable. Beef had loads of fat in it. "I don't eat beef myself." Waxy was with me again, bearing a five-page booklet about how the cattle were killed. "I mean, would you want to die that way?" The eyelids drooped in desolation.

Frank came over on the morning of our date. "We have to be there early," he said. "Peter Luger is wildly popular." That night we rocketed down the West Side, across Manhattan, over the Williamsburg Bridge, the taxi finally drawing up outside a rusty building with the name written in black Gothic script. Inside it was, I supposed, like a Beer Hall in Munich, a place I knew only from the movies. The maître d' barely greeted us, although he seemed to know Frank in an offhand kind of way, and he seated us at a scrubbed wood table. The waiter, a dumpy sort wearing a bow tie, didn't waste a smile on us. He asked Frank, "For two?" Frank just nodded. The waiter dropped a basket of rolls on the table as he passed, and said out of the corner of his mouth, "Sides?" Frank said, "The usual, spinach and fries." The waiter ambled back and asked, "Red wine?" and Frank said, "Yes."

Frank, I noticed, was undergoing a personality change. Gone was the friendly Boy Scout, and in his place was a beef fanatic. Frank had at his fingertips the entire story of American beef. He conjured up the landscape of the West, with its snow-capped mountains and endless plains, and the more he talked, the more it became clear how he bonded with beef. No wonder the waiters were so chippy; they were serving food for the gods, an attitude not unlike the old-line French waiter in New York who used to sweep the breadcrumbs off the table with a disdain that included the customers too, as if they really weren't up to the food.

Once Frank had set the scene, he told me in detail about the food we were to eat. The steak was not only Prime, the U.S. Department of Agriculture's top grade of beef, but the highest classification within Prime, something known only to butchers and the savvy steakhouse buyers, who call it "wasty" because it is so wasteful, since only 35 percent of the meat is retrieved from the surrounding caul of fat. The average consumer couldn't even buy it.

As far back as the 1930s, *The Joy of Cooking* warned readers that the great steaks were hard to find because most of them were reserved for restaurants and hotels. Prime beef was always a luxury, the way foie gras was a luxury—more so because it is much harder to produce Prime beef than foie gras. Beef quality is in the genes, as Robert Bakewell knew, and breeding is never a surefire thing. Out of a hundred candidates for Prime, regardless how much corn they're fed, only two or three will make the cut. This renders Prime breeding very expensive for the ranchers.

So I learned that the only way to ensure getting a real steak was to go to an old-fashioned steakhouse, one that dry-aged the beef.

Dry-aging, sighed Frank, was on its way out. The meat-packers, who now dominated the industry, had moved the slaughterhouses closer to the farms and feedlots for quicker processing. Then, instead of sending whole carcasses out to customers, they butchered the meat right on the spot, packing the edible parts into heavy sealed vacupaks. This was a big saving in shipping costs, and butchers loved it because far less meat was lost in wet-aging than in dry-aging.

Frank shook his head sadly. Wet-aged beef sat in plastic packs and decayed in its own juice; there was none of the flavor-producing microbial action. The bacteria couldn't get at it. No self-respecting beef connoisseur would have anything to do with wet-aged steak, which tasted at best like tin, Frank told me, and which was to dry-aged steak as a blended Scotch was to Glenmorangie. The dry-aged beef did not have one single taste; you had to roll it around in your mouth before you bit into it, and only then were the tastes and subtleties within those tastes revealed.

We didn't have to wait long for our dry-aged steak. It was enormous. A Porterhouse, weighing in at around three pounds, the kind of steak, Frank said, "I could saddle and ride right out of here." A steak, he informed me, was only good with a bone in it; the flavor leached from the bone marrow was particularly good. The Porterhouse was cut from the top or short loin of a steer, the location of the most tender steaks, the club or Delmonico, for example. Other steaks—well, Frank was a tad condescending. Flank steak and London Broil were fine on the barbecue as long as they were rare and sliced razor-thin. The Porterhouse had the best of all beef. A rib divided the short loin or strip steak from a gelatinous nugget of fillet, the softest piece of meat. The strip was a good bite of steak, the flavor spilling out with the juice, an iron taste with an aftertaste of rye whisky, not Scotch. The fillet had not much taste but it cut with a fork, and dipped into the juice, it was like a bonbon.

The waiter turned up to divide the steak, giving much more to Frank than to me, but that was fine with me; I'd never eaten more than six ounces of steak in my life. Then he turned over a side plate and placed the steak plate on it at an angle so the juices ran down to the rim. The juices were scooped up and dripped over our meat. This was the house tradition. Frank cut a piece of steak, dipped it into the juice, and sighed. I can't remember the side orders; they just fell into the steak's shadow. It was a fine steak.

Next day, Waxy wasted no time in signaling me to come into his office. "So, how was it?" "Great." I was about to

embark on what I'd learned at the beef seminar, but his eyelids, which had started to droop, shot up. "I can't believe it.
No one else has ever said he was any good at all."

The Calvary of Beef

My visit to Peter Luger took place in the 1970s, when beef
was coming down from the high point in its history. In the
1960s, the halcyon years of beef, almost half the U.S. population ate beef, including 200,000 hamburgers a minute. But
that would all change over the next twenty-five years as the
media reported first one, then another, and finally a third
fatal illness from eating beef.

The saturated-fat scare started in the 1970s as more and
more medical research linked saturated (animal) fats to heart
disease. Mad cow disease or BSE (bovine spongiform
encephalopathy) was identified in the 1980s; and in the
nineties, a new terror microbe—*E coli* O157:H7—was identified in beef cattle.

As media reports about the dangers of saturated fat grew,
public demand for beef slipped. The industry went into a
panic, and then with great fanfare virtuously declared a war
on fat. In 1976, and again in 1987, USDA grades were
changed to reflect a new, leaner beef. The breeders would
start crossing the old trusty breeds like Angus with exotics,
the skimpy French breeds, and the profile of American beef
began to change. This took time because about three years

are necessary to assess the meat of a new crossbreed. But by the 1990s, the highest level of USDA Prime no longer appeared, and there would be 20 percent less of the Prime and Choice grades. All grades would be leaner.

Many consumers believed the grades to be an impartial rating by the Department of Agriculture. In fact, the meat-packers pay for the grading system which, when it was established in the 1920s, was designed to promote meat to consumers. But almost immediately, the meatpackers asked for changes in their favor. Fattening cattle costs money; it's cheaper to produce lean meat. Just as the war on fat played into the economics of the dairy industry, so it did for the beef industry.

Consumers started to grumble. The new beef tasted like the grass-fed beef imported from Argentina. Argentinian beef has a fine taste all its own, but it wasn't as satisfying as that of the rich corn-finished American beef that consumers liked best, and it was on the tough side. The new beef cooked up dry. In 1995, a really black year for the industry, complaints multiplied; the Marriott hotel chain said that 30 percent of its customers had complained about the quality of the steak.

Paradoxically, even though beef sales fell, the number of steakhouses rose. One reason was that customers were so confused by the way beef grades had changed that they preferred to rely on steakhouses' expertise to get a good one.

Beef had always been treated generically, its quality defined only by the USDA grades. But in 1978, the first brand-name beef appeared on the market. The American Angus Association started the Certified Angus Beef Program (CAB), which guaranteed consistent quality (Choice plus) to consumers confused by the wavering USDA grades. CAB would be followed by other brands, such as Sterling Silver and the Cattleman Collective, but so far it is still the most widely recognized. Alain Ducasse, the global French chef, picked a CAB steak for a column he wrote in the *New York Times* in 2002. Then he ruined it by proposing a marmaladish garnish, something no true beef lover could go along with. In fact, Escoffier too liked to gussy up a steak. He chose the little tournedos cut from the end of the fillet and then disguised them. Of course. I can see Escoffier being so bored with steak, a food with limited options. The taste was too assertive: eaters wanted to get at a steak, they didn't want it disguised. *Tournedos Henri IV* is a grilled tournedos served with Béarnaise sauce on a slice of French bread fried in butter, topped with an artichoke bottom garnished with potatoes the size of hazelnuts and cooked in butter. *Tournedos Rossini* is fried, placed on a fried-bread slice, and topped with slices of fresh foie gras that have been dredged with flour, fried in butter, and garnished with a slice of truffle. I can remember a version that had pâté de foie gras placed on top of the meat, and I think the garnish was an olive, but as I had never tasted a truffle, I found it very good.

But the war on fat was nothing to what followed. Ever since breeding for beef began, breeders have gone all out to make cattle a reliable commodity. Beef cattle are now Frankenoxen, bred in the lab, where the last words in reproductive techniques are applied—from artificial insemination to in vitro fertilization, alteration of a cow's menstrual cycle, embryo transfers among cows, even embryo splitting, not to mention cloning and sperm sexing. Cattle are given antiobiotics against disease and to spur growth; and they are bulked up with an FDA-approved protein mix of restaurant leftovers, out-of-date pet food, and chicken litter. Spray-dried cows' and pigs' blood is mixed into the cattle's drinking water.

In Britain, the cattle feed included animal remains. (The practice of animal cannibalism as a low-cost protein boost was pioneered in 1865 by the chemist Baron Liebig.) But during the 1980s, a change in processing the feed—done, ironically, for health reasons—apparently allowed the sheep disease scrapie to enter the food chain.

At first, only the cows went mad, pathetically staggering around the farmyard before falling into a coma. Scientists were sure that mad cow disease or bovine spongiform encephalopathy could not infect another species. Humans were safe. Then, in the early 1990s, the Creutzfeldt-Jakob Disease (CJD) Surveillance Unit in Edinburgh spotted a suspicious statistic. CJD was the human variant form of mad cow disease, although up to now nobody had thought of it that way. It had been identified as a brain-destroying disease in Germany in the 1920s, but scientists knew little more about it because it was so rare, infecting only one in a million people. Nobody knew how people became infected. But in

1993 the Edinburgh researchers noticed that 109 patients diagnosed with CJD were 13 times more likely to have eaten veal regularly than people who died of other diseases.

Over the next two years, a mysterious illness was reported in Britain among people under forty. The victims displayed puzzling symptoms: depression, loss of balance and coordination. CJD was tentatively diagnosed until the brain scans of several of the patients were studied. Yes, the patients did have brain disease—the mad cow kind.

The report traumatized Britain. At first the government denied it; in 1995, Prime Minister John Major said there was no evidence that mad cow could be transmitted to human beings. That was true. Nobody knows how the disease is transmitted. On the other hand, the evidence that the victims had mad cow disease was irrefutable.

The British beef industry was almost destroyed: British beef was banned, but British pedigree cattle had been exported far and wide, and the disease began turning up all over the world. In Florence, they had to stop eating the famous local bistecca cut from giant Chianiana, and in Spain, victorious matadors were no longer permitted to toss the bull's ear into the crowd for fear of infection. In the Camargue, the wild marshes at the mouth of the Rhône in France, the ancient dish of black bull stew that tastes like ink had to be withdrawn from menus.

More significant for the future, the British themselves lost confidence in food science. After years of false alarms, the scientists had missed the real thing. They had assured people there was no danger, and now they were admitting the possibility that perhaps millions could die horribly. From then on, the British became Luddites in their opposition to innovations such as genetically modified food. It was all very well to be told over and over that transgenic food was now eaten daily by North Americans with no bad effects reported. Trust in the health authorities was dead.

Mad cow disease was not caused by a bacteria but by a mutant protein, a prion that turns the brain into Swiss cheese. At least, that is the current thinking. But it was a bacteria, the newly emerging *E coli* O157:H7, that cut a vicious swath through the North American population, killing consumers, and often leaving survivors without the use of their kidneys. In her book *Secret Agents*, the medical writer Madeline Drexler describes how the pathogen took several years gathering force, a death here, a death there, before it made its breakaway move, infecting more than seven hundred people and killing four children after they ate Monster Burgers at a Washington State outlet of the Jack-in-the-Box chain. The Monster Burgers were advertised with hyperbole that for once was warranted: "So good they're scary."

Scarier still was that the conduit for O157:H7 is cattle excrement. There are almost 100 million cattle in America and they produce at least 1 trillion pounds of manure a year. When the bug started turning up in unpasteurized apple cider, in children's wading pools, in water systems, suspicion fell on the factory farms, which were leaching animal wastes into the streams and underground aquifers.

Mad cow disease and O157:H7 have disturbing implications. No source for either disease has yet been confirmed, and nobody therefore knows when the diseases may strike again. Scientists acknowledge they have only identified a fraction of the bacteria that exist, and how the prion invades the brain is as yet not understood. After mad cow was considered vanquished in Britain, it suddenly appeared in Canada in 2003.

The American cattle industry immediately banned Canadian beef as unsafe and then held its breath. It knew—even if the public didn't—that the U.S. and Canadian industries are inextricably linked: the United States imported 1.2 million head of cattle in 2002, and Canadian beef represented 40 percent of U.S. yearly consumption. Both countries were cavalier about the chances of the cattle coming down with BSE. On May 27, 2003, Tara Parker-Pope reported in the *Wall Street Journal* that the United States and Canada considered the threat of BSE so low that they never adopted the strict safety standards of Europe, where animal cannibalism is now banned. In North America, cattle cannot be directly fed other cattle's remains, but the parts can be fed to chickens and pigs, which in turn are made into cattle feed.

The other shoe dropped at the end of 2003, when a Holstein in Washington State was diagnosed with BSE. So, after all, Texas ranchers' public enemy number one, Howard Lyman, had been right back in 1996 when, on *The Oprah Winfrey Show*, he said that BSE was already in the United

States. Lyman now told the *Los Angeles Times*: "Anybody who thinks we have only one mad cow in America is smoking the number one crop out of California."

The media, hobbled in the past by the litigious cattle industry, used BSE to lay bare the gruesome details of cattle rendering. It turned out that sickened "downer" cows were routinely killed for food, and that an ox may be recycled in unimaginable ways—into lipstick, cake frosting, sour cream, canned ham, candy, soups, and gelcaps for medicines, and cattle bones are sometimes used to make gelatin. In the 1990s, the industry started using an advanced meat recovery (AMR) technology that employs hydraulic pressure to strip carcasses. Consumer groups complained that ground beef was turning up in pizza toppings, and government scientists discovered spinal cord tissue (which may be a source of BSE) in some meat. Even so, the government still refuses to ban the technology. McDonald's, having won Sir Galahad's spurs when it rescued the martyred hen, is now doing battle for consumers: it has banned all AMR meat.

As for the prevalence of 0157:H7, cattle processing provides opportunities for the pathogen at every stage—and particularly in the slaughterhouse. In 1906, Upton Sinclair wrote a novel, *The Jungle*, which laid bare the squalor of the Chicago packing plants, and prompted the establishment of safety regulations; but a century later, slaughterhouses aren't much better. Cattle go to slaughter with their hides drenched in manure, and as the skins are stripped off, the manure infects the carcasses. The meatpackers have promised hyper-hygienic measures—cattle washed and washed again. Obviously, that wouldn't be enough. The only sure way to destroy the bacteria is to cook your ground beef to boredom. The interior of a hamburger should be gray. No more Steak Tartare, which has only just got back on the menus after raw eggs were declared safe. *Pot-au-feu* may finally find friends in North America: stewing beef, after all, should be safe—or rather, safer, because realistically, beef will never again be completely safe.

Even if it's irradiated. Irradiation bombards beef with gamma rays, which annihilate all pathogens, *and* the meat's flavor. Some beef is already being nuked in America. Like pasteurization, irradiation may be effective as far it goes. The subsequent handling of the food, however, may negate its effects just the way the pasteurization of milk may be rendered useless by how milk products are handled.

Today, the safest beef is probably beef from naturally raised cattle: organic cattle. For many years, the Queen of England has been eating the lean, clean beef from her own herd of Highland cattle, a breed of Teddy bears that come in *feuilles mortes* colors; and she's not alone. Highland meat is sold by hobby farms all over the world. It is naturally tender and has a non-assertive taste of hay. The beef scares have also spurred beef boutiques, their products available by mail order or on line. Some of the beef is called "natural" and some "organic"; some corresponds to USDA Prime, some is leaner. Antibiotics are only used when the cattle are actually ill, and growth hormones are banned. The feed is free from animal detritus, and in every case, the beef has been personally cared for from birth to a slaughterhouse that isn't run by a commercial meatpacker.

One of the first American beef boutiques, the Niman Ranch in Oakland, California, describes its cattles' bucolic surroundings: the animals browse on self-sustaining pasture; they're treated humanely and killed only when their time has come. A similar operation exists in Scotland on the Duke of Buccleuch's estate. Is this how beef was two hundred years ago, before the inexorable industrialization began?

In the late 1990s, I wrote an article for a Toronto newspaper about the state of steak after its twenty terrible years. To do so, I visited several steakhouses in Toronto, and came away depressed. The old-line steakhouses seemed so grungy; none equaled the great Brooklyn steakhouse where I had learned all about beef. All the steak was wet-aged. The new steakhouse, part of a national chain, was worse. It was a Potemkin steakhouse. When I stepped into the tiled courtyard with its large stained-glass skylight, I entered a steakhouse theme park. The maître d' was friendly, the waitpersons as pristine as Disneyland guides, the decor as pretty as one of the frog pond restaurants in Manhattan. USDA Prime was headlined, but the menu also offered fish and a vegetarian plate. Now I knew just how scared the beef industry had become. A steakhouse could no longer set its own terms. Peter Luger had a waiter, so it was said, who told customers: "Order steak; 150 percent of our customers do."

The new steakhouse style was *über*-salesman. It used to be that customers were expected to know what they liked and order it; that's no longer enough. Now waiters are salesmen. First the menu is treated as a tipsheet that is followed up by a pitch from the waiter. You order, and then a culinary Sherpa, sometimes different from the waiter, guides you to the higher level, explaining exactly what you are going to eat. Our Sherpa pitched fillet steak: "I have to tell you how good the fillet is." In an era of leaner and often tougher beef, the tender fillet is tops among customers, the industry is working to give all beef that old-fashioned melting mouth-feel—but without the fat.

The future may well be beef like Nolan Ryan's Tender Aged Beef brand (named for a Hall of Fame baseball pitcher), which is available in grocery stores in Houston, Texas. The Beefmaster ox is a cross between Herefords, Shorthorns, and Texas Brahmans. But breeding no longer determines quality. Once slaughtered, the carcasses are shocked with a tenderizing 400 volts of electricity and evaluated by something called a BeefCam, which rates the color of the ribeye and gives the beef a tenderness score. The top scorers are slapped with the Beefmaster Premium label.

In the meantime, the founding beef, British beef, is back on the markets. The French had held out, but they finally capitulated early in the twenty-first century. Prince Charles flew to Paris as ambassador. Prince Charles may yet become a food king—he has his own herd of organically raised Black Angus. The Entente Cordiale was remade as the Prince enjoyed a steak with a glass of St. Emilion, and he even remembered to give the nod to John Bull, saying: "This wonderful piece of beef is not just a delicious lump of meat we enjoy eating—it represents an entire culture."

The Late Great Offal

"Hath a calf, which is the emblem of stupidity, brains?" asked E. S. Dallas, the author of *Kettner's Book of the Table*, a dictionary that only an idiosyncratic Victorian could have written, full of encyclopedic trivia. It has always been debatable whether an intelligent animal's brains would be edible, which is why calf and sheep brains were favored, although recent experiments indicate that sheep are not such duffers after all and can actually recognize individual humans in a wooly sort of way. But in the nineteenth century, the dumbness of animals was beyond doubt, and Dallas said that it was one of the glories of cookery that it recognized good in everything—even a calf's intelligence, which happened to be the best part of a calf.

He was writing at a time when anything that could be eaten was eaten and enjoyed. Today, it's hard to find brains on the menu, and when I did, I wished I hadn't. I had ordered brains from an Italian restaurant in Toronto. A large gray pancake appeared, run through with tiny black lines—capillaries, I suppose. I couldn't believe it. I had ordered them with a particular picture in mind. In London my parents used to frequent a pretty little gilt-edged Italian restaurant—London had the best Italian restaurants in those days—decorated with curly Venetian glass mirrors and populated by charming Italian waiters who wore starched white cotton jackets. We always went to the same restaurant to eat brains, *Cervello dore*, golden brains, a Roman recipe, little crisp beignets lapped by bronze butter with a snap of vinegar in it. Their texture was soft and slightly spongy, and they tasted, of course, of the delicious butter; they were also highly digestible.

My mother loved brains but refused to try to prepare them at home. Brains have to be soaked and cleaned, bringing one into almost too intimate a contact. After soaking the brain for a couple of hours in cold water, you have to pull off the membrane that covers it, which means you must actually get inside the squiggles of the brain. Sometimes the membrane is left on, as I think it was with the brain I was served, and that makes the dish tough and gray. The brain must also be cleaned of any spots of blood. You can see why this is not a popular home recipe.

The brain is then simmered for almost half an hour and allowed to cool in the liquid. For *Cervello dore*, the pieces are butterflied and sliced, dredged in flour, and sautéed in butter until it has a crisp crust. The morsels are served on a platter with butter bronzed in the frying pan, a sprinkling of vinegar, capers, and parsley.

Offal always sounded better in French. In the days when

it was understood that a little knowledge was a dangerous thing, anything unpleasant about food was avoided. In England, this meant that a French word was used, the way Escoffier called frog's legs *nymphes* so frog lovers wouldn't be distressed or snobbish people feel that eating a frog was beneath them. For the English, a French menu glossed over all unpleasantness, and the ingenious chef Ali Bab's braised and stuffed *rognons* didn't look like kidneys at all. The taste for kidneys is declining, not just because kidneys have such an aggressively earthy flavor to the timid modern palate but because people now know too much about how kidneys process bodily wastes. Nowadays, even in England, the ripe old steak and kidney pie has become steak and mushroom pie, and deviled kidneys are glimpsed no more on the breakfast sideboard. Still, there are wonderful old recipes for both.

· ·

STEAK AND KIDNEY PIE

Serves 6

2 lb sirloin/rump steak

1 lb veal kidneys

2 Tbs all-purpose flour, with salt and pepper added

1 large onion, chopped

3 Tbs unsalted butter

2 cups beef stock or 1 cup stock and 1 cup red wine
   with high alcohol content

1 cup mushrooms, sliced
Bouquet garni
6 oz of 12-oz frozen packet of puff pastry
Optional: 12 oysters
One large egg, beaten

Day One

Preheat oven to 300°F.

Cut steak into 1-inch pieces and core and slice kidneys. Sprinkle with seasoned flour. Cook the onion until lightly browned in 1 Tbs of butter, then add the meat, brown it quickly, and transfer to a Dutch oven.

Pour the stock/wine into a frying pan and boil it for 5 minutes. Then pour mixture over meat.

Fry mushrooms in the remaining butter and add them with the bouquet garni to the Dutch oven. Cover, and simmer in oven at 300°F for 90 minutes. Cool the Dutch oven and let the stew rest overnight in the refrigerator.

Day Two

Preheat oven to 450°F.

Roll out pastry. Cut off strips wide enough to cover the rim of the pie dish and hang down a little inside it. Add the cold stew to dish. If you are using oysters, add them now. Brush water lightly over the pastry rim and cover the pie with remaining pastry. Brush pastry cover with beaten egg.

Bake at 450°F for 15 to 20 minutes, then lower heat to 325°

and leave for another 45 minutes until the pastry is golden brown.

Serve with boiled potatoes and green beans.

. . . . .

CHARLOTTE'S DEVILED KIDNEYS

Serves 4

6 lamb kidneys
2–3 thin rashers of streaky bacon
1 medium onion
4 Tbs unsalted butter
1 Tbs vegetable oil
½ cup button mushrooms
1 Tbs plain flour
1 Tbs warm water
1 tsp red wine vinegar
1 tsp strong English mustard, made up
1 Tbs red currant jelly
Sea salt and pepper

Halve and core the kidneys. Using scissors, snip the bacon into small batons. Cut the onion into thin slices.

Add butter and oil to a sauté pan and brown the kidneys. Add the bacon, onion, and mushrooms, and sauté briefly over a high heat.

Sprinkle in the flour and stir the contents of the pan, adding warm water slowly to make a smooth sauce the consistency of single cream. Add the wine vinegar, and blend in the mustard and red currant jelly. Season to taste with salt and freshly ground pepper.

Simmer briefly until the onion and kidneys are cooked.

Serve on plain boiled rice.

. . . .

Like kidneys, sweetbreads assume a delicacy in French, and gourmets could eat *Ris-de-veau à la financière au vol-au-vent*—a mouthful to say as well as to eat—the large pastry case stuffed with sautéed sweetbreads, truffles, and mushrooms, all bathed in Béchamel sauce, without any anxiety about swallowing vital parts of a calf's digestive system, in this case, the pancreas and thymus.

The first time I ate a sweetbread, in France, I thought it was a marshmallow, sweet and squashy. *"Guimauve?"* (marshmallow), said my hostess incredulously, and looked at her son, Yves, darkly. What savages was he consorting with? She had taken us out to a Sunday lunch with her family; we must have been a party of about ten, including Yves's grandmother, a nephew, a married daughter, even a silent child. The restaurant had a covered terrace that overlooked a stream. It was a lovely early summer day, and we were in the countryside somewhere near Blois.

Jack was already fretting. He had come along under protest. To Jack, an Englishman who had fallen in love with steak when he lived in Los Angeles, relocation to Paris had been a mixed blessing. French food was all right, but how he wished his wife, Pat, would stop going on about it. When Pat had suggested that she and I spend a week exploring the Dordogne, he was quite happy to stay home and eat steak— that is, provided he could find a decent steak. The French served only silly little steaks. But then Pat read that the Dordogne was a place that attracted women of a certain age. "Widows!" she cried in horror. We were still young.

So Jack was corraled to accompany us, with the promise of three-star meals. "I bet they don't have steak." And then Yves, another friend, entered the equation. He so wanted us to see Blois, his home, and it was on the way, which is how we came to be eating this enormous lunch with his family. The menu was large and various, although Madame did the ordering for us in a quick, commanding way, saying as she did so that she knew the menu's strengths and weaknesses, and after a few of bottles of Savenniere—a tingling Loire white—were opened, even Jack cheered up.

Course followed course in leisurely succession. The lunch went on for hours. Its mood changed as does a play with three acts, each dish creating different emotions, trains of conversation snaking off in all directions. We English found we were able to talk amazing French—yes, yes, how fine the spiral staircase is at the château—banal but pleasing chat, only to be given in return a complete tour of the bloody political history of Blois, Yves smiling with satisfaction. We had *rillettes*, a pork pâté that was like eating solid fat, and crayfish in a cream sauce; and a wonderful leg of lamb, fragrant and pink and garlicky, served with *flageolets verts*, the little green version of kidney beans, the first time I had ever eaten that particular combination of meat and beans, the beans sopping up the juice from the lamb. I think it was after the lamb that we ate the delicate salad with what looked like toasted croutons and I made my gaffe comparing them to marshmallows.

Jack promptly stopped eating, fork suspended over his plate. He knew it. Just when the lamb had lulled him into feeling so good. Worse was to come because we had eaten far too much and were exhausted from the food and the emotions that went into it. The tiny fraise-des-bois and the luxuriant meringue cake were too much, and the rest of the day passed queasily.

The Taboo: Chevaline

If beef goes, what will the replacement be? How about horse? There are plenty of horses going begging, as it were. Claude Bouvry of Bouvry Meats, a horse-packing plant in Calgary, Alberta, is the leading North American exporter of horsemeat round the world. He sells 2 million servings of meat a week and he says he has no difficulty getting horses. "There are millions of horses. We buy them everywhere— all kinds of horses"—horses that have been abandoned by their owners, horses whose life in the shafts of an Amish buggy are finished, horses who have run their last race, hunters who've jumped the last hedge, and horses put out to grass, all destined for the knacker's yard because it is a rare horse that dies naturally.

Horse is excellent food. It is more nutritious than beef, 27 percent protein versus beef's 21 percent; it has 5.7 percent fat compared to beef's 12 percent; and horses don't get sick the way cattle do. They don't get foot and mouth disease (which may not affect humans but lays waste to the herds), or mad cow disease, or tuberculosis. So far, no rogue toxin has tainted the meat, and here's the clincher: horses taste like beef, like grassy Argentinian beef more than Prime beef, but the millions of people the world over who eat horse regularly like it just fine.

The only glitch is that in parts of North America and Britain, there is still a taboo about eating horse. A horse is designated as a companion animal, almost a human. A horse is a pal, like a cat or a dog, and do you really want to eat a significant other? On the other hand, the animal shelters are full of abandoned significant others which have to be regularly euthanized (the animal lovers' evasive word for death), so if a horse has to die anyway, why not eat it? But people in the grip of emotion are rarely rational.

We didn't have a cook in London, so my mother did all the shopping, and one day she returned from Soho with a large rump steak. It was reasonable, she said, pleased with her bargain. It was not well marbled, but we didn't care. I don't believe I had ever seen a piece of marbled beef at that point. The test was obviously to be in the eating.

After she rubbed it with Worcester sauce, she broiled the steak under the gas grill so it was rare to medium rare. Then she stroked it with a clove of garlic. The verdict was unanimous. It was tough, a little, but tasty, very tasty, we judged. Pressed to describe the taste of good sirloin, I think of iron filings. Some of that tenderizing powder helped—the kind that I believe was found to be potentially carcinogenic and eventually recalled. My father added to it his own mélange of mustards, a mixture of Dijon and hot mustard.

After that, we had steak once a week until the fateful day when my father accompanied my mother on a shopping trip. My mother couldn't help herself. She had to show my father her steak place. After she had eagerly guided him to the magical butcher's where she joined the end of a long queue, my father wandered outside, and he noticed something that my mother, who perceived the world through an obliging blur, couldn't see. In the corner of the plate-glass window, in almost invisible characters, he saw the word "*Chevaline*" and a tiny silhouette ("I almost needed a magnifying glass") of a horse's head.

Selling horse was legal—the British government encouraged it, in fact, because of the shortage of beef. My mother was quite sanguine about horse. But the rest of us weren't. "Well, really, we could have eaten Patsy," my father said when they got home, and he added that perhaps we should have, but of course he didn't believe it. Patsy had been my pony, a feral animal who first showed me what true alienation was. Still, eating her would have been taboo.

Why we eat what we eat is a curious mixture of need and myth, and the needs and myths vary from country to country and time to time. Once, a friend of mine from Beijing offered to cook a Chinese New Year dinner for me. On our way to Chinatown, he began going over what would be needed. A fishhead, a big one, he began, and black chickens, and a lot of canned food. I had had no idea how the Chinese relied on cans, and there was I thinking that the whole meal would be organic. I did give a warning that whatever he chose was okay as long as there were no paw-paws in syrup, and he replied, blank-faced, "Cat good, dog better." So it was true. My father passing a Chow in Eaton Square had commented, "They say Chow in syrup has a unique texture, like slipper satin." But of course no one in England would contemplate eating a dog.

How deep the English taboo against horse ran was more questionable. As the long queue at the *Chevaline* butcher showed, the English ate whatever they could when they were hungry. Horse eating had been routine in ancient times. When Caesar conquered France (Gaul), his soldiers lusted for the taste of horse. In those days, the unindustrialized ox was no doubt inedible. Western Europeans continued to eat horse without a qualm until, for no special reason, the Catholic Church banned eating horse—and beaver—in the Middle Ages. But need overran scruples, and horse eating crept back. The food king Louis XIV banned horsemeat, but only because he was always at war and he needed horses for battles. That ban ended with the French Revolution. In 1812, as the starving French retreated from Moscow, they had to eat their horses; there are grisly stories of dying French soldiers, their faces smeared with horse's blood, and of a camp follower feeding her baby horse's blood.

Within a few decades, the French, always practical, were considering the horse as a source of animal protein. The French do nothing by halves. A distinguished committee— scientists, philosophers, gourmands of note—was struck to test the taste of horsemeat. In 1868, the year the first little boutiques *hippophagigues* opened in Paris, invitations went out for a dinner in Paris featuring *Rosinante*—oil mayonnaise, roast fillet of Pegasus, and patties of *Bucephalus* marrow. The diners were unanimously pro-horse. The horse bouillon was better-tasting than beef bouillon, and the roast fillet of horse scored over a beef fillet.

The same year in London, the Society for the Propagation of Horse Flesh as an Article of Food organized a horse banquet. The menu included chafed withers and horse got a modest boost, a few horse butchers opening in London. But they didn't last long. The idea of eating a horse, the animal that had given mankind its greatest freedom until the automobile was invented, was abhorrent, particularly when you considered how the horse had sacrificed itself for man, taking the brunt of battle. This moral dimension is often evoked by animal activists. The horse was a martyr to human folly. Men might choose to fight and die, but horses had no choice.

Despite the taboo, I had liked the horsemeat steak, so

when I first saw a horse butcher in Paris, I didn't shudder and look away. The butcher on rue Lepic in Montmartre was positively elegant, a red door with a little gold horse's head hanging above, and gleaming white marble counters within. It was tidy and hygienic. Plastic covered a sidewalk spread of horse cuts. I never thought Patsy had a heart, but I saw now that horses had them. Liver, brains, kidneys, tenderloin, and rump . . . the paler cuts must have been from colts.

After mad cow disease was discovered to affect humans, beef sales slumped in Europe and sales of horsemeat started climbing, peaking in 2002. Horsemeat, which had been declining as pork and lamb were so cheap, was now seen as blessedly safe. And all over the Continent, horse-meat returned to the menus—from Belgium and the Netherlands to northern France, Paris, of course, Italy, where the most horsemeat is eaten, to Spain and Switzerland where *Fondue bourguignonne*—cubes of horsemeat deep-fried in oil, and served with aïoli, the garlic mayonnaise—is much liked.

Quack and Track

The restaurant looked just like a French bistro. It was among several small restaurants clustered together in Kensington Market in Toronto's multicultural heart. Horse was not on the menu—just in case someone might be offended. I asked about *Chevaline* and the cheery waiter said, "Quack and

Track? A duck leg and a horse fillet." I ate the rare fillet with my eyes closed and I could have been eating any low-fat beef, only the horse was more tender. The chef told me he hadn't had many negative comments and no angry ones. Opponents were sorrowful more than anything else; one customer said he felt that eating horse would be like eating a friend. Horse, I found out, was being served at several restaurants in Toronto, and of course routinely in certain Japanese and Italian restaurants. And when it went on the menu at The Fifth, the city's most glamourous restaurant, customers ordered it without a qualm. I checked with the local animal activists to discover their attitude. The reply was that while they were against any animal being eaten, at least horses were treated better than the industrialized cattle, lamb, pigs, and chickens. These were the truly pathetic victims of man's greed.

The Last Word for Pork and Lamb

In Shillingford, after the war, our pig was a despised creature. For one thing, it never grew. My father, who checked on it regularly, was convinced that Katy, Dick the farmer's wife, had swapped our pig with her own. Failing that, she had cast a spell on it. Katy, who gleamed with shiny glasses and clinked with large bracelets, believed in "the other world," and she put down the slightest disarray of her house to the fact that it was haunted by a poltergeist. Sometimes at night there would be these bangs, and the next day, a piece of Staffordshire was on the floor, flung from the alcove where it had once sat safely, or Dick's favorite armchair was overturned. What is a poltergeist? my sister finally asked. Katy replied; "A wicked German spirit." There had been German prisoners of war working on the farm, but they seemed nice country boys and had made the most cunning toys for the village children. But there it was. With typical Katy histrionics, she wailed to my father, what should she do? Should she perhaps ask the vicar?

My father smiled disbelievingly. He doubted very much, he said, whether the vicar was up to exorcizing a poltergeist, or any German spirit, for that matter. The vicar was a pacifist; no doubt a vegetarian. He was all for turning the other cheek to the Germans, enemies just yesterday. My father, who was responsible for reading one of the lessons at the Sunday service at the church in the adjoining village, tried to counter the vicar's pusillanimity by choosing the most bloodthirsty lesson from the Old Testament each week, leafing through the books for something along the lines of the destruction of Korah, Dathan, and Abiram. "And the earth opened her mouth, and swallowed them up, and their houses, and all the men that appertained unto Korah and all their goods. . . . They . . . went down alive into the pit, and the earth closed upon them: and they perished from among the congregation." The vicar didn't seem to notice; he smiled benignly as we left the church.

My father hurried home still in war mode, the lines from "Don't Let's Be Beastly to the Germans" humming in his head. He relished a favorite record, Noël Coward's mocking retort to the lefties who wanted to make peace with the Germans as early as 1943.

> Let us treat them very kindly
> As we would a valued friend
> We might send them out some bishops
> As a form of lease and lend . . .

And the triumphant finale:

> Let's let them feel they're swell again
> And bomb us all to hell again
> But don't let's be beastly to the Hun.

Apparently these last lines were added after Coward sang the song for President Roosevelt, who loved it and said if anything it could be stronger.

My father was away in London when the pigs were killed; my mother shuddered and refused to have anything to do with it. She had never become used to the bloodthirsty English taste, symbolized by the Chamber of Horrors at Madame Tussaud's Waxworks Museum. We children loved the Chamber of Horrors—actually, I never knew a kid who didn't. There lay Marat in his bloody bath, Charlotte Corday poised above him, knife in hand. The emphasis on the French Revolution came from the founder herself, Madame Tussaud, who had escaped to London with a few relics—an actual blade from a guillotine and several severed heads. Small tableaux set in the wall continued the violent themes. For a threepenny bit, you could push a button and behead Mary, Queen of Scots, yourself as she kneeled before her executioner, who would raise his ax and bring it down, the Queen's head rolling across the floor of Fotheringay Castle. It was most satisfying.

But the execution of the pig was different. As my sister and I walked up the road to the farm, we were joined by other children, for this was the real thing: death. The vet arrived with the local butcher in the butcher's van; he wore a flat cap and a gray raincoat, and he carried a gun. While shotguns were everywhere, we had never seen this kind of gun before; it was more like a revolver. A humane killer, we were reassured. A steel bolt would be driven immediately into the pig's brain and he would suffer no pain. The pigs were docile, although as the most intelligent of food animals, they tend to fight to the death on the assembly killing lines, often jumping off and attacking one of their killers—like humans, they do not want to go alone into the void. Luckily, we had no idea of the pig's metaphysical state that day in the farmyard, and there was no noise at all as the pigs, one by one, their ears flapping, sank silently onto the frozen ground. Then the butcher stepped forward and ripped the carcasses down the middle, reached inside, and plucked out the bladders. He blew them up and tossed them to the village boys, who started kicking them around as footballs.

We had no trouble eating our slain pig. How good the bacon was, how excellent the roasted loin with crackling. Today, you have to order crackling specially as the pigs are skinned when they are killed, the producers quite confident that fat is proscribed. But the crackling makes all the difference to good roast pork.

. . . .

ROAST PORK AND CRACKLING

Serves 8–10

1 6-lb boned loin of pork with the skin (you usually have to ask for such a loin in advance. Specify that you want the skin cut off from the meat and ask the butcher to score it for you)
Fennel seeds, sea salt, and white pepper
3 lemons, squeezed, the juice mixed with 4 Tbs olive or cooking oil

Preheat oven to 450°F.

Grind up a handful of fennel seeds, sea salt, and white pepper, and rub the mixture all over the meat.

Tie the scored skin onto the loin, and put the meat into the oven in a roasting pan (use a meat thermometer to check the interior temperature—160°F is recommended). Wait for the skin to start browning, then start basting it with the lemon juice and oil mixture. Keep turning and basting the meat for 35 minutes, then turn off the oven and let the loin rest for ½ hour. Carve, making sure everyone gets a slice of crackling. Serve with *jus* from the pan and mashed sweet potatoes.

. . . .

Now it was revealed that my mother's favorite meat was ham, not beef. Our single ham arrived cured, as the bacon was; she marinated it in cider and spices, then baked it, covered in brown sugar. The sugar was rationed, but even so, it had to be acquired with enormous difficulty from Mrs. Pratt at the village shop, Mrs. Pratt being of the old school of shopkeepers who didn't like to sell anything and thought sugar an unwarranted extravagance.

Once beef was again available, I never sought out pork. Now I think it was because pork was often overcooked, which makes it disagreeably dry. The reason was that pork was an early victim of the political manipulation of food science. Originally, pigs fed happily out of garbage pails, which is what made pork such a democratic food; anyone could keep a pig without cost. The downside was that like all wild food, the pig could pick up parasites. In the late nineteenth century, a German scientist found that uncooked pork harbored a roundworm, *Trichinella spiralis*, which infected humans by burrowing into their muscles and sometimes killing them. The best way to kill the worm was to cook the pork to a tough and tired faretheewell.

Trichinella was an annoying worm with a low kill rate, but once trichinosis was identified in pig, it became a weapon in the ongoing food wars. In the late nineteenth century, because U.S. pork had a higher rate of trichinosis than European pork, Europeans refused to import it, and a trade war erupted. Panic is the only way to describe what followed. The American pigs' diet was overhauled and continued to be overhauled until only a tiny fraction of 1 percent of pork may have trichinosis today. In fact, the overcooking of pork is unnecessary: while the Centers for Disease Control recommends cooking pork to 170°F, it acknowledges that that temperature "substantially exceeds" the heat required to kill any lingering *Trichinella*. The worm is dead at 140°F, in fact, and rosy pork is no longer a threat, although most cookbooks still recommend 160°F.

The French, amazingly, also overcook pork. Pork doesn't feature in the classic cuisine except in pâté, where pork fat is of course essential, and pig is even more essential to the cured meats and sausages of the charcuterie; but pork is not for the gods, it is hardscrabble cuisine. Chinese cooking would be lost without pork, which is the very best meat to put into Hot and Sour soup. There is nothing better than pork chitterlings, or pork sausages, pork and sauerkraut, pork short ribs; roast pork, of course, with the ineffable crackling—food for the soul and the body in every way.

Pork is so good that cannibals apparently said it was as good as human flesh, as soft and easily bruised. This sounds like the way the rest of us regard Kobe beef, which sits in a pool of fat and is so soft it might as well be Jell-O. A roasted sucking pig is one of the truly great dishes, better even than roast loin of pork, but it's going begging these days.

Lamb, the other great industrial meat, isn't as versatile as beef. The most popular cuts are the expensive rack of lamb, or little loin chops; the old chump chop, cut from the neck, is rarely seen any more, and mutton—old lamb—has virtually vanished. Now all sheep's meat is young lamb because mutton induces horror in many North Americans.

Apparently, rank mutton was served to the U.S. and Canadian troops during World War II. When the soldiers came home, they refused to look at mutton again. This was fine with the lamb industry because it could get a higher price for young lambs.

What went out along with mutton for the British was Shepherd's Pie. After the war, most of the meat we saw in Britain was mutton. We liked its gamey flavor, although we tired of its regular appearance at Sunday lunch—a poor substitute for beef. Any mutton left over was either served cold—and cold mutton is very good eaten with pickles—or the cook ground it up for Shepherd's Pie. Shepherd's Pie proved too attractive a name for a dish to be given up because of muttonphobia, so beef started to be substituted for lamb. The beef Shepherd's Pie sold well frozen. Now, of course, beef is suspect and lamb has made a comeback in the pie. It's ever so much tastier than beef.

I comfort myself that should beef go, and horse not catch on, there will always be Shepherd's Pie to fall back on. I just hope nothing is found to be wrong with sheep.

. . . .

CHAPTER FOUR

THE LOST
KITCHEN GARDEN

Six years of war and an errant German bomb had pretty well finished off the kitchen garden at Shillingford. How desolate it looked. All that was left of the three greenhouses was broken glass and tangled wreckage in a forest of weeds, which had grown like a jungle, obliterating the order of what was once a proper Victorian kitchen garden. Mr. Haggie, Edward VII's rich tailor, hadn't stinted in designing Shillingford Court's kitchen garden, because a kitchen garden was a status symbol. It made the owner self-sustaining in food—and the food was something to show off.

Mr. Haggie's garden was a quarter-acre rectangle filled with beds of fruits and vegetables. There must have been rows of peas and green beans, Brussels sprouts, kale, and cabbage, potatoes, beets, carrots, raspberry canes, lots of gooseberries, red, black, and white currants, rhubarb, and strawberries—many kinds, of course—all bordered by walls and trees. Cardoons, the thistly artichoke so liked by Victorians, and scorzonera too, a black salsify. Windsor Green fava beans, All the Year Round lettuce, Purple Cape cauliflower, and the Long Red Surrey carrot were surely planted. The greenhouses housed tomatoes and cucumbers, melons and grapes, figs, nectarine and peach trees.

Surveying the wreckage, Sheridan Russell—a precursor of the organic movement, although we didn't know it—looked on the bright side, telling my father, "Now you can completely renew the earth."

Normally my father would have been impatient with this kind of thing, but Sheridan had such supple charm, and he was such an old friend. When he said that he ate only eggs from hens he knew personally, and only true whole-wheat bread, not that imposter Hovis (much promoted at the time), which was just dyed white bread, my father was relieved. He said it simplified social life in such foodless times. Sherwood could always be asked to dinner safely because he wouldn't come.

Instead, Sheridan, a regular guest at the house of friends who lived a few miles away, would bicycle over between meals to chat with my mother, whom he felt was more sympathetic. Once he brought her a book from which he had drawn great inspiration: Sir Albert Howard's *An Agricultural Testament*. Sir Albert, a scientist, had evolved a whole earth philosophy that called for organic and self-sustaining agriculture, and his book had been published during the war.

The rot, according to Sir Albert, started in 1879—a terrible year for agriculture—with the import of cheap corn from America and the way it had been processed. Sir Albert, a natural headline writer, called it the murder of our daily bread. Gone was the whole-wheat loaf, so naturally nutritious, and in came chemically treated white bread, which had a longer shelflife. White bread lasted longer because the wheat germ had been removed: the wheat germ, the soul of goodness, was alive and decayed like all nature, like us, so the bread became rancid. For country people, who still made their own bread, this wasn't a problem; but the growing urban masses had to have mass-produced, reliable food. The deracinated white bread was a clear break between humans and their food, because bread was no longer part of the natural food chain. It was a commodity divorced from its health-giving source.

The next thing Sir Albert said was even more prescient: although people were being fed, there was a famine of quality. More and cheaper food could be produced with chemicals, but it would be less and less nutritious. That's what we have today: hot and cold fast food available 24/7 and an epidemic of an illness called obesity.

Sir Albert's philosophy sounded familiar to my mother, one of whose dearest friends had married an anthroposophist. Lavinia was sitting on a bench in Central Park, she wrote my mother, feeling low about her divorce, and this charming man sat down beside her. Kurt was balm to Lavinia's troubled soul. He was a follower of Rudolf Steiner, the founder of anthroposophy (the science of the spirit), and he was absorbed by biodynamics, a way of growing food organically according to the lunar calendar: seeds are best sown a couple of days before the full moon.

Most people took organic with a big pinch of salt. "Catch me planting potatoes by the light of the silvery moon," joked our local farmer. Britain was embracing modern farming techniques, welcoming fertilizers and pesticides, because never again would the country be caught short of food. The idea of returning to the old ways of farming by rotation and using only natural fertilizer was sniffed at. That was all very well for the exhausted earth of India, the inspiration for Sir Albert's demand for sustainable land, but his recipe for a good fertilizer sounded bizarre. It consisted of garden rubbish, clothing, leather sacking soaked in water, animal, bird, and human excrement, and even human hair (it takes 15½ pounds of human hair to produce 2¼ pounds of useful nitrogen, which shows how essential inorganic chemical nitrogen is for the professional grower), earth itself, and water—all thrown together in a pit and allowed to stew in the sun, slowly turning into soft, rich black soil. Sir Albert claimed as well that this organic soil would repel weeds and disease. But almost immediately experiments showed this wasn't the case, and pretty soon, organic growing went into the national crackpot file, along with Gurdjieff, Ouspensky, macrobiotics, Annie Besant, Madame Blavatsky, Bertrand Russell and Bernard Shaw, and the flying Duchess of Bedford.

The Natural Way

Our Nanny was organic without knowing it. Nanny came from an ancient Sussex village, where her family had farmed a smallholding, a piece of land passed down father to son for a thousand years. The family had a pig, sometimes two; a cow; chickens, of course; a few crops. The five children learned their lessons on the barn: their father would white-wash its sides, and when the sides were filled up, he would whitewash it again. We children loved the image. What a school!

Nanny inculcated us into the country ways of Shilling-ford. Time had paused in Shillingford, change so incremental as to be invisible. Nobody fussed over the disappearance of the wharf next to our house and the fact that the hamlet's road now ran straight into the river. The fields were odd-shaped, with names like Home Meadow and Three-Quarter Field. The cows ambled to the water meadows to drink and the river was thus undoubtedly polluted, but who knew or cared. We children still swam in it without getting ill.

The farm was the main employer. As my sister and I walked home from school, we would pass the farmworkers on their way home. They wore old clothes, the men's cor-duroys patched and their shirts darned, but their boots were real leather and had thick leather soles, and they wore cloth caps to shade their faces from the sun. They smelled of the earth, a sweet smell of stored apples, and their hands were grooved with dirt. They spoke Oxfordshire, an accent with glottal stops, the skipping of a consonant here and there. In the spring, men would come to the riverbanks and cut the willows to make the whips into baskets, and more men would be slicing off hazel branches and splitting them to weave wattle fences.

The countryside was packed with wildlife. The hedgehog—Mrs. Tiggywinkle, of course—was a friend. So were the two baby brown squirrels we found abandoned; Nanny showed us how to feed them with fountain-pen fillers charged with milk. A marauding snake was killed by Nanny, armed with a big stick. Then, in front of us, she skinned it and set out to dry its handsome paisley-patterned skin, which she later made into a belt for my sister.

When Nanny decreed that summer pudding should be made with wild blackberries and nothing else, we believed her. Some people said that summer pudding can be made with whatever berries are available, but Nanny was quite firm about the superiority of the blackberry. The hedgerows where the blackberries flourished were the country people's market garden. In the autumn, the hamlet children picked their way along the hedgerows that bordered the old rights of way cutting through our property, hurrying to beat the birds, as Nanny said. There were hips and haws, which made such a good tea or jelly, and elderberries for elderberry wine. The blackberry produced a royal purple pudding. I think a summer pudding is as good as any fruit tart mainly because it's fruitier.

. . . .

SUMMER PUDDING

Serves 4–6

About 7 slices well-risen white bread (not soggy cheap
bread), a day old, with a texture that is loose and
absorbent. A farmer's loaf is good
2 pint baskets blackberries
½ cup white sugar
¼ cup cold water

Cut crusts off bread and slice into oblongs to line a pint-
sized traditional English pudding bowl, chopping up triangular cuts to fill any gaps and using whole pieces at the top
and bottom.

Saving 5 or 6 berries for decoration, put remaining berries
in a saucepan with the water and sugar, bring to boil,
remove. The juice will have turned black.

Pour berries and syrup into the bread-lined bowl. Fit a
plate over the top so it presses down on the pudding and set
a 2 lb weight (such as a large can of tomato juice) on top.
Leave in the refrigerator for a day.

Unmold onto a plate. The juice should have soaked the
bread completely. If not, put remaining berries in a saucepan
with 2 Tbs water and bring to a quick boil. Take off heat, mash
blackberries and water, and pour over unmolded pudding.

Whipped 48 percent butterfat cream is the best garnish.

. . . .

Everyone in Shillingford had a garden of some kind; the villagers had "allotments" in the farmer's fields, where they grew a variety of plants. Oxfordshire was farming country, grain and livestock. Our area didn't have a special crop the way they did in Hampshire's Hamble Valley. On the strawberry coast, as it was called, a strawberry culture flourished. The local schoolchildren wore blazers with strawberry emblems on the pockets, and the school houses were named after the local strawberry varieties—Duke, Sovereign, Paxton, and Bedford. In June, the great month for strawberries, armies of pickers would take to the fields at four in the morning so there would be plenty of berries for the early trains to London, where they were rushed to Covent Garden Market. The train was called the "Strawberry Special," and the farmer who took the berries to the train was the Strawberry Knight.

In our village, vegetables were runners-up to flowers—with the exception of the vegetable marrow. Vegetable marrow is a summer squash that only the English seem to love: it is a watermelon-sized zucchini. Villagers competed fiercely to grow the largest vegetable marrow and capture the prize at the local flower show. My mother had no patience for it. "No one can eat such a big marrow," she complained. "Why don't they pick them when they're small and then they'd be delicious!"

Of course, the French would have done that; but then, the French garden differently from the English. The English garden to dream, the French to eat. The greatest garden at

Versailles is Louis XIV's *Potager du Roi*, twenty-two acres laid out with the precision of a military tattoo. Carême must have taken his inspiration for his foodscapes from Versailles. The fruit trees were cut into pom-poms and marched around the borders of precise vegetable beds. The *Potager du Roi* was a horticultural laboratory where plants were bred, cross-bred, and grown in huge amounts. In a good season, four hundred figs were harvested a day, enough to feed the huge court. The *Potager du Roi* is still going strong today. Visitors can buy the produce from an amazing variety of plants. Of the fifty original varieties of pears, forty-nine still exist.

But not far away from Versailles is the château of Malmaison, where once flourished the wondrous rose garden of the empress Josephine. She dreamed like an English gardener. In 1804, she began to collect roses from all over France and all over the world. Within ten years, Malmaison was a hub of the nascent French rose industry. Even the British, then at war with the French, gave her their roses, and by 1814, she had 250 species. That however was the year she died, and the garden died, too. All that is left are the watercolors she ordered up from Pierre-Joseph Redouté, and they of course have never been equaled.

At my mother's dismissal of the giant marrow, Nanny's face would go blank. It was annoying to her that my mother, who so obviously knew nothing about nature, should know the best time to eat the marrow. What a waste. Allowed to grow, the marrow had many uses. First you could stuff it with a mixture of breadcrumbs, beans, and herbs; should

there be a scrap of meat, that could be ground up and
included as well. A fine, nourishing meal. Marrow chut-
ney—the best! Nanny also fried the marrow. She cut it into
slim slices, doused it with salt, and left it to drain. Then she
dipped the slices in flour and fried them in a little dripping.
Bland, but Nanny considered the child's palate was perfect
and should be maintained by the simplest food, without
strong flavors. Escoffier couldn't have said it better.

. . . .

FRIED VEGETABLE MARROW
(OR ANY SUMMER SQUASH OR
OUTSIZE ZUCCHINI)

Serves 4–6

The taste of squash is in the skin, so cut a summer squash
into ¼-inch slices, remove the seeds, sprinkle sea salt over
the slices, and let them sit for 30 minutes to drain.

Dry with paper towels, then dredge the marrow in flour,
and fry in 4 Tbs unsalted butter, turning quickly. Sprinkle
with salt and pepper and serve.

. . . .

The vegetable marrow fritters were delicious. Even my
mother had to say so, although she kept muttering about
the size.

The Great Seed Laboratory

Nanny looked over the remains of Mr. Haggie's garden with sorrow. A gardener herself, she itched to get her hands in the soil. She could remember what the garden had looked like, the raised beds of strawberries and beans, the raspberry canes, the fragrance of the flowers that bordered the beds, and the drowsy sound of bees as they pollinated the plants.

She could remember the gardener, too. His name was Ted and he lived in the bungalow—a grim one-story building that squatted between the kitchen garden and the river-bank—picking up local help as he needed it. Ted would have grown mostly heirloom seeds, the old varieties that repro-duced true to type, so the seeds from one year could be used for the next. Victorian gardens contained hundreds of heir-loom vegetables, and hundreds of just one vegetable: enough varieties of green peas so they ripened in sequence, assuring a supply all summer long. My mother loved fava beans and Ted, Nanny was sure, planted several kinds, so there would be a long season for them. I wonder if he crossed his own seeds to make hybrids—all gardeners are scientists—because hybrids would have made a change from the stan-dard plants.

Hybridization, the crossbreeding of like species to pro-duce a larger, more beautiful, tastier vegetable, created the commercial seed industry. Hybrid seeds don't reproduce accurately, so the seeds have to be bought each year. Thus the commercial seedsmen promoted the hybrid over the heirlooms, and the heirlooms began to die off. Today, all hybrid tomatoes are derived from the same variety. Should some scourge wipe out the variety, the tomato would survive only because seed banks have luckily saved many heirlooms such as Alicante and Gardener's Delight. Otherwise the tomato might go the way of the monocultural potato in Ireland.

I don't suppose Ted was concerned about biodiversity (not yet a media worry) in the 1930s, nor did he have to worry about needing fresh vegetables to grow year-round as my parents were only in Shillingford a few months of the year. But the Victorian gardener manipulated growing so that a fresh vegetable or fruit was always on the table. In February, the vegetables forced in hotbeds and pits and under glass included melons and cucumbers, carrots, turnips, early celery, eggplants, peppers, and tomatoes; and successional crops of kidney beans, cauliflower, Brussels sprouts, early potatoes, asparagus, rhubarb, and sea kale. The Victorians nurtured exotic fruit: a pineapple called Charlotte Rothschild was the pride of the greenhouse. Was it as good as the Costa Rican pineapple today? Melons, hanging in little baskets in the greenhouse, were very popular, and apparently a lot better-tasting than most of the melons that show up all year in my local Toronto supermarket. The Victorian country house owner was persnickety about melon. Should it fail to please, he returned it to the gardener with a terse note: "Not good enough"—the best kind of quality control. If only I could do that in a supermarket.

Strawberries were grown for Christmas. Danish gardeners had discovered how to bring along the wild strawberries by planting them in July and August and then forcing the plants slowly in pits with pitched roofs. The market gardeners in Paris were famous for the vegetables they forced in the very early spring. They used heavily insulated cold frames containing manure to keep the soil warm, covered over with glass and even lighting to produce *primeurs*. The gardeners planted the seeds layer by layer, the first-maturing radishes and lettuce on top of carrots and cauliflower, then finally spinach. It was extraordinarily efficient, a dazzling if expensive promotion for restaurants, and the vegetables tasted delicious.

Now I know that when it comes to fruit and vegetables, small is best. Taste benefits by compression, and I've also learned that a good tomato needs time to mature. But the Victorians wanted larger, faster-growing vegetables. When, in the nineteenth century, the chemical nitrogen was discovered to be a potent fertilizer, Victorian entrepreneurs wasted no time in hunting for sources. Soon the British were digging up old battlefields like Waterloo and the Crimea to recycle bones into nitrogen, and they cornered the guano (seagull excrement) market in Chile, a seagull haven of guano cliffs. The Great War forced an opening of the market: the nitrate in guano was extracted to make explosives—for both sides.

Guano's effect on vegetables was equally explosive. Two ounces of guano per yard sprinkled over onions doubled their size compared to untreated onions. Inorganic chemicals of course were even better, and soon nitrogen was being synthesized for both bombs and fertilizer.

The Threat of the New

Although organic growing had no followers at our local farm, the idea that science was changing the earth for the worse came up again and again. Usually, it was the Americans, with their new-fangled ideas—"Look at the atom bomb"—who were to blame. The Gothic anti-American in our neighborhood was Mr. Barrett. We called him that because he was an ogre who treated his family the way we understood Mr. Barrett had treated his daughter Elizabeth Barrett Browning—like a slave. However, there was one subject that was safe to talk about. Music. Mr. Barrett himself played the cello, and had once dreamed of a musical career, so now he dreamed of making his son, Jo, a Sir Thomas Beecham, by God, because Jo had great gifts. He himself had trained Jo's perfect ear, had prepped and tutored him, and found the right mentors. Now Jo was seventeen and on the brink of the career that Mr. Barrett knew he would follow.

So why was Jo spending all his time at our house playing our piano, and, what's more, playing jazz? Not that we put two and two together right away, because Jo was morose. He would come over during the school holidays and spend his time leafing through the old copies of *Life*, a magnet for all our friends; he particularly admired the pictures of basketball stars. Then he would ask my mother if he could play the piano, and of course she said, yes, yes, she loved jazz, and he was really very good at improvisation. It was a pleasure to listen to him.

My father didn't like Jo quite so well. "Who is that young man who plays the piano in a dazed stupor?" He asked. It was true. Jo did nod and moan as he fumbled for the right notes, the right riff—not the kind of stuff that my father, whose idea of light music was "Take a Pair of Sparkling Eyes" from *The Gondoliers* by Gilbert and Sullivan, really understood. One day I would live with a jazz pianist, and as the relationship cooled, I found myself echoing my father. Does he *have* to look like that to play at all? Still, Jo became a fixture for a while, and perhaps would have gone on being one, if we hadn't gone to dinner with Mr. Barrett.

It was an informal family party, I recall; my father was in London. Mr. Barrett was in a praising mood and ran off some of his children's accomplishments, most of them musical, and when he got to Jo, he positively glowed. He had great news. Jo was going to get the chance to work with a certain famous conductor in the summer, and my mother, who had been wool-gathering as she so often did around Mr. Barrett's angry presence, said, quite without thinking, oh, she thought Jo was going to be a jazz pianist.

Conversation stopped. "Jazz pianist?" said Mr. Barrett, his eyes narrowing into slits. "Where have you heard him play?" And then of course my mother had to say she was so pleased he used our piano, and Mr. Barrett appeared to swell before our eyes. Now we knew why Jo came to our house to play the piano. The angry father launched into a slashing attack on jazz, and before we knew it, was lambasting the cultureless Americans. "Everything bad in the world is the fault of the Americans," he cried, and then hastily added, "But of course not you, Izzy." (My mother's name was Isabelle and my father, with his dislike of nicknames, never shortened it, another strike against Barrett.) Why was the countryside culture vanishing, hedgerows dug up, farms mechanized, the old ways of growing food done away with? It was the Americans' fault: they believed everything had to be made to be sold. Today I realize how ridiculous this was because Mr. Barrett was a banker, a money merchant himself.

While we hated Mr. Barrett, one thing we knew was true. The land *was* changing. But it wasn't the Americans' fault, it was the Labour government's fault, and not just because our father said the Labour government was to blame for everything, but because it had brought tragedy on Nanny's family. The government had appropriated—that was the word it used, but my father said "stolen"—the family farm, a thousand years old, for a road. And Walter, Nanny's brother, had gone out to the barn, got down his shotgun, and killed himself. This family tragedy echoed through the dying countryside.

The Supermarket That
Swallowed Food

The moment I arrived in Los Angeles, I forgot all about England and fell in love with supermarkets. When I stepped inside my first supermarket, I thought I'd fallen into Aladdin's cave. I had never seen so much food in my life— even at Harrods—or such beautifully burnished food: food that glowed like jewels, food temptingly presented, even the packaging itself looked edible, and it was all so cheap. I was taken to the Farmers' Market where big was extra beautiful, jumbo fruits and vegetables piled high. The grapefruit, I swear, were the size of basketballs, and the oranges as large as melons. They shone with cleanliness. It was hard not to be bowled over. At a coffee shop I ate a mile-high sandwich stuffed with fresh tomato and avocado, a fruit that was still called an alligator pear in England and considered exotic. It didn't matter that the fruit didn't taste of much. Coming from England, to me the bounty was all, a horn of plenty. It never occurred to me that within a few decades, the supermarket was going to emerge as the single greatest threat to the taste of food.

At first, supermarkets seemed benign. They were so cheap, and there were enough different chains to provide variety. But then, as the supermarkets began to telescope into fewer and fewer and larger chains, the food buyers started to think globally. They didn't search out toothsome vegetables to tempt the customer. Instead, they drew up criteria for the fastest-moving food and then ordered it grown. Whole varieties went to the wall, and the supermarket began offering only a fraction of the accumulation of fruits and vegetables once grown in even a modest Victorian kitchen garden, with its supersized onions and giant leeks. The supermarket vegetable is above all telegenic and tough—like a Hollywood movie star. It may be that corn only tastes good when rushed from the field straight to the grill or pot; but supermarket corn must be bred to survive for weeks. Iceberg is the model industrial lettuce because it stays crunchy indefinitely in the fridge.

Greens to the Rescue

Just when many people had surrendered their palates to industrial food, there came along this hippie who preached organic food. Alice Waters had been seduced by the simple food of the Mediterranean, by the Elizabeth David lunch: fresh bread and local cheese and wine, sun-dried olives and tiny tomatoes drying in the heat of a vine-cloaked terrace. In 1970, she opened her restaurant Chez Panisse (named for the the baker in Marcel Pagnol's bucolic trilogy), where she served only local and seasonal organic food. The restaurant was in Berkeley, fountainhead of sixties' rebellion against Amerika, the military-industrial complex and all its works, including fast food. Macrobiotic food was the rage, about as far from McDonald's as could be imagined.

Alice Waters had no time for the elitism of the classic cui-

sine. Taste itself was personal and thus relative. Cooking
was feeling: only if you love to cook will you cook well, and
techniques can be picked up as they're needed. As she wrote
in the *Chez Panisse Menu Cookbook* (1982), "I don't believe
that all the gourmet equipment and utensils are vital. To
begin with, the terms 'gourmet' or 'gourmet cooking' have
all the wrong associations for me. It is far easier to cook with
good sharp knives, but you *can* cook without them."

Waters's *nostalgie de la boue* would sweep across North
America and Europe. Even the French were impressed. The
Louvre offered her space for an educational and inspirational
restaurant, but the French government squelched the idea—
that was going too far. Waters's timing was perfect. She
appealed not only to fellow hippies but to the richest generation so far in history. When yuppies and boomers traveled,
they came home with new ideas about food and wine and were
ready to pay for good food. The environment was a hot-
button issue, too, one that was beginning to cross over into the
media mainstream. And in a world dominated by instant
news, the word went out faster than ever before that there was
a new Eden, this new religion on the shores of the Pacific.

Like several of my neighbors in downtown Toronto, I
was a true believer. When an organic market set up its stalls
of a Saturday morning a couple of blocks from my house, I
was overjoyed. How virtuous we felt as we got up early to
buy organic raspberries, so succulently crimson that the
farmer had to ration them. The farmer told me he sang to the
Lord as he seeded his fields northwest of the city. Next year,

he vowed to revive that old heirloom gooseberry the size of the bowl of a Champagne glass, one that I remembered as a star of the Victorian garden. Although I didn't particularly like gooseberries, I loved the idea of such a large and rare one. Even the potatoes from the market tasted better, I swore, and there were stripey green tomatoes, obviously heirlooms, that looked so decorative on the plate. The first time I saw a giant puffball mushroom harvested from the fields at the market, I knew I would never find it anywhere else. Those were the days when I thought organic had all the answers.

And Max confirmed it. Max was the local organic guru. He never explained his conversion to organics, but something catastrophic had changed his life, forcing him to confront himself—to confront food. He came to the conclusion that only his own homegrown vegetables would do. So he began digging up his garden and replacing the soil with compost made from the vegetables thrown out by the local organic food co-op.

Max was regarded with awe. Toronto in the 1990s was fervently green, and our little downtown patch greener than most, a cluster of small two-story houses under the shade of rangy maples. In the summer, the loudest noise was the sound of gardens being watered, and the smell carried by the breeze was first of lilacs, then orange blossom and roses, and in the fall the astringency of chrysanthemums. It was hardly like being in a city at all. Toronto had issued plastic compost kits—composters—free to homeowners with instructions on how to make compost. The recipe was innocuous; there was no mention of life-giving human excrement or old clothes or human hair. Even so, composting bared the weaknesses of gardening in the city. Urban life being what it was, disordered and confused and without the reassuring rhythms of country life, the wrong things got composted, and in no time, rats were seen bounding out of the mix and young mothers threatened to sue the city.

Max, on the other hand, was serious and committed. He composted properly in a wooden frame, and he boosted the vegetables with a good shot of liquid human manure bought from the local sewage plant, which sounded a great idea until his garden was strangled by bindweed, the seeds having passed through both the human and sewage systems, the kind of thing overlooked by Sir Albert Howard.

Max persevered, and his garden eventually started to produce cucumbers and carrots, kale and leeks, and obviously tomatoes. They were good, I thought, but as a gardener myself, I believed I could do better. Heirlooms weren't two a penny as they are today: an heirloom then was on the cutting edge of gardening.

The names of the old tomatoes were mouth-watering: Marizol Purple, Soldaki, Brandywine, Cherokee Purple; and what of the Giant Tree Tomato, or those Victorian favorites, Gardener's Delight and the little Alicante? What of Radiator Charlie's Mortgage Lifter, a three-pound monster? Perhaps I should choose a yellow tomato, the tomato's original color. In the end, I picked a Giant Belgium from a Missouri

catalogue. It looked like Baby Jane, crinkled and craggy—
the opposite of the perfect hybrid. I absolutely believed that
this tomato would taste far, far better than any other tomato.
I had to sign a customs form to import the seeds, and when
they arrived, I prepared for them a bed of dried sheep
manure. I didn't use any pesticides, and only occasionally
plucked off a giant tomato hornworm en route to its dinner.
I worried whether to cut the sprawling plants or let them run
wild as Max insisted. Eventually, I left them to flourish in the
sunniest spot in the backyard.

The tomatoes grew and grew, redder and more gnarled
every day. They gave off that insistent citrus fragrance that
makes being close to a tomato plant so pleasant. I knew better than to get closer and eat the leaves, which are poisonous.
Finally, the day arrived to pick them. I was excited. I had a
couple of friends who owned restaurants and I imagined
asking them over and offering them a few of these supreme
tomatoes to spike their menus.

Reverently, I snipped off the largest, rosiest tomato. One
and a half pounds, I reckoned. I sliced into it. The spurt of
juice was very satisfactory. I lifted a slice to my lips. Nothing. I lifted another slice to my lips. Still nothing. The Giant
Belgium was a bust. It tasted bland and meaningless. The
flesh, too, was disappointing: thick and grainy, not slippery
and juicy.

Shaken, I had to rethink my food philosophy. Where had
I slipped up? I knew what a great tomato tasted like. It was a
homegrown tomato, and not just any homegrown tomato. It

grew in a walled kitchen garden in one of the folds of the
Cumberland Valley, where the summers are hot and steamy.
My friend Hilary, whom I had known from school in England, and who now lived in Pennsylvania, had a great vegetable garden, asparagus and beans and a weird Italian
marrow called *Trompetti* that curled around like a rambling
pretzel. She had smuggled it in from her mother's mountain-
side garden in Liguria. But it was her tomatoes that year in,
year out were so reliably good. Surely she had a secret? Yes:
modern hybrids from an Agway catalogue with names like
Early Girl, Better Boy, simple old Cherry, and the Roma, a
tomato that didn't taste at all until it was cooked into a rich
paste. The Roma was a reminder that a century ago, the
tomato—still relatively new to European and American
palates—was routinely cooked to get rid of its suspiciously
raw taste. Now we know that when cooked, the tomato
releases the cancer-busting chemical lycopene, quite a
change for a vegetable once thought to be poisonous.

The plants were allowed to spread out. One way or
another, they all delivered the requisite tomato fix: a fizz of
acid upon the bite, followed by a rich, deep sweetness. Their
structure was firm without being pasty or mealy. The
smaller ones were the juiciest, their flavor compressed and
thus more intense.

This model in mind, I scoured the local Farmers' Market,
and discovered two things. The field tomatoes so plentiful at
the height of summer were rarely any good at all. Field
tomatoes, I found out, are invariably picked when unripe,

even the ones from local farms, and this is death to tomatoes. A tomato is like a raw milk cheese: once the cheese is cut, it stops ripening. The same thing happens to a tomato. It will never improve after it's picked.

The fancy heirloom tomatoes brought to market by organic growers looked sensational—purple, tiger-striped, deep orange—but taste as I might, I never found one that came near Hilary's Early Girl. The good ones came from smallholders who picked tomatoes only when they were ripe. None of the tomatoes that I liked turned out to be organic. The best growers told me it was too much bother, too expensive and labor-intensive. "Tomatoes just need good soil, and lots of sun. It doesn't matter what fertilizer you use, the plants don't know," said one, and others echoed the point. After sampling several growers' tomatoes, I picked one I really liked and asked what its name was. "Aranca," the grower said. "It's Dutch, costs a dollar thirty [Canadian] a seed, and it's grown hydroponically."

The Holland Tomato

A dollar-plus seed! The tomato puzzle was solved. It is cost, of course, that ensures a tomato tastes better. The field tomatoes, whether local or Californian or Spanish, are the Holsteins of the tomato industry. They are fast growers and big producers. Dozens of better-tasting varieties exist, but they aren't so profitable, the seeds are more expensive, and the tomatoes are not so prolific, and when you're producing tomatoes in bulk, the farmer thinks only of the bottom line. The bottom line is that field tomatoes are cheap, the cheapest tomatoes on the market.

But what about a tomato raised in water in a greenhouse? In a reversal of all that I believed, it turned out I was better off buying a space-age tomato than a fresh seasonal tomato from local fields.

The idea of growing plants in water is thousands of years old, but as far as food was concerned, mostly as a scientific curiosity. Only in the 1930s did hydroponics, Greek for "waterworks," receive serious consideration as a commercial possibility for parts of the world like deserts where crops can't be grown. The first tests came during World War II, when hydroponic systems produced fresh vegetables for American troops stationed on barren islands in the Pacific. Hydroponics has been considered a possible system for feeding the first moon settlers, and today greens are grown hydroponically in submarines on long underwater journeys. Still, the technology hardly seemed worth a heavy investment for California, with its miles of sun-drenched fields and its cheap tomatoes and lettuces.

But the Dutch live in a waterlogged country, where land has to be constantly retrieved from the sea. Growing anything demanded ingenuity, and that led to the Dutch starting the first commercial greenhouse industry, and thence to hydroponics, which happened to offer the perfect environment for the tomato, a vegetable from the subtropics. In fact, the first greenhouses in Europe were built for just this purpose, to acclimatize exotics like the Chinese orange—a fruit with an intensely sweet fragrance that sent Europeans wild with desire—and tomatoes that shriveled and died in cold climates.

The greenhouse reached its apogee in England in the middle of the nineteenth century after the glass tax was removed, that is to say when the timber used to make glass was no longer needed to make warships, a neat example of the inexorable progress of technology. The Crystal Palace, a million square feet of glass, was built to house the Great Exhibition in 1851, and it was a gardener's vision of a future world with everything under glass. Joseph Paxton, the head gardener of the great eight-acre kitchen garden at Chatsworth House in Derbyshire owned by the Duke of Devonshire, was the designer. There would never again be so audacious a greenhouse, or so prophetic a glass vision, foreshadowing the American skyscrapers, because once glass became available, increasingly mundane uses followed, and commercial greenhouses were not far behind.

Hydroponics is much more efficient than greenhouse growing. It is completely clean; no herbicides or pesticides are needed. The plants are grown in water, or in rockwool or perlite, sterile media that don't need fumigating the way greenhouse soil does. The plants feed on a computer-controlled mix of nutrients and water.

A flourishing hydroponic crop turns the greenhouse into the *Little Shop of Horrors*, crammed with forty-feet vines.

The only creature seen in a hydroponic greenhouse is the pollinating bumblebee. Tomatoes are self-pollinating, but often need help under glass. Originally, battery-operated vibrators and toothbrushes were used to spread the pollen, but the bumblebees with their sonfication (buzz) technique ran rings round them.

The hydroponic tomatoes and lettuce sit pristine on the shelves. But the taste! "The lettuce looks like green tissue paper and tastes like it," cried my sister Lynn. "And the tomatoes are watery." That is true of the inferior hydroponic, and the Dutch admit that ten years ago their hydroponics failed the taste test. It took a tomato depression to change all that.

Around 1993, there were just too many round, red tomatoes on the world market, and the Dutch couldn't compete. One grower simply gave up; he couldn't afford to have his tomatoes picked, so he chopped up the vines and sold the tomatoes as they were. "It wasn't genius," I was told by Fried De Schouwer, a Holland tomato grower now transplanted to Arizona, where he's trying to replicate the Holland tomato's success with an American brand, Eurofresh. "One lucky yo-yo just didn't let the vines hang there covered with ripe red tomatoes. He thought, 'I'll save myself picking them one by one and sell them as they are,' and then everyone went berserk over them."

The cluster tomato on the vine caught the public fancy. It became the tomato that everyone wanted, and growers everywhere were quick to grow them. Before long, the markets were full of cluster tomatoes, not all Dutch and not all good—I never see a supermarket today without them.

At first, the vine tomato looked good but failed the taste test. Was it their food? Quebec hydroponic growers feed their hydroponic tomatoes more salt, with good results, and so do some Dutch growers. But the big difference turned out to be a combination of nature and nurture—breeding and the length of time the tomato is allowed to grow. The key to taste, I learned, is to torture the tomatoes by keeping them thirsty. That's why a garden tomato tastes so good—home gardeners are always forgetting to water them! One Dutch grower compared a tomato's growth to the slow, steady way a human builds muscle. Seed and time cost money, and a slow-growing tomato is not a natural profitmaker. But the Holland tomato now has a niche in the North American market.

The Holland tomato actually smells of the sun and lemon, although not quite so intensely as a tomato grown directly in the sunlight, and not so sweetly as the sublime industrial, the Canary Island tomato. The Canary Island tomato is a little orange apple, firm, and with a spritzer of citrus juice; it is a cross from the old Pommes d'Amour, which the Spaniards took from Peru in the seventeenth century to their islands in the Atlantic just off the coast of Africa.

The hydroponic tomato is the future. Already Southern Europe is going hydroponic with large areas under glass, and hydroponics has finally caught on commercially in North America. The control factor is what is so attractive. The tomatoes can be controlled the way field tomatoes cannot; they are more uniform not only in appearance but in taste; and they are environmentally friendly (although heating the greenhouses may eventually prove a problem). And then there's the coup de grâce, the deployment of bumblebees as pollinators—an environmentally friendly touch.

Organic tomatoes, on the other hand, are inconsistent in taste, just as expensive as the best Holland tomatoes, and they have fallen afoul of the food police because manure may carry the toxic O157:H7 strain of *E coli*. The consequences could rock the organic movement to its roots. Just how much manure from organically fed animals is available?

Frankenfoods

But hydroponics can only go so far. There's a new super-industrial tomato on the way, which may completely revolutionize the nature of the tomato.

The new food is already taking shape in the test tube. It is genetically modified—whether it will taste good is a toss-up. However, it will be incredibly good for you, and it will last a long time on the supermarket shelf. The new tomato will be "enhanced." It may include a gene from yeast that will ripen slowly and thus allow the tomato to accumulate more of the cancer-busting lycopene. It could include a smallpox vaccine, or it might have Omega-3, the good fat that has now been added to eggs to make them extra healthy. One thing it's not going to be like is the Flav'r Sav'r. The first gauche effort to modify the tomato, the Californian Flav'r Sav'r was crudely commercial. No attention was paid to taste; the plant was modified so its stems could be easily snapped by picking machines, and when this didn't happen, the model tomato was junked.

Since then, food scientists have grown savvier. They started out as naifs in laboratories, cocooned from the brutish world of food politics, and they made their pronouncements as if showering the world with miracles. The centuries-long struggle to grow food was over. They would soon solve all the world's problems: we'd have more food, safer food, food that didn't need chemicals or pesticides, foods that would contain vaccines and supervitamins. It was the all-important win-win. Corn was the first successful commercial application: a major crop that had to be soaked with pesticide to eliminate a pest called the European corn borer. By splicing a gene from a microbe, *Bacillus thuringiensis*, into corn, scientists created a protein that was toxic to the borer. This had huge implications both for the industry and for the environment, which would no longer need to be sprayed with so many pesticides.

You would think that environmentalists would welcome the potential to lessen chemical poisons in our food in the shadow of Rachel Carson's work and the annihilating DDT that is still in the land years after it was banned. Our food is still not free of DDT and the other organochlorines that are now inextricably part of the food chain. More than a quarter of the food that carries the certified organic label in North America still has chemical residues in it. But instead of celebrating the possibilities of genetic modification, many environmentalists attacked the food.

In North America, 70 percent of our food is probably transgenic. Although only three crops are in production—corn, canola, and soy—these are present in a wide variety of foods, from breakfast cereals to canola oil, candy, and cakes. But to extreme environmentalist movements such as Greenpeace, transgenics are a radical, sinister break with nature. The mad cow disease outbreak in Britain turned people against the food industrial complex. To the British, assurances that transgenic food is safe ring as hollow as the politicians' claims that beef was safe. In Europe, transgenic food is represented as yet another power grab by American business trying to reap a fortune from seeds that must be bought each year.

A new food war has erupted. With cheese, the battle is between traditional raw milk cheese producers and the industrial cheese industry, and the tool is the scary bacteria. With plants, the positions are reversed. It is the environmentalists who use scare tactics about transgenic foods against the scientists and the food industry, and of course against America, the source of everything new and unknown.

When genetic modification was called "crossbreeding," nobody feared it, and horticulturalists were proud of their successful experiments. Without crossbreeding, we might still be eating peas hard as bullets and carrots with leathery skins. Crossbreeding was a hobby for amateur gardeners, who became aware of their limitations quite quickly. Unless species had compatible chromosomes, crossbreeding failed.

Today, scientists are able to move genes among species, with novel and unpredictable results. For example, transgenics has the potential to clean up the strawberry, currently the most heavily contaminated fruit, laced with something sinister called endocrine disrupters. But the public might freak out. One scientific gaffe was to announce an experiment in which a gene from the Arctic flounder was spliced into an industrial strawberry in order to help it survive frost. Fishy strawberries—the future looked bleak.

As Asian as Apple Crumble

All self-respecting English country houses had an orchard, and Mr. Haggie's property was no exception. The orchard at the end of the long driveway of chestnut trees bloomed scores of pink and white candles in the spring. From 1939 to 1946, the orchard went to seed, and the only apples we children found were small, green, and hard. When we bit into them, they tasted bitter, so we fed them to the ponies, or let our neighbor David use them as targets for his pop gun. He would climb over the fence, his gun pointed down while he recited: "Never let your gun / pointed be at anyone," then fire away.

The pictures of Adam biting into the apple suggest he had

no trouble finding one. In fact, an apple is an exotic every-where but Central Asia. Apples did not spring up sponta-neously anywhere else. They were brought to the West along the Silk Road from Kazakhstan, where wild apples still grow copiously, mostly yellow and orange and tart to the taste. It took a good deal of work to acclimatize the apple, but its taste so entranced Europeans that they crossed and cosseted it to produce any number of varieties. Apples were bred to be eaten alone, or so they cooked well, and their tastes varied according to when and how they would be eaten.

We children knew the little green apples were not the real thing. For England, the greatest apple in the world was a Cox's Orange Pippin—every nation feels this way about their favorite apple. The Cox is a modest-sized, yellowish apple, with irregular pink markings and some russeting, or rough skin. It doesn't look like anything. Only when you bite into the Cox is its greatness revealed. Then, as with wine, or cheese, or strawberries, the flavor opens up. A Cox may be compared to a vast, ancient soprano, who seems totally unsuitable as Mimi until she opens her mouth and starts to sing. Then, of course, reality falls away and she is the most beautiful woman in the world. First comes the spark of acid; then the firm but not too crisp flesh and the subtle fragrance of orange blossom that you smell and taste simul-taneously; and finally, a mellow aftertaste. These were the apples our aunt grew.

I never knew why my aunt decided to grow apples, and

she didn't care to explain, at least to me, but she gave indica-
tions of boredom with the ceremonial role of diplomat's
wife. She and my uncle lived on the Isle of Oxney in Kent,
in a mellow brick Queen Anne rectory. The house had been
transformed by the Edwardian architect Edwin Lutyens into
something proconsular, an imposing edifice with a garden
facade that had a line of French doors opening onto a stone
terrace, flanked by rosebeds, a wide lawn, and a view extend-
ing over the marshes toward the sea. You could throw a formal garden party at the drop of a hat.

Beyond the garden was the orchard, a snowy cloud in
spring, which stretched away in every direction in carefully
tended rows, in and around old footpaths, the odd cherry
tree, and barn. My aunt never did anything by halves, and
she took her apple growing very seriously, picking her crop
with care. Cox's, of course, were the top crop. She had no
trouble getting rid of them locally. Apples grown this way in
a small orchard were a calling rather than a profit crop. As a
photograph of my aunt sorting apples along with village
helpers shows, apple growing and harvesting were communal and organic pursuits, followed in similar orchards all
over Britain. We got a box of Aunt Peggy's pre-industrial
apples at Christmas, and they were fresh to the bite. In the
space of a few decades, the great Cox would be on the
endangered apple list.

My cousin Philip Mallet eventually inherited the house
in Kent, keeping the orchard—which remained a calling,
not a profit center—and the apples were still snapped up

locally. Philip kept to such classics as the Egremont Russet, which was probably what the little green apples in our
orchard had been originally. The Egremont Russet, bred
as a dessert apple for the Victorians, was not too sweet,
and tasted of hazelnuts, a perfect accompaniment to a
glass of port. In those days, the high point of apple eating
was after dinner. Queen Victoria was a lifelong lover of
an American apple, the Newtown Pippin, a big yellow
apple that tasted disarmingly of pineapple. At first bite,
the Queen found the Newton Pippin so good that she
directed the import duty on it lifted. Those were the days
when a monarch still had real food power. If only science
had been more advanced, the Newtown Pippin might be
more than a hobby apple today. But it declined because
nobody understood that the tree, which grew hugely,
leached all the calcium from the soil, and without calcium
it couldn't thrive.

In the past couple of decades, Philip has had more and
more difficulty selling his apples. The local shops in nearby
towns shut down one after another as the supermarkets took
over. The supermarket grip on food distribution is even
tighter in Britain than it is in North America, because Britain
is smaller. Today, only a handful of chains sell most of the
food, and they've closed down almost all competition. The
supermarket buyers don't listen to customers, of course, but
buy the apples that make the most profit. Nowadays, these
are the apples approved by the European Union as the only
"real" apples—they must be a minimum of two and a half

inches in diameter and come from an approved list of varieties. Red and Golden Delicious, Fuji, Royal Gala, and the Jonagold which, although American, has become the national apple of Belgium. The Cox is a miserable failure: it doesn't look like a beauty queen and it sometimes doesn't conform to the EU's size standards. All over Europe, the old varieties are being discarded. Until the 1950s, the Finkenwerder Herbstprinz—a juicy red russet—was the most loved variety grown in the orchards around Hamburg, one of the big apple-growing regions in Germany. But thirty years later, the Prinz had almost disappeared from production because the supermarkets didn't want it. Thus, an apple unique to a region is no longer good enough, and local tastes are trampled on. The result is predictable: many varieties are dying. Britain still grows more than seven hundred varieties, but for how long? Even the most enthusiastically patriotic supermarket stocked only ten varieties, all the usual suspects, in 2002.

Philip still grows Bramleys, the unique English cooking apple. Philip's wife, Mary, made an heirloom Bramley apple crumble for lunch. It was really good. The English, unlike North Americans, differentiate a cooking from an eating apple. The Bramley is named for a nineteenth-century butcher and it meets the EU template for a large apple, but that still hasn't got it onto the EU list. It is a big green apple with pink streaks, and it is creamy, grainy, and acid. As it is cooked, it melts down into a thick purée. The nearest thing to a cooking apple elsewhere is the Granny Smith, the slightly sour soda pop apple originally from Australia.

Philip tried to keep up with the trends. He planted Fujis and Royal Galas, a Cox cross that could be called Cox Lite, designed for the modern palate, which is addicted to sweets.

Sugar is the industrial narcotic, so bland is preferred over any taste that causes the mouth to pucker even a tiny bit. This is increasingly true of all the new fruit: some huge new Bing cherries called Lappins taste like a candy bar. Even the superior Rainier, a blush cherry that tastes of strawberries and cream, has only a tiny spike of acid.

Rating the Pop Apples

In the fall in Toronto, I count the varieties of apple in the markets. I live in the heart of good apple-growing country; the little villages that still survive amid spreading exurbia have apple fairs and cider tastings, and some heirloom apple orchards still sell the resolutely untelegenic Cox. In a small Korean market, I saw fourteen kinds of fresh apples in baskets on the sidewalk. I selected seven modern hybrids, Golden Delicious, Royal Gala, Jonagold, and Fuji, as well as McIntosh, Red Delicious, and finally an Elstar—a Dutch apple I'd never heard about. They all looked rather alike, I thought, pink and green, so under the suspicious eye of the storeowner, I marked each one with a felt-tipped pen.

Then I went home, chopped the apples up, and ate slices in sequence.

I started off with the Golden Delicious, the apple grown most frequently through the world. Golden Delicious (not related to the Red Delicious) was a seedling that grew in the Appalachians in West Virginia, and it is highly variable. Depending on where the apple is grown, it is either anemic or robust. Reportedly, the taste is exceptional in the Auvergne in France. My Golden Delicious was pale yellow. I thought it tasted watery, and its bite was far from crisp and inviting.

When I bit into the Royal Gala, there was a world of difference. Royal Gala is bred in New Zealand, and it is a cross between the Golden Delicious and the great Cox. The Royal Gala had just a hint of acid in its bite, and the flesh was firm; an immensely edible apple that melted in the mouth. However, it didn't have the Cox's orange aroma or the Cox's complexity.

At first I thought Jonagold filled every taste requirement. A spurt of acid on the first bite, the crunchy flesh, and then a pleasant melonlike flavor. After letting the aftertaste linger in my mouth, however, I decided I didn't like it as much as the Royal Gala.

Fuji, the most expensive, was a letdown. This Japanese apple, another Golden Delicious cross, had abrasive skin—I felt I had to fight to eat it. It was very sweet. When I read later about Fuji, I learned that the apple "improves" if kept for a month. It grows sweeter!

I compared two red apples, McIntosh and Red Delicious, directly. The McIntosh is brusque to the bite, then turns to mush. It makes a good cooker, and seemed better than the Red Delicious. The Red Delicious, like the Fuji, had a defensive skin, and only a faint, watery taste.

Then I tasted the Elstar. The champion, I decided. Nothing to look at, a disappointing bite, flesh on the soft side—but none of that matters. The Elstar's taste has legs. It begins crisp, even chippy, then mellows into a satisfyingly loamy flavor. Beside it, the Royal Gala tasted flat, and too sweet, as were all the other apples. I have never again found an Elstar.

When I told a grower how much I had liked the Elstar, he said, "Oh, you like an acid apple, so you'd love Pink Lady." I tried Pink Lady, a new breed that growers have great hopes for, but it was just as sweet as any of the soda pop apples.

The Other Side of Paradise

Philip's troubles in England are magnified a thousand times in Washington State. Once proclaimed apple grower to the world, the home of the mighty Red Delicious, Washington has been brutally humbled by a combination of bad science, supermarket economics, and the rise of an apple empire in China.

North Americans never ate as many apples as Europeans,

and now they're eating even fewer. Apples just can't compete with manufactured snack food or the ease of opening a plastic pack. You have to be proactive to eat an apple, and, of course, the modern apple bought from the supermarket doesn't taste very good. Not only do supermarkets have a very small selection but they are mostly the same innocuous varieties approved by the European Union. Further, the apples have mostly been picked unripe, which means they will never fulfill their potential. They are usually old. Ripe or not, the industrial apple is picked in the fall; most are then put into cold storage and brought out when necessary to restock the shelves throughout the rest of the year. When you buy an apple in July, you are buying a senior citizen. It will taste stale, its initial crispness lost. And it will invariably taste bitter because the apples are buffed with something like furniture polish, which cannot be washed off.

Lastly, the supermarket owners couldn't care less. They pay very little for apples now because they are in the catbird seat. They force farmers to grow the apples they want to buy and then make them compete to sell them.

The only apple supermarket owners really want is the Red Delicious. It is the brand-name apple that sells regardless of how it tastes, though it's hard today to find a single apple eater who doesn't complain about the taste.

The melancholy fall of the Red Delicious traces the life and death of the American industry itself. At first, apple growing was an all-American pastime, innocent and life-giving. More than a century ago, homesteaders started growing apples in the fertile Wenatchee Valley in Washington State. It turned out that the Wenatchee had one of the most perfect apple climates anywhere, comparable to the apple's original home in Central Asia. The soil is volcanic, rich in nutrients, the whole region irrigated by the inexhaustible Columbia River. The valleys themselves are protected from the Pacific damp by the Cascade Mountains, the dawn unfolding into sunny, dry days, and the dusk heralding the cool nights so essential to bringing a blush to the apple's cheeks. The air was clean and so was the water. The region was a paradise—before the Columbia River became so polluted that neither human nor salmon could swim in it safely, and even wet-suited Para-Sailors and sailboarders feared being dunked in it.

The first farms were small, some as small as twenty-five acres, and apple growing was as much a calling to the families who grew them as a profit center. They were immensely proud that their Red Delicious, an apple developed in the Middle West, found its true home in the Wenatchee. In those faroff days, the Red Delicious did not merely look tempting, a blood red molar, but actually tasted good as well. Apple historians speak of a snappy bite, a cider sparkle. The Red Delicious was never as good as the Golden Delicious, an entirely unrelated American apple, which has a more complicated taste, honey and lemon mixed, at least when it's picked ripe. But the Red Delicious was so beautiful, so popular, that it became first the state apple, then the national apple.

There was one problem about the Wenatchee. It was
hours from any large population center; obviously the farmers couldn't eat all the apples themselves, and far too few visitors came to the region. So they had to send their apples
miles away, to supermarkets across the mountains, across the
country, and beyond. Even so, there were plenty of food outlets then, and many of them couldn't get enough of the
Wenatchee apples. By the fifties, the farmers' standard of
living was not only good but getting better all the time. The
export market in particular looked rosy. America at this time
was number one in apple production. And so, the first worm
i' the bud.

Wenatchee's success drew Goliath growers—outsiders
who saw a good thing in apple speculation. Big companies
began to muscle into the market. There was no land left in
the Wenatchee for them to buy, so they went south to the
irrigated lands around Spokane, where the climate was not
so good for apples—a small but significant step toward
lowering the state's apple standard. The Red Delicious
would start to lose its luster as it became more and more
commercialized.

Most apple eaters have never known, and apparently still
don't know (or perhaps don't want to know), just how difficult it is to grow an apple. Even a small orchard has to use a
range of chemicals if its apples are to survive to maturity
without being consumed by a multitude of pests or falling
prey to any number of diseases.

Industrial growers, who need the highest possible percentage of perfect apples, drench the trees with chemicals. In the past, up to four hundred chemicals might readily be used to grow an apple tree. Even organic farms use poisonous natural pesticides, since organic soil, despite the claims of the founders of the organic movement, cannot repel either disease or pests. An apple tree cannot be left to grow by itself: it needs constant attention. Left to its own devices, it will simply produce masses of small apples, the more seeds the better, since its main intention is to reproduce itself, not satisfy consumers.

To produce an apple large enough to bite into with satisfaction, or to match the European Union apple template, the grower must take a firm hand and routinely thin the trees. If you're producing apples for sale on a large scale, you need a good deal of help, not only to thin the trees but also to pick the apples once they're ripe, before they've fallen and lie rotting on the ground. The answer is chemicals. Alar, a chemical hormone designed to stop apples falling prematurely from the tree, was used extensively.

Alar proved to be the industry's downfall. The Alar case was a perfect storm of ambiguous science, extreme environmentalists, government foot-shuffling, and ignorant consumers ignited by mass media sensationalism.

Every processed food we eat has chemicals in it, and chemicals often change as they are processed. When Alar-treated apples were cooked for applesauce and apple juice, a toxic byproduct formed. Scientific analysis of unsymmetrical dimethyldrazine (UDMH) revealed that it was mildly carcinogenic. Even so, the risk was considered slight by the National Cancer Institute. But in the eighties, the National Resources Defense Council (NDRC), an adversary group, pressured the Environmental Protection Agency to conduct more experiments on UDMH. The results were inconclusive. Fifty-two mice were fed UDMH in amounts analogous to a person drinking 19,000 quarts of juice made from treated apples daily and for life. Eleven mice developed cancerous and non-cancerous tumors, while eighty died prematurely, poisoned by the massive dose of UMDH—which it turned out was a key ingredient of rocket fuel.

The Alar scare was unsubstantiated by any peer review journal, yet the media swallowed it whole. In 1989, Phil Donahue—a crunchy granola in his own right—said on his daytime talk show in his folksy way, "Don't look now, but we're poisoning our kids. I wouldn't lie to ya." The claim was repeated on CBS's flagship show *60 Minutes*, and beamed to a prime-time audience. Immediately, Alar was fingered as a killer. That was all it took for the apple's innocence to be lost forever. Celebrities rushed to condemn it. Once, an endorsement by a movie star for anything but Chanel No. 5 or Obsession would have been dismissed out of hand. The public used to know a fantasy when they saw one. They liked their movie stars to be fantasies, the way John Wayne was a fantasy, and Marilyn Monroe. But as movies declined, the stars began to take themselves seriously as tribunes for the common person, using their fame as a platform from which to air political views.

Meryl Streep, a concerned mother herself, went before Congress pleading for all mothers whose children were being threatened by the carcinogenic apple. She was put up to it, according to the investigative journalist Robert James Bidinotto, writing in *Reader's Digest* (October 1990), by the National Resources Defense Council. Bidinotto writes that Streep "came up with the idea of setting up a group called 'Mothers and Others for Pesticide Limits,' which was an NRDC front operation from the word go." Before and after the *60 Minutes* segments, Streep also played a prominent role in speaking out against Alar in the media.

Panic ensued. Schools went on an apple-dumping spree. Naturally, the bottom fell out of the apple market, and the financial reverberations have never stopped since.

Did the crusading movie star wish to put an end to family farming? Because that is what happened. Despite the fact that a consensus of scientists cleared Alar, the chemical was withdrawn in America although, interestingly enough, it is still used in green Europe. The victims of the Alar scare were the family farms, built by the original homesteaders. When the market shrank in the mid-1990s after the furor, the small farmer was left at the mercy of supermarket buyers as the chains became fewer and exerted more power. The supermarkets, sensing weakness, wasted no time in putting pressure on the growers, playing Goliath against the Davids of the family farms, pushing down prices as low as they could. More and more, the small growers were squeezed out of a diminishing market because the big producers could survive the downturn better. Today, less than half of the growers in the valleys are small growers, and they grow the best apples.

As the small growers go broke, the supermarkets make money, even though apple sales are not what they were. The supermarkets can now buy apples so cheaply that they make more money from them than they do from selling Coca-Cola or potato chips. And they don't want to rock the boat. Recent consumer research for the Washington Apple Commission shows that consumers are not wedded to the Red Delicious or, for that matter, any red apple. They want crisp, juicy apples, regardless of color. But the supermarkets don't want to take chances. The computer printouts show that overall, red sells best. The grower can do nothing about it. The supermarket pays higher prices for red apples, so the growers, their backs to the wall, continue growing them. The growers can actually grow far better Red Delicious than are found in the supermarkets, but they aren't red enough.

One Wenatchee grower, Ron Skagen, has been quoted as saying, "You have this disconnect between financial returns and what the consumers want." This is the unacceptable face of industrialized food, the middleman deciding what consumers will eat based on his profit margins.

The last straw was the downturn in the export market. All industrial food is now produced to be exported; that's where the largest profits lie. But as more and more countries become players, the game has grown as daunting as chess, a series of moves and countermoves often leading to deadlock. Every self-respecting country has an armory of trade barriers that it juggles to suit the political mood. The European Union's rule that a banana may only be called a banana if it's straight is one way to keep out curved bananas from the Caribbean, all part of the United States vs. Europe banana war, and, said an EU official, to prevent bananas from being mistaken for a "bicycle wheel."

The Americans had counted on the Japanese market, always tough to crack, opening up to their apples; but the Japanese were wily. They rejected the proposed exports for, among other things, not being sweet enough for Japanese taste. This seemed at first plausible as the Japanese are sugar junkies. They have their own sweet organic apples—Kinsei, Orin, and Shizuka—large, golden apples that sell for five dollars apiece. And the Japanese produce their own Fujis, whose sweetness they love. They eat their apples peeled, thus eliminating the tastiest part of the fruit. On the other hand, the rejected apples were hardly tart: the Red Delicious and the Golden Delicious are both sweet and bland. Stalemate.

The Washington growers turned this way and that in desperation. They tackled head-on the problem of chemicals. They followed an integrated pest management schedule that lessened chemical use, even coming up with sex traps to stop insects breeding, and they achieved some success. But one insect simply couldn't be got rid of, and it was the most lethal.

Of all the pests that attack apples, the most destructive is the codling moth, as devastating to apples as the European corn borer is to corn. The codling moth emigrated along with the apple; it flourished because it had no natural predators outside Central Asia. In Kazakhstan, native wasps feed on the moth. As a result, only a small number of apples there have the telltale mothholes in them. So, American scientists have mounted wasp-catching expeditions to Central Asia, returning with several species of predator. But the wasps are sensitive. They haven't been happy in Washington State—the food, the water, who knows? Anyway, they don't gobble up the codling moth the way it was hoped.

If ever a crop cried out for genetic modification, it is the apple. And in fact a recent discovery could change the apple's fortunes. The gene for the peptide protein that prevents tooth decay has been identified, and one suggested application is to splice it into apples. An apple a day keeps the dentist away! No sooner had this news got out than there was what seemed now the de rigueur protest from Europe. A transgenic apple would not be the right kind of apple; it would no longer be our old familiar apple (as if the Asian apple was ever really ours).

The future looks bleak for Western apples. In a few years, the Chinese apple will be as supreme as Chinese apple juice is now. The big question is, when the Chinese achieve a monopoly, just how many varieties they will think it necessary to grow. The Red Delicious, or the Fuji?

Before the apple returns to Central Asia, there are recipes that mustn't vanish. Who knows, the Kazakhstan apple might become a tourist attraction, Westerners journeying to Central Asia just to taste it, and bringing home a box or two of the precious fruit. Then, as the apple becomes more and more desirable, some bright fellow will say: "I believe we could grow apples here . . ." And the whole cycle will begin all over again.

The Millionaire's Pear

Before apples vanish, the pear will already have disappeared from North America, where consumers eat a meager two pounds each a year. The pear has its own peculiarity. Most fruit should be picked ripe. The pear, however, should be picked unripe and then ripened personally. It demands the kind of participation that modern eaters are loath to engage in. My father used to say that a pear is ripe for precisely ten minutes. Before that, it is hard and dull; afterwards, it is like damp cotton balls.

The ten-minute-pear theory was established by the Victorians—at least I assume so, because it was the rule of my father's generation.

When it came to the green Cor erence pears that grew on a tree espaliered against the sou h wall of our house, my father laid out the scheme. The pears would be picked as soon as they attained a decent size and then laid out on newspaper in the attics under the skylights. My sister had to check them each day. The way to judge a pear's ripeness is to pinch its neck. When the neck is soft, the pear is ready for eating. Do not be distracted by the rest of the pear, which in terms of ripeness is irrelevant.

As I survey the bushels of pears in the market today, I know it's going to be a gamble to find a good one, another reason for this fruit's lack of popularity. It should be easy in the fall to spot a good Bartlett (a Bartlett is a European Williams) that streams with juice when you bite into it; but industrially speaking, a Bartlett is too juicy for its own good. It often looks beat-up in the market, its skin torn from traveling, brown spots marking its fragile surface; and even if the neck pinch says it's ready, it may be bruised and mushy.

The only reliable way to get a good pear is to buy one of the firm, grainy, fibrous pears, a hard one like Bosc, while it is still unripe, and ripen it yourself in a brown paper bag (itself a disappearing species), pinching its neck at regular intervals. A Bosc is even better cooked than eaten raw, and there are several good ways to cook them.

STEPHEN'S BOOZY PEARS

This recipe was given to me by Stephen Temkin, a friend who also makes wonderful wine. The pears are potted in 1-quart Mason jars. Once cooked, they can be kept for months. You will need 2 pears per Mason jar. Choose large, underripe fruit; Anjou and Bosc are equally good.

For 1 jar of pears:
⅔ cup white sugar
1 cup water
1 bottle deep red wine, a Syrah perhaps
2 pears, peeled, cored, and halved

Boil sugar and water to 240°F (soft ball on a candy thermometer), then continue cooking until it is a deep caramel color (this usually takes 5–10 minutes).

Add the wine, stirring with a long-handled spoon as the mixture will spatter.

Pour the liquid into the Mason jar and add the pear halves.

Seal jar, set in a canner (any large saucepan with lid), and boil for 20 minutes. Remove the jar, cool, and store. The pears are best eaten after a year. Stephen makes chestnut ice cream to go with them.

The finest pears come from Oregon, once the pear capital of North America, when orchards flourished all along the Hood River. But now, with consumer enthusiasm flagging and a flood of cheaper imports, the Oregon growers are demoralized. It was the New Zealand growers who produced the new taste sensation, a Comice called Taylor's Gold. In North America, the best way to enjoy a good pear is to send away for a box of Royal Rivieras. Formerly the cream of the Comices, the Riviera, big and biscuit-colored, is a sumptuous fruit—more so than any apple, and yet not quite attaining a great apple's complex taste. A Comice's flesh is smooth, its taste mildly herbal. The Royal Riviera doesn't come cheap. One grower is asking $26 for a box of seven. Better snap them up before the pear vanishes completely.

. . . .

CHAPTER FIVE

A Good Fish Is
Hard to Find

We went fishing today, or rather we visited Ralph on the Wye where he has a beat of the river. That's what they call it. The Wye is quite beautiful, or rather the surroundings are because the river isn't great although they make a big fuss about it. It's like so many things in England. The most insignificant things turn out to be the most important, like the shabby golf clubs with the terrible food, they are by far the smartest. If the Wye was a shining body of water I would have been impressed, but it's just a country stream really. Nobody picks up a rod and goes fishing in the Wye because it's all private, and fishing is let out to shareholders and only they have the rights to fish, and then only on the bit of the Wye they have paid for. The Wye is a rich man's river because it is a salmon river, and salmon is a rich man's fish. Can't anyone else fish for salmon here? I asked, and the answer was no. Don't you love it? It's so English. I thought of asking whether I could just drop a line into the water, say can't women fish here, but then I realized while to me it's a joke, it isn't to Ralph and he is Seaton's oldest friend and so I might offend everyone and it wouldn't be worth it. . . .

My mother wrote this after she arrived in England in the late 1920s. She was newly married to Seaton, her first husband, who had not prepared her in the slightest for the country life she encountered. In those days, there was no name for the feeling of total alienation that might steal over an ignorant American faced with the intricate mores of the British. To an American, fishing was just that: Tom and Huck threw their lines over, caught bass and catfish, and fried them right away with bacon. They had never tasted anything so good because of course the fish were fresh. The truth about fish is expressed so simply: All fish is wonderful when fresh. But quickly my mother learned that fishing in England, like everything else, was determined by caste, that the countryside was like a club to which you had to belong. "Imagine the whole country as a club," is how she put it to her brother Leigh, as iconoclastic as herself. He saved the letter, half laughing at the privilege it revealed.

The New York my mother had left behind was in ferment. She worked for Ben Huebsch, a pioneer publisher who was the first to publish James Joyce in America. But she never mentioned that to her new in-laws, county gentry embedded in Norfolk, or for that matter anyone else, because James

Joyce was regarded with deep suspicion outside avant-garde circles.

Nothing had changed on the Wye after World War II. It was still fished privately, and Phil Sencourt, one of my father's oldest friends, a childhood friend in fact, had a little shack on the bank of his beat to which he retreated in the summer when the salmon were running freely. We stayed with friends nearby and would go over to share sandwiches at lunch while Phil demonstated the lore of the fly-fisherman—for Phil, the only kind of fisherman to be. A storklike figure, Phil wore high waders and a waterproof vest over a thick sweater, had flies hooked into his tweed hat, and he lived and dreamed fish, this much he would allow. Because Phil wasn't much for words. To me, he was Dick Hannay in person. I had encountered Hannay, thanks to David, our surrogate brother who when he tired of playing tennis with us would read from his favorite books. *Dracula*, full of vampire bats and werewolves in the suburbs, seemed absurd. Sherlock Holmes was too rational. But *The Thirty-nine Steps*: John Buchan knew how to frighten, because he wrote about us, people who were protected from the anarchy of the real world, who knew of guns only from books or in the hands of hunters and farmers. When Phil said "poacher," his nose wrinkled in disgust. Poachers were locals who deprived us of our salmon, fishing for it at night. They came under cover of darkness and snagged the salmon with nets—or rather, killed them—because this noble fish was never caught as an ordinary fish might be, it was "killed" or "taken," and the idea that it should be trapped surreptitiously was an affront.

Phil's attitude to the salmon was one of brotherhood. The only fish that humans got really close to emotionally was the salmon, to be precise, the Atlantic salmon, dubbed the King of Fishes, and thus an equal, indeed, almost human—not because it was kind or gentle, but because it could fight.

Of all fish, the salmon moreover was comprehensible. Because it spawned in the rivers, its life pattern could be observed by those who fished for it. They noted the immutable rhythms of salmon life, the mnemonic that called the salmon home from the sea, then the great leap upriver against the odds and swimming for miles and miles to its birthplace, and finally apotheosis, the reproduction of the species, the reason for living. All of this touched salmon fishermen deeply; few other creatures inspired prose bordering on poetry from their predators. No one penned an ode to a sheep. But then, the salmon was still wild and out of human control.

The salmon was thus given royal status, and named for every cycle of its life. Once it had spawned upstream, the little fish were called "alevin," then "fry"; at four inches, they became a "parr," which doesn't look unlike a trout. By the time they drifted down to sea, they were "smolts"; and if they matured fast, they might return to the river prematurely as "grilse"—very tasty, say those who've eaten grilse, on the delicate side. Only after a few years of bulking up at sea do the fish grow into the title of "salmon." The springers, or

spring salmon, come into the rivers first, before spring actually arrives, and these are the best of all to eat, because they
are in their prime, although fish continue to return to spawn
throughout the summer.

The salmon campaign was a crafted affair. Phil, a tall,
gaunt man with Ben Franklin glasses, whom we rarely saw in
London, would spend hours tying his own flies and dream-
ing of the special salmon that was lying in wait for him.
What a fight that would be. Straight from the sea, the salmon
would be fit as a boxer, its teeth sharp, its hearing sharper,
and it would be hurrying upstream and therefore a little care-
less. It would be hungry and easily annoyed. Phil would tie
on a red fly, a bundle of filament to disguise the hook, and
then cast it far into the stream. A wet fly, it sank into the
water and could be pulled along under the surface. The idea
was for it to look like a prawn, a favorite salmon tidbit. Red,
too, was said to irritate salmon, to be an invasion of their
space, an interruption to their holy crusade to reproduce.
Phil moved up and down his patch of river casting far for
irate fish.

He offered us a few gnomic tips on the arcana of fishing.
He was most articulate on the subject of the first bite. The
tradition was that, after the first thrilling bite, the fisherman
would pause long enough to say, "God Save the Queen," and
only then tug at the rod. The fight began as the salmon
leaped and jumped and swam furiously trying to find refuge
or a way to snap the line. This was when a fisherman's Hannay characteristics came to the fore: he had to be as doughty

as his prey because the rod could bend double; the line, once so inexhaustible, was now running out; and the fish was tireless. A fighter of a fish would run, feint, and hide; it had a bag of tricks. Only the wiliest, the strongest of fishermen, could kill such a foe.

Honorable salmon killing was not limited just to rod fishermen. Democracy and history demanded some local participation, even though the fishing rights on the rivers were privately owned. Netting was allowed in some rivers, and sometimes fishing by coracle. Coracles are delicate-looking craft of antique conception, tarpaulin stretched tight over lath, and so light that a child could carry one, balancing it on his head. They are still seen upended outside cottages in the little villages along the salmon rivers. Coracles were the ancient workboats, ferrying people across the Irish Sea between Ireland and Wales; a two-man crew sat on the only seat, each with a paddle, the little shell loaded with luggage and bouncing on the waves.

We children had a coracle, too, and so understood how volatile a craft it could be, skidding across the water at the touch of a paddle. To cross a choppy sea in it seemed unimaginable, as was the idea of landing a large salmon in it. But on the lower reaches of the Teifi, the great river of Wales, coracle fishers were licensed yearly to fish for the springers with nets as they dashed up the picturesque stretch of river between Lechryd Bridge and Cenarth Falls, the first major leap of the salmon. Like poachers, the Teifi fishermen went out at night so that the salmon, which incidentally have excellent eyesight for fish, couldn't see the nets. It took two coracles to net a salmon. The fishermen used one hand to paddle and the other to hold the net between the boats.

"They make a lot of fuss about catching the fish and then all they do is poach it," wrote my mother to her brother in one of her bulletins on the sporting life. It is true. I never ate anything but a poached salmon, but I never minded. A whole poached salmon à l'anglaise was the finest of dinners. It might be served on a blue-and-white platter with a creamy Mousseline sauce and cucumbers sliced to translucency, sometimes spread over the fish itself like celadon fish scales, and the newest of small boiled potatoes flecked with fresh parsley, perhaps some samphire as well. An Atlantic salmon was very fatty—the reason for its sweetly rich taste. In the 1980s, the Omega-3 in a wild salmon was found to contain two fatty acids (DHA and EPA) that help prevent heart disease, cancer, Alzheimer's, depression, even hyperactivity in children.

The recommended method of cooking salmon a hundred years ago was to boil it and so prevent the fat from turning to oil and thus running out. The salmon was stunned; a transverse cut was made just below the gills; then slashes were cut in the fish's side, and the salmon was held by the tail so the blood could run out. It was plunged into ice-cold water and subsequently boiling water. The result was a wonderfully creamy salmon, or so it is reported. Escoffier thought this barbaric; but in fact a salmon is always bled alive so the blood runs out because the blood cannot be allowed to clot, disfiguring the flesh. All fish caught by commercial fishermen at sea are gutted alive for the same reason.

The wild Atlantic has been a star for more than twenty centuries—its tender scarlet flesh and faintly brackish flavor eliciting cries of delight. Except from those in jail. In the mid-nineteenth century there was so much Atlantic salmon that it was fed three times a week to prisoners in England, who threatened to escape if they were made to eat more salmon.

How ironic this sounds today when wild Scottish salmon costs $45 a pound in London. But then, the fish so plentiful 150 years ago has all but vanished. Wild salmon can still be found in certain streams, but only four countries, including Scotland and Norway, have enough wild fish to be sold, and each year there is less. As far as the average consumer is concerned, wild Atlantic salmon is extinct. There is no one reason for its death. Overfishing, pollution, industrialization, global warming—everyone has a favorite theory. But it shouldn't come as a surprise. For the past couple of hundred years, the salmon has been on the way out, and there have been plenty of warnings.

The First Fish Farmer

Once, the Thames River had the sweetest of all salmon, in the opinion of Izaak Walton, the eighteenth-century philosopher of fishing, who wrote, "God never did make a more calm, quiet, innocent recreation than angling." But by the nineteenth century, the gilt glint of salmon was rarely glimpsed in the Thames, and the reason was obvious. The countryside was being overwhelmed by industry. Factory runoff leached into the rivers; dams stopped the salmon on its run upstream. Its death might not be far off, reckoned one observer, Frank Buckland—an army surgeon turned amateur naturalist who, after writing a bestseller called *Curiosities of Natural History* in 1837, was much in demand.

Natural history was a best-selling subject in the early nineteenth century. The public, once alerted to natural history, was hungry for more information about the amazing animals and plants with which humans shared the world. Buckland's admirers kept up a brisk correspondence with him as both agony uncle and educational resource. Once, he was sent a bottle found floating in the Atlantic that contained the two front feet of an armadillo—how, his correspondent asked, could they have got there? A stumping question. And he was famous for tasting everything, so one reader sent him some edible snails. Buckland fattened them on lettuce leaves and pronounced them not as good as whelks. He did an experiment of his own, boiling the head of an old porpoise, then frying slices of it. Porpoise, he concluded sadly, tasted like "broiled lamp wick." A toast of mice was delicious, but earwigs horribly bitter. Panther paws were soft at the edges.

But Buckland's obsession was fish. He saw the growing threats to their continued existence: the pollution from factories, overfishing by trawlers, above all the indifference of government and the fishing industry. Fish, thundered Buckland, were a public resource—they belonged to everyone, and the government must regulate fishing. Why, he asked, couldn't the mesh in fishing nets be larger, so the little unmarketable fish could escape them? The seas should be explored to find out the "dark and mysterious habits of food fishes."

Buckland also wanted to know, and he thought everyone should know, what the occasional red appearance of the sea meant. He was referring to the so-called red tide of plankton. Plankton are bacteria, essential nutrients for fish, that bloom in warm waters. They are mostly harmless, but like all bacteria, they are sometimes toxic to humans. In 1793, Captain George Vancouver left a chilling account of a member of the crew of his *Discovery* dying of paralytic shellfish poisoning five hours after eating mussels. The seaman's lips went black, his face and neck swelled up, he became faint, suffered numbness and tremors.

Fish farming was at the heart of Buckland's work. When he looked out at the sea, he saw the oceans emptying of fish and wondered how to replace them. He hatched fish from eggs (fish hatcheries lengthened the life of the Atlantic salmon long after its death sentence had been pronounced). He stocked other parts of the world with fish against the day when they would no longer be seen in British waters. He sent some trout eggs to New Zealand, hoping they would become acclimatized and expand the amount of available trout. And he wanted the public to see the fish before they vanished. He

was a superb communicator and he knew that once the public caught sight of real live fishes, it would love them. Buckland was right. When, in 1863, he put on an exhibition of a
fish hatchery in the window of *The Field* magazine's offices
in the Strand, Londoners were bewitched. Most of them had
probably never seen a fish moving before. Incidentally, it
was P. T. Barnum who opened the first aquarium in the
United States in the 1880s.

After Buckland's death, his work was dismissed by Dr.
Thomas Huxley, the eminent scientist. Huxley pooh-poohed
the idea of emptying oceans. He said the first job of government was to help fishermen catch more fish. Huxley's scientific training, reported an admiring subordinate, made him
ridicule the modern notion that it was possible to stock the
sea by artificial methods. Imagine stocking the North Sea
with artificial cod, or herring!

But in the United States, scientists took the threat of
extinct fish much more seriously. Atlantic salmon was
declining on the East Coast, and there were signs that even
the rich fisheries on the Georges Bank were no longer deliv-
ering the expected catch. Moreover, the rest of the country's
fisheries weren't even mapped. America didn't have an
inspired Buckland, but it did have more responsive scientists,
and after much wrangling a Fish Commission was established in 1871. Its first act was to set up a fisheries laboratory
in the Gulf of Maine, the home of some of the world's
largest fisheries, at Woods Hole in Massachusetts. Its brief
was not so distant from Buckland's economic culture of fish.

Basically, it was to discover what was happening to the fish, and how to grow more of them.

Today, when environmentalists are so concerned about the farming of Atlantic salmon in the Pacific, it's useful to look back, to see how such fish colonization started and why North American waters are now full of migrant, sometimes immigrant fish—or, as they are often called, invader fish. Fish have been global travelers for a long time.

To try to boost the diminishing stock of Atlantic salmon, chinook eggs from the U.S. Breeding Establishment on the McCloud River—another innovation—were sent to the East Coast; but they died off. Rainbow trout, however, traveled splendidly around the world, and Pacific halibut found a home in the Atlantic. Sometimes an accident altered fish-scapes. The Elkhorn River in Nebraska got a whole new population of eastern fish when a freight train carrying cat-fish, eels, bullheads, perch, bass, trout, and lobster to Cali-fornia crashed into the river after the bridge beneath it collapsed. Central European immigrants homesick for their favorite fish, the freshwater carp, smuggled it into North America with disastrous results: the carp promptly domi-nated the ponds, eating up the local species, and it kept on doing so, because a carp is long-lived. The ancient carp caught the fancy of the novelist Aldous Huxley. In his novel *After Many a Summer Dies the Swan*, he describes how a nobleman lived for three hundred years on carps' intestines.

Invader fish would become more common as the world's waterways opened up to shipping and fish species were introduced inadvertently into new environments. The lamprey was one great example. It stole into the Great Lakes as they were opened up by the St. Lawrence Seaway and annihilated the indigenous fish. A fish is wild, after all, and lives only to chase other fish.

The Buckland Salmon

One hundred and fifty years later, Buckland's dream has come true: salmon farming is a huge industry. A handful of conglomerates are predominant. The largest is Nutreco Holding, a vertically integrated Dutch agribusiness giant that started as a feed company, then bought Marine Harvest, the second largest salmon-farming company in the world, and now accounts for around 20 percent of the world's farmed salmon production, which is expected to surpass 1 million metric tons a year in the next two years.

The Norwegians pioneered salmon farming in the early 1970s as a way to take the pressure off the wild salmon. The idea was to raise farmed salmon for sports fishermen. As it turned out, the fjords of the rugged coastline proved ideal for the industry. The fish were protected in their pens, and the tides washed in and out, gently bringing in nutrients and briskly taking away waste. It wasn't long before the Norwegians discovered how easy it was to farm salmon, and eventually so many fish were produced that salmon prices sank spectacularly. By the late 1980s, salmon had gone from being a luxury fish to an absolute steal. Consumers couldn't buy enough farmed salmon. In no time, other countries jumped aboard, often with Norwegian help. The Scots had an ideal coastline for farming, too, full of jagged inlets; the Irish started producing bio-salmon, firm-fleshed, the nearest salmon to a real one.

The Canadians began farming Atlantic salmon on their craggy Pacific Coast. Another big producer was Chile. If you turned the world upside down, Chile would be exactly where Scotland is, and it has a similarly indented coastline. By 2000, farmed fish were forging ahead of wild fish; fish farmers raised 860,000 metric tons of Atlantic salmon— more than 1 metric ton for every surviving wild salmon caught in the North Atlantic. In 1999, British Columbia's fish farmers were cultivating $292 million worth of farmed Atlantic salmon, more than eleven times the value of Canada's wild Pacific salmon catch; and the wild salmon fishermen in Alaska, a determinedly environmentalist state, were being undercut by cheap Chilean salmon, even though the Chilean salmon is generally considered to taste no better than fishmeal. The survival of the Copper River Salmon, the aristocrat among Pacific salmon, was even at stake.

The New Salmon Template

A juicy farmed Atlantic salmon lies on my plate. I taste it carefully, armed with notes from an expert, Bill Gerencer, a

fish buyer for Foley's of Boston. I found Bill by logging on
to a chefs' chat room, where I learned from a couple of post-
ings that Foley's farmed salmon was recommended. He has
told me that although farmed salmon can be as generic and
bland as some shrimp, "it often has a better flavor than many
wild salmon. People forget the history of salmon farms.
When only the Norwegians did it, farmed salmon beat out
wild because of flavor, consistency, freshness, quality, and
year-round availability." Foley's, Bill says, once sold a lot of
wild salmon in season, but it was always a struggle to get
good-quality fish. So, when the first farmed fish came along,
they easily replaced wild as the fish of choice for restaurants
and retailers. I myself did a sampling of wild and farmed
salmons for friends. I served the vivid Copper River, a wild
Coho, and two different farmed salmons. Most guests liked
the farmed better. They didn't like the highly touted Copper
River half as much: the flesh was so dense, and it tasted like
herring. Even so, a manufactured salmon is a tragic creature
to anyone in thrall to the old wild salmon's leap upriver to
reproduce.

The word is eugenics. The process starts with the selection of the handsomest wild salmon from the local hatchery.
The fish are grouped in families. The finest individuals in a
family are singled out for further breeding. What might be
called species cleansing ensues as certain characteristics of
the wild fish are bred out. The grilse, the early maturing
salmon, is weeded out, for example. Grilse tend to breed
other grilse, and while a grilse tastes fine, it does not con-

form to the standards of industrial salmon. The salmon's mating dance is gone as well. Instead, the sexually mature female is anesthetized and her eggs squeezed out of her, and the same thing is done to the male fish in order to retrieve his sperm. And something else: the industrial salmon is bled to death just as the wild salmon was—in order to avoid unaesthetic blood clots.

Its food is the key to the flavor of farmed salmon. The first farmed salmon were fed ground-up herring, anchovies, sardines, vegetable protein, and fish oil—and some still are. The cost of feed has been reckoned to total as much as 50 percent of the cost of raising farmed salmon, but it was worth it in terms of taste. Then, as feed companies like Nutreco, the Dutch giant, took over some of the larger farms, the agenda changed. Feed has to be economic first and foremost. "This means focusing on growth and production," says Bill. "They falter when they forget the goal here is flavor."

Some salmon seem flabby, and this has been put down to the farmed fish's lazy life. A farmed salmon loafs in a pen waiting to be fed. But the flabbiness of a fish could mean something else. The fish may have been fattened up too soon before being harvested—a common problem among farmers anxious to increase their yield. A fish doesn't chew food but swallows it whole, and the digestive enzymes do the rest. When a fish is gutted, the enzymes that automatically go to work on the undigested food are confused as they come into contact with the fish's own flesh, so they begin breaking that down too, and the flesh goes mushy. Ideally, a fish should be starved for a couple of days before it is harvested; but then it wouldn't weigh so much and would command a lower price.

Color is very important. A wild salmon eats rosy crustaceans as it swims along, which makes its flesh a delectable pink. But farmed salmon flesh is gray. That is hardly going to lure consumers to the fish counter. Even a pale pink salmon is not particularly appetizing. So a dye called cantaxanthin (organic farmers use an organic pigment antaxanthin) is added to the fish feed. Cantaxanthin rang a bell with me: it is one of the dyes used to deepen the yellow of egg yolks and tint chicken flesh. In Britain, a tanning pill that contained cantaxanthin was withdrawn in 1987 after the chemical was found in the retinas of several users. The FDA considers the small amount included in animal food safe, specifying only that the food should be labeled. I've never seen an egg or a salmon so labeled, however.

The color is chosen from Salmofan, a color swatch from the chemical giant Hoffmann-La Roche. And the choice is considered very seriously. Fish are compared to color charts, and any off-color ones are thrown out. The most popular color is a nice healthy orange.

Consumers, however, don't care how salmon is reproduced and eat it as if there were no tomorrow—happy that for once they can eat delicious fat without guilt because farmed salmon, like wild salmon, contains health-promoting Omega-3 fatty acids.

But the farming industry's amazing growth has been

matched by problems. From the first, environmentalists objected to the idea of raising farmed fish in pens in the ocean. What would happen if hundreds of thousands of farmed fish escaped from their pens and went after the remaining wild fish? If, for example, a hungry sea lion tore a gaping hole in the nets that surrounded the fish? The industry was reassuring: Even if the fish did escape, they would never survive in the wild.

But the fish did escape. In a single example, at least half a million Atlantic farmed salmon escaped into British Columbian waters in the 1990s and began to compete for food with the wild fish. They also survived. In 1998, researchers found that the Atlantics had actually spawned in the Tsitika River on Vancouver Island.

That wasn't all. Just as cattle and chickens became diseased when industrialized, so too with the salmon, jammed like the other animals into far too close quarters. A typical one-pound farmed Atlantic salmon swims within fifteen inches of its neighbors. Infectious fish anemia, hemorrhagic kidney disease, swept through the pens, and spread to the wild fish. Of course, the fish are fed antibiotics to make them grow faster: the medicated feed then enters the food chain in the sea and affects other sea life. Fishermen near the farms have reported a deadly black sludge on the bottom of the ocean. Sometimes the cure seems worse than the illness. Norwegian authorities have opted to poison twenty-four rivers with rotenone—which kills all aquatic life—in an attempt to eradicate sea lice and a lesion-causing disease spread there by farmed salmon.

Finally, there's the common detritus of industrial animals: excrement. It is estimated that a salmon farm of 200,000 fish releases an amount of excrement that is roughly equivalent to that for a town of 62,000 people, which creates a dead zone on the sea floor.

Today, organizations like Audubon and the Sierra Club, which have been among the most vociferous on the subject of saving wild fish, are actually advising their members to choose Pacific wild salmon and Arctic char over farmed salmon, because they say the farmed fish pose a menace to wild fish.

"Extra! Extra! Farmed Salmon Is Toxic!"

The really bad news arrived in the January 2004 issue of *Science* magazine, which published a study showing that farmed salmon in Europe and North America had higher levels of toxic organochlorines than wild salmon. Synthetic organochlorines are part of humans' Faustian pact with industry. They are chemical compounds essential to modern life, appearing in all manner of useful things from plastics to paper, pharmaceuticals, pesticides, electrical insulation, you name it; but the cost lies in the unknown risks. Many organochlorines are toxic or throw off toxins that do not break down easily, if at all, in the environment, instead embedding themselves in the soil and water, plants and animals. Just how and if humans are affected by these pollutants, and at what levels, is the subject of controversy. The poster toxins are PCBs (a group of now-banned polychlorinated biphenyls), and they were found to be seven times higher in the caught farmed fish compared to the caught wild fish. The reason, it was speculated, was because farmed fish are fed too much fish oil (to increase the valuable Omega-3, of course) and therefore are more susceptible to chemical residues.

PCBs have been found to cause cancer in laboratory animals fed large amounts of the chemicals. Up went the red flag all over the world. The media leaped on the story: banner headlines warned of the danger of eating farmed salmon. One of the researchers, Dr. Barbara Knuth, chair of the Department of Natural Resources at Cornell University, maintained that "the vast majority of farm-raised Atlantic salmon should be consumed at one meal or less per month."

Cardiologists blanched. Farmed salmon, full of heart-protective Omega-3 fats, had been urged on patients—after all, one out of every two Americans dies each year from heart disease. Now what? The FDA immediately pointed out that the levels of PCBs in farmed salmon are well below the FDA safety limit. The fact is that chemicals are part of the human diet, the way other natural poisons have always been; we just have to be careful not to ingest too much of them.

"We certainly don't think there's a public health concern here," said Dr. Terry Troxell, director of the FDA's Center for Food Safety and Applied Nutrition. "Our advice to consumers is not to alter their consumption of farmed or wild salmon."

It was the unsubstantiated Alar scare all over again. In that case, an environmental advocacy group charged that the chemical used on apple trees caused cancer in animals, and an industry was brought down. This time, environmental advocates had the farmed fish industry in their sights. Funny thing. When, in the 1980s, leaders of the Egg Nutrition Center begged for reputable researchers to clear the egg's reputation, they were turned down by scientists who refused to participate in an industry-sponsored study. But the salmon study was funded by the Pew Charitable Trusts, an influential environmental advocate, and one of the report's authors was Dr. David Carpenter, of the Institute for Health and the Environment in Albany, New York, who had spent years claiming that PCBs caused cancer in humans—without, however, offering any actual scientific proof. Even so, *Science*, a peer-reviewed journal, had no compunction about publishing the study.

In the ensuing roundup of expert opinion, it emerged that PCBs' interaction with nature, with each other, and with humans remains mysterious, despite endless speculation about their potential to cause cancer.

The final word came from the National Cancer Institute. Asked if there was an existing study that showed PCBs caused cancer in humans, the institute's answer was: no. There is no study.

Bill Gerencer at the Portland Fish Exchange had the real last word. "The problem with all this 'shocking study' press release stuff is that it will eventually dilute the credibility of this kind of information to the point where it truly endangers the public health. The public may eventually treat legitimate warnings as cries of 'wolf' at the wrong time."

But What Other Fish Are There?

If consumers cut back on farmed salmon, and for that matter, all farmed fish, what fish are going to be there for them to eat? The oceans are emptying out. Just as fish has been declared the most nutritious, healthiest food, the fish themselves are vanishing.

In the 1970s, I lived in a small Connecticut village on Long Island Sound, which had the only surviving fishing fleet in the state. I would have a front-row seat as commercial fishing collapsed.

The village, like so many fishing communities, lived at the mercy of the weather, poking out unprotected like a gnarled finger, surrounded on three sides by water. Hurricanes had battered it for centuries and danger was always there, hovering offshore waiting to strike. Even in the eighties, the great hurricane of 1938 was recalled as if it were yesterday. The storm had arrived unheralded on a late August afternoon and swept away, among other things, a beach colony on Napatree Point that was just across Little Narragansett Bay from the village. All that remains today is a curling arm of firm yellow sand, a fine beach, and an Audubon bird refuge. On a summer evening, Napatree glimmered in an opalescent light that, after a glass or two of white wine, was sometimes compared to that of Venice. Standing on the bleached sand in the midday sun, it was hard to imagine a bright afternoon turned suddenly to midnight, or the cottagers who survived, those who climbed onto the roofs of their houses and were then carried by the storm miles inland, all the way up to the Pawcatuck River—a frightening, roaring trip that took hours in pitch darkness and ended in deserted marshland.

The village had the rhythm of fish—one of its original attractions for me. I might not be a true fish eater, but I loved the sea, and I liked the idea of a working fishing fleet, a string of wooden draggers painted in the rich dark colors of the Azores, whence had come the fishermen. Once, the fleet supplied markets as far afield as the Fulton Street Fish Market in New York. That was in the days when the village was a transportation hub, trains from Boston coming right in because the passengers changed to a steamer to take them on to New York. A trolley ran all along the coast as well. The village then must have been not unlike the English village I grew up in, except that this village was dominated not by a farm but by industry—first, the Atwood Machine Company, once the world's largest maker of silk thread; then its successor, a plastics company, and just outside the village itself, a velvet mill, and of course the key industry as far as villagers were concerned, the fishing fleet.

Unlike the farmworkers, who had an affinity with the land they worked, and knew and even loved the animals they tended, the fishermen feared, even hated the sea. Village history was pocked with stories of death and injury and of heroic survivals in devastating storms. Each year, "the Blessing of the Fleet," a harbor service for those lost out fishing, underlined the dangers. Fish themselves were just a living; there was no interest in them as a species, and their taste was never the subject of conversation. I lived for a while in the house of a fisherman, and occasionally a slab of haddock or flounder was left outside my door. I once asked the fisherman's wife how she cooked it. She replied, "Anyhow." Her kids hated fish and longed for hamburgers. She thought I was odd that I chose to sit out on a deck facing the harbor. Her family, she told me, liked to sit overlooking the street. It was safer. They couldn't wait to leave the village and find a house inland, and then eventually retire to Florida, near Disney World.

The village of fishermen awoke early. Around four in the morning, the men congregated at Ernie's on Water Street for a bowl of spicy Portuguese soup before setting out on a day's fishing, the big glass café windows steamed up from the cooking, Ernie also producing a hefty fried breakfast. Pachie, I still remember, was the archetypal fisherman, a gaunt figure in a streaming black oilskins working his way

along Water Street over the cracked paving stones. Then the
men headed out past the breakwaters guarding the harbor,
out beyond the Fishers Island that sat a mile offshore, out of
Long Island Sound, and into the Atlantic toward Block
Island. If you looked hard enough and dreamed, you could
see them on their way to Ireland. As the day declined, they
would be back, a procession of black silhouettes against the
setting sun.

Naturally, I thought it would be easy to buy fresh-caught
fish from the dock. I was wrong. The fish caught by the fleet
was immediately trucked elsewhere. If I wanted to find
something caught the same day, I had to drive a couple of
miles to a small fish market, and once there I found the
choice limited. Other than lobster, there was no shellfish
because signs were posted all along the shore warning of
polluted waters. First it was the sewage flowing from the
growing village; then, after the sewage plant was built, the
pollution came from chemical runoffs, like that from a hardware store on the edge of the marshes. The store burned to
the ground, the chemicals on the shelves spilled into the wet-
lands, and they were then swept along the coast by the currents and tides so that the coastline was completely tainted,
even the little inland ponds that were watered by the estuaries. It didn't help that the estuaries themselves were being
built over by developers.

The local fish were three—yellowtail flounder, haddock,
and bluefish—the only ones that swam freely in local waters,
not fish I particularly liked. Should I eat the fish because it

was there? That was how it always used to be, when there were no options. Haddock was a favorite because it was the local fish; the local people didn't know a mackerel might taste better as they never saw one. Today I know that I should have eaten the local fish because starting in the late 1970s, the fish began to decline and the industry fell apart. Even sportfishing was disappointing. It was becoming frustrating trying to fish off the rocks; and the fish were deserting the once plentiful reef in the bay, on which scores of small boats descended at sunup. So I took my nephew Moby out on a commercial fishing boat that promised the thrill of sea fishing and plenty of bluefish. But as the boat bucketed over the waves, the fish resolutely refused to bite—or rather, they just weren't there. The old salt running the trip kept shaking his head unhappily and repeating nostrums: "It's never been like this before . . ." But of course he knew it had. Fishermen even more than scientists, who came so late to fish, have always known that fish are dynamic: they change all the time because they are always on the move as they chase each other. Sometimes they overeat, just as humans overfish, and wipe out too many of their prey, so they must go elsewhere for food. Why did the bluefish decline in the harbor in the 1980s? Once, the blues swept into the harbor at the height of summer in such strength you only had to hang a hook over the town dock to catch one and take it home to be grilled over fennel twigs. Then they declined. Then they reappeared somewhere else, in waters where their favorite food was.

But this time, it was surely more serious and prolonged. There was much muttering of disapproval at the town dock when a freelancer imported two large steel-hulled shrimp boats from the Gulf of Mexico and sent them out for a week or so at a time. The boats went far into the Gulf of Maine and out to the Georges Bank, one of the richest of fish patches, a sure sign that the global fish war was beginning to have a deadly impact on our little fleet.

Out on the high seas, the fish equivalent of a world war was going on. Just as Buckland had foreseen a century before, the oceans were emptying. As the fish began to disappear, they became more valuable, and nations fought over them. No one talked conservation. The nations that could extended their borders two hundred miles into the sea and subsidized ever larger fleets. Clashes became frequent because wild fish refused to keep to the boundaries. Why should they? The sea was theirs. Countries tried to claim as theirs the fish that spawned in their waters, but they had no control over fish that moved of their own accord. The majestic tuna, the swordfish swim the oceans at their own convenience.

The trawlers and draggers were small fry now. In the 1980s, Russian factory ships appeared in New England waters and emptied fisheries at a rapid pace. Today, the greatest threat to fish are the pirate ships, which slip under the radar and fish where and when they choose. SMERSH, James Bond's evil antagonist, is running the oceans: I envisage the typical pirate ship like the one in the Bond movie where the bow opens up like a jaw and gobbles everything in sight.

Haul In the Nets— Fishing's Off

It wasn't until the seas around our village were almost bereft of fish that the fish conservation laws got some teeth. That was in the early 1990s, and then it was thanks mainly to lawsuits brought by environmental groups—lawsuits that continue today, and which if successful will put the whole New England fishing industry out of business, leaving the remaining wild fish to swim freely.

Almost anticipating the end, not many of the old fishermen or their wooden boats are left at the town dock. Most fishing is for scallops and lobster, the supply of which seems to vary. The boats now tied up are prepared to go the distance, kitted out for a week or more at sea, able to move into the Gulf of Maine for the elusive fish. But not often. The fishermen are strictly limited in the number of days they can be at sea fishing, depending on the species, and they have to use nets with holes large enough to let the unwanted catch escape; a fisherman customarily throws away something like a third of his unwanted catch. And should he head off to the Georges Bank, he will have to consult a grid that has been placed over the Gulf of Maine, showing which fisheries are still fishable, since some are open only on a sequential basis and others are closed permanently due to overfishing. Depending on who you talk to, this either isn't enough or it's too much.

Along with fishing regulations come the lists of pro-scribed fish, those that environmental groups of varying credibility consider endangered. Some politically alert chefs won't serve them: "No, you can't have swordfish. It's on our list." Not being a regular fish eater, I began to wonder just how many types of fish are available for sale.

Plenty of Fish?

I live in landlocked Toronto, hundreds of miles from the sea, so when I went out on a Saturday morning in summer to check on the availability of fish, I didn't have very high expectations. My impression was that most of the fish I ate was frozen and that the choice was limited. For that reason, I had been unadventurous in my choices. Now I had a mission to find out how the decline in fish is affecting its supply and variety.

I turned again to Bill Gerencer, the fish buyer for Foley's. I had a preconceived notion of a fish buyer as a fishmonger, someone who evaded hard questions and emphasized the deliciousness of the available fish. "No cod today, but I've a nice piece of haddock," was the familiar patter. Now I realize that the patter is environmentally correct, because it underlines that fish are not there solely for the customer's pleasure; the fish chooses when it will be available. The customer, moreover, is obliged to try another fish and so extend his or her knowledge.

Bill Gerencer turned out to be a biochemist. I should have guessed. But then he broke the scientist's mold.

After college, Bill worked on a dragger trawling the Georges Bank fisheries two hundred miles off Cape Cod. That's where he got the feel of fish, as it were, hauling aboard shoals of groundfish, flounder and pollock, haddock and hake, learning as he went along where and when the fish tasted best. Why does a Georges Bank cod taste so much better than a cod from Brown's Bank, just a few miles away? They're both technically in the Gulf of Maine, but they are separated by currents carrying different nutrients—plankton, crustaceans, herring. You won't find many fishmongers today who have that kind of information at their fingertips.

Fish is distributed in North America through fish auctions. When Bill got married and decided to find a job shoreside, he was hired to buy fish for Foley's at the Portland Fish Exchange in Maine, the largest auction on the eastern seaboard. Five days a week, Bill puts on a pair of overalls and goes out "to squeeze the tomatoes," as he calls it, covering himself with fish in the process.

"We buy fish as close to the source as possible," he told me. "In Portland, I buy the northern cold-water fish—cod, haddock, pollock, greysole, sea dabs, hake, ocean cat, cusk, redfish." For fish from farther away (and more and more fish comes from distant places) such as shrimp from the Gulf of Mexico, wild salmon from Alaska, farmed salmon from Scotland, Bill makes routine pilgrimages to view the local situation firsthand, and to build up the kind of relationships that ensure the fish ordered is always up to standard.

Bill knew all about the feel and smell of fish he had just hauled into his own boat, but it took a while for him to learn the tricks of the trade. The fish from local waters are three days old when a fishing boat comes in; however, they may be older than that, depending on the temperature at which they've been stored. Bill explained for me the two-degree rule. For every 2 degrees Fahrenheit above 32 (freezing point) that you store fish, you lose an extra twenty-four hours of shelf life.

Not that an old fish is easy to spot right off. Fillets of fish may be brined so they don't smell, and tuna is sometimes gassed, which is known as modified atmosphere packaging (MAP). "You can't tell how old it is," Bill says. "That's just the problem. It looks too good. You don't find out until you taste it. If it's cherry red versus the deep red of fresh tuna, avoid it." Such duplicity saddens him. "There are many great reasons to live in the USA," he says, "but sometimes we forget how to eat."

Now I learn that a fish caught out at sea and flash-frozen immediately may be much better-tasting than a fish called fresh, one that has taken a few days in a fishing boat's hold to get to the auction.

With Bill's advice ringing in my ears, I go to Mike's, the largest fishmonger in Toronto's St. Lawrence market. On a

Saturday like today, I learn that Mike's sells a metric ton of fish; in fact, the store sells out all its fish, an excellent sign. The first surprise is that while I've been told that fish is declining, there's no shortage here. The second surprise is that a lot of the fish is fresh. Not right from the sea, but flown in from the sea and no more than a few days old. Some fish I see has been flown in from thousands of miles away. I always thought fish was transported by truck, but that's passé. Fish is now jetted round the world, and so much fish travels that way that plane travel is relatively cheap—for a fish, that is.

Of course, it's hard to see that what's on display is actually fish. The modern fish eater, like the modern meat eater, does not want to know whence food comes, so the fish are beheaded, gutted, and otherwise rendered anonymous. Few are left on the bone, and fewer still have skin showing, and that's a pity because it is the bones and skin that give a fish its taste. Only a rare white fish such as Dover sole can survive filleting with its taste intact. Otherwise, white fish is often reduced to what my father used to call "light hospital food," something even a baby couldn't hiccup over.

The skin is particularly important because it contains oil, and, as with every other food, it is the fat that gives fish flavor. Dark fish, bluefish, mackerel, and of course salmon are fattier and tastier than white fish. The tastiest fish is usually the busiest fish; muscles improve taste, and the tastiest part of any fish is near its tail. Another tip: buy small fish over large fish. Not only are small fish less likely to be full of pollutants, but overall, they taste better.

I can't help comparing Mike's counter to the fishmonger in London where I went as a child. That was a tantalizing glimpse of the deep. We lived across the road from a busy fishmonger, which we patronized rather than nearby Harrods, where the fish looked wonderful but cost far too much. MacFisheries' fish spilled out onto boxes on the sidewalk, a display of brightly gleaming neon creatures, wispy silver whitebait or baby herring, the blue-striped mackerel, sharp-nosed whiting, smoked haddock the color of mustard, and the pickled herring. History lay there, too. The herring—a slim, shiny fish with cousins like the shad and the sardine—was so plentiful in the Middle Ages that the North and Baltic Seas ran silver with them. The silver meant money, and the fish begged to be caught. Entire nations lived off herring. Entire communities lived and died herring. One of those Scottish sayings that batter with consonants was popular: "Ye may ca' them caller herring/Women ca' them lives of men."

Of all food, fish was the most political, and the herring was perhaps the most political of fish as it was so plentiful—great shoals moving around the seas in a tantalizing way, even causing fleets to collide. The smashing of the Dutch herring fleet by the English in the seventeenth century is sometimes said to have changed the course of both empires.

As for its edibility, the herring was tasty, but a little too many bones for the aristocratic taste. Still, for everyone else, it was excellent cheap protein. On the marble slab, the Empire-smasher looked humble: to the fore were the pickled

herrings—rollmops, those blue gilt packages of raw fillet
rolled around cucumber and soaked in vinegar; and Bis-
marck herring, sweet and sour squares of herring in vinegar
and onions. These were the staple of the hors d'oeuvres
trays. But such little dishes of hors d'oeuvres, served in
British restaurants, were scorned by postwar gastronomes,
who remembered the days when hors d'oeuvres meant
beluga and lobster mayonnaise. We children loved them.
They were the best of grand hotel food to us. The little
dishes came on trolleys with shelves that could be swung
out, allowing customers to choose for themselves. And they
offered just a taste; you didn't have to tackle a whole course.
Pickled beetroot, potato salad, Russian salad, peas and carrots and mayonnaise, eggs mayonnaise, *haricots blancs*, all
kinds of pickled fish, sardines and anchovies—food for
grazers. I've only once or twice seen a restaurant attempt to
revive such variety, and then with no commercial success.
Instead, the fashion now is to offer a series of *amuse-bouches*
before the meal. At one particularly imaginative restaurant,
I was given a glass of foamed egg white with vodka and lime,
red cabbage gazpacho with a spoonful of mustard grain ice
cream, a *pousse-café* in a little glass cup, layers of crab
mousse, pea purée, and pigeon jelly. Good indeed, but not
the same thing as a trolleyful of choices.

Sometimes a huge ray lay on ice at MacFisheries, its omi-
nous wings flat and dead, with a great tail that curved around
several fleets of flat fish—Dover sole in their drab over-
coats, dab and flounder squinting upward, the big octagon of

turbot, the smaller halibut. There were tubs of cockles, mussels, and winkles. A scarlet lobster, already cooked, was an unimaginable expense, and so was a dressed crab. Oysters, the small Portuguese, however, were abundant—layers of barnacled shells, and a dozen could be shucked immediately and taken home. Rosy scallops sat in their elegant shells, with their pink roes intact. Stacks of bronzed kippers, too. The kipper is perhaps the finest taste to be had of herring, smoky like Scotch whisky, and a treat with scrambled eggs. The fishmongers wore boaters and seemed a little like carnival barkers with their nonstop patter: "Nice piece of cod that" . . . "How about some plaice, then? Yes, the lobsters are pricey. The trout are tasty if a bit small . . ." Or, "Salmon, you say," and the fishmonger would go to the back of the shop and emerge with a big salmon, cradling it in his arms like a baby.

Although there's no such handsome display at Mike's in Toronto, the store has more kinds of fish than I ever saw at MacFisheries. The fish in London was mostly local, trawled in the North Sea down to the Bay of Biscay. In those days you had to travel to eat anything different such as the extraordinary percebes, those gooseneck barnacles that look like large horny toenails at the end of a fleshy toe. The barnacle uses its toenails to kick food into its mouth. They are among the unique delicacies of the Atlantic coast of Portugal and Spain, and they're still there. Once you get over the horror at their appearance and learn how to peel off the thick skin, they have the chewiness of lobster meat.

Groupers and the Quixotic Swordfish

As for eating tropical fish, that was out of the question. But here, a thousand miles from the Caribbean, I see a mound of fillets of fresh grouper, a fish caught off coral reefs in sea the color of mouthwash. Groupers are a big species of polka-dot and striped fish; they are pleasingly chubby, maybe four foot in length, and can weigh in as high as fifty-five pounds. They used to be called jewfish before they were recruited from the deep to fill the gaps at the fish counter, and had their name changed. Nobody knows where the name grouper comes from, since groupers are loners. They only get together for social and breeding occasions; otherwise, they like to brood alone among the coral, keeping an eye out for toothsome prey. They have huge mouths and their lower jaws drop open so deeply they can easily accommodate a lobster. Funny thing, though, they don't taste that good. The tastiest, the Nassau grouper, which looks as if it's just swum in from a Miró print, is now endangered. The grouper has a confused sexuality. If there are too few male groupers, the females change sex to even things up. This makes estimating fertility difficult, and presumably saving the grouper difficult. I don't know whether I should eat grouper.

I pass on quickly to the swordfish. Those handsome hunks of thick white meat are the nearest thing to a piece of beef in terms of mouthfeel, but the steaks tell me nothing about a fish with a sword as long as a third of its body. The swordfish is an endearing fish, a romantic. It has Cyrano's nose and Don Quixote's dreams. It has an irresistible impulse to attack anything larger than itself, routinely slashing away at boats, often leaving its sword in a hull and swimming away in a huff. A swordfish once charged a submersible, thinking it was a whale, and sunk its sword deep, only to be caught when the sword got stuck.

Until the 1960s, the swordfish was fair game: it was hunted with a hand-thrown harpoon and had a fighting chance to get away. Now, it's been subdued by modern technology in the form of deep-sea lines. Because the sword swims where it wants, the fish is difficult to track. There is still sword-fishing off the Grand Banks. Only twelve U.S. boats have the special permit necessary to fish for swords off the Grand Banks, and they must carry special gear to prevent sea turtle mortality, as well as an observer to make sure they're fishing fair. The swordfish war is particularly bitter, and the Spanish fishing fleet's predatoriness has inspired a joke among the fishermen in the Gulf of Maine: "Ask a Spanish swordboat where the turtles go? Hint: 'Is it soup yet?'"

The swords are now about 65 percent of what they should be in the Gulf of Maine. Even so, if this were early fall, I might be tempted to buy a steak because it could have come from a Block Island sword, which Bill says is especially good since the fish will have spent the summer bulking up on seas packed with food.

. . . .

PAN-FRIED SWORDFISH

Serves 2

1 fennel bulb, cut into wedges
2 small red onions, also in wedges
3 Tbs olive oil
1 large tomato, cut in wedges
12 sun-dried black olives (preferably from France)
Salt and freshly ground pepper
2 8-oz swordfish steaks

Heat the oven to 350°F. Toss fennel and onions in 2 Tbs of the olive oil, put in a roasting pan, and cook for 20 minutes; add the tomato wedges and the olives, and season. Cook for a further 10 minutes.

Heat a heavy frying pan. Rub swordfish steaks with the remaining olive oil, season, and cook for 3 minutes to a side. Check to see if it is done. Serve with the roasted vegetables.

. . . .

"Sushi Quality" Fish

Chunks of pinkish tuna in a dish are marked "sushi quality," which I thought meant expensive. If this was the tuna Bill spoke about, wasn't it suspiciously red; might it be old? If it *were* old, say five days on ice, it would have turned a rusty brown. To me, tuna is a squashy, gelatinous fish that is over-rated. I don't fancy canned tuna, either. My mother, being American, ate tuna salad sandwiches, but she ate alone. She could never bring us over to that taste.

There have been reports that the mighty bluefin is in short supply. The bluefin, and the bigeye, and the yellowtail tuna, all are now fished on a quota, and the checklist from the Gulf of Maine says they are not endangered. In fact, schools of sportive juvenile bluefins have been tracked up and down the East Coast, one of their favorite trolling lanes. The tuna like to winter in the Caribbean, then start chasing the mackerel up the East Coast in the summer. They are caught on the way up and on the way south again, and they are still har-pooned, although the deadly drift nets and long lines with their myriad hooks are used as well.

I prefer to think of the fish being harpooned because then an enraged tuna (the tuna has a hot temper) has a chance to escape the fisherman. A full-grown tuna can weigh eight hundred pounds, a fearsome beast. One indelible memory from my childhood is the sight of two great tuna slung up on a New England dock, looking like a couple of steel torpedos. The huge fish were an unwelcome insight into what the sea contained. For years, I preferred a swimming pool. Just the salty smell of the sea reminded me that it was full of the unknown. The bluefins that are landed in the fall in Boston are jetted immediately to Japan, because the Japanese prefer the big, fat tuna above all else for sushi.

When I ate sushi for the first time, I was amazed. The tuna proved reliably delicious so long as it was eaten with soy sauce (pure salt), wasabi—that spicy green horserad-ish—and accompanied by the astringent pink ginger. In Toronto, the entire sushi mystique was eventually revealed to me by Miki-san, a Torontonian steeped in Japanese culture.

When I first went to a sushi bar in Toronto with Miki-san, he was at once knowledgeable and reverential. We sat at the counter, of course, so Miki-san could chat up the chef in his excellent Japanese and learn what was fresh and what was not, and to check out the chef himself. "It's okay," Miki-san told me. "He's genuine." I did not know that there are many non-Japanese masquerading as sushi chefs in Western envi-ronments. I was then surprised to discover that the fish in the sushi bar was mostly frozen. Tuna is a typical example. Tuna is one of those fishes that turns poisonous soon after it is caught, so it must be kept at freezing temperature if it isn't to spoil. Even so, it is frozen routinely for sushi and sashimi because it is easier to cut that way. I have been told over and over again that this isn't true in Japan, that the tuna there is fresh; but then I see pictures of white-frosted tunas lying like mothballed subs in the Tsukji Market in Tokyo. Clearly, this is one more fish story that, like *Rashomon*, comes in different versions.

The people who run restaurants often say a fish is fresh because they don't realize a flash-frozen fish may be better; they only know that consumers hang on the word "fresh." Consumers will never know the state of the fish they are served unless they ask—and then the waiter probably won't know, either. In London, once, my niece Larissa, on a fish diet, looked down the list of local fresh fish and ordered red snapper. When she checked with the waiter where it came from, he replied, "Sorry, the Seychelles." In fact, it was probably farmed, because red snapper is increasingly being farmed.

Miki-san gave me the drill. Skip the package deals, and order sushi individually. An order consists of two pieces, and they vanished immediately. Like many novice sushi eaters, I overate horribly the first time: sushi is addictive. The addiction can only be cured by massive overeating. One addict I know found a restaurant in Japan that offered all the sushi he could eat for $50. The result was bittersweet: he has never touched sushi again.

Skipping the package, I also missed the cooked shrimp, pale and listless. Some chefs wish that customers would boycott shrimp altogether because, with rare exceptions, it is always frozen, and a shrimp doesn't take kindly to freezing. If not soggy, the frozen shrimp is tough. But it doesn't seem to matter because shrimp is one of the glamour shellfish. In North America, the sight of a shrimp seems to evoke the same knee-jerk reaction as the sight of a Red Delicious apple.

Miki-san advised me to always start eating sushi with that flabby slice of scrambled egg that is attached to the rice by a black seaweed band. I didn't like it, but I ate it because I was told this was the first stage of sushi connoisseurship. By eating something so bland I would be able to judge the quality of the rice, and the quality of the cook.

Rice, said Miki-san, is sacred to the Japanese. They are proud of their rice, which is polished to the nth degree, and which, for sushi, must be steamed to perfection, each grain separate and just cooked to the bite. The second lesson I learned was to pick up the sushi roll with my fingers, turn it over, and dip the fish into the little dish of soy sauce. Never, never dip the rice side into soy sauce. Miki-san said he personally did not cringe, but his Japanese friends did when they saw round-eyes dunking the rice side of their raw fish sushi roll into the soy sauce. This is taboo. A lot of trouble has been taken to polish the rice to a nacreous hue. It should not be sullied.

I learned to start off with tuna, and only then to proceed to white fish. I learned that Anglos like strong fish while the Japanese go for subtler tastes. I learned how easily we all rationalize the superiority of our cultures. I learned how to hold the sea urchin against my hard palate so I could absorb its jellylike consistency. Miki-san, pleased with my progress, suggested Engawa, the cartilage of the fin of the fluke—two little pieces of reddish flesh with a faint herringbone pattern. A true delicacy. Had it been winter, he said, he would also have suggested an appetizer of monkfish liver.

Miki-san warned me against quickie sushi chefs. "In Japan, making sushi is a way of life, and the sushi chef spends his years perfecting his art." He starts by learning how to wash the vegetables and will have at least fifteen years as an apprentice; and a great sushi chef is never too old to adjust infinitesimally the angle of his curved knife to achieve a finer slice.

Miki-san told me that he could tell how sharp the knife

was when he ate the cut fish. But, he sighed, in North America, sushi is so sought after that good sushi chefs are becoming as endangered as some fish. There aren't enough chefs to fill all the openings, and often the domestic chef doesn't have the patience to hone the aesthetic. It's the American way: get some experience in the rudiments, good enough, and start your own sushi bar.

Female sushi chefs now exist in North America, in direct contravention of the ancient belief that women's hands were too warm to shape the precious rice. Of course, men and women who shake hands routinely have always known the truth. Men's hands are muscular and thus warmer, while women have cool, fatter hands. But what a way for a great food tradition to end—in an argument over the comparative warmth of male and female hands.

Of course, said Miki-san, it was good that a myth had been exploded; but, he added wistfully, he was a traditionalist, and when it came to food, he preferred tradition to reality. On the other hand . . . He laughed and pointed out that the Japanese were very like the French. Both nations have a philosophy of food of which they are justifiably proud, and yet they can't help themselves, they undermine it. The French were responsible, for example, for pasteurization, the enemy of taste. The French actually buy the loathsome ultraheated pasteurized milk, the kind that lasts months before rotting. The French also invented homogenization, the process that further renders the taste of modern milk inferior; and of course margarine! And the pressure cooker!

The Japanese, after venerating the male hand as the only implement that can properly shape the rice for sushi, have invented a rice-cake machine.

The Japanese are succumbing too, Miki-san noted sadly, to the Western habit of adaptation, and they allow sushi to go around the world in some very un-Japanese ways. Americans have taken sushi and run with it: they are hiring Chinese, Filipino, Korean sushi chefs who really don't know what they're doing and often deliver a below-par sashimi. Miki-san assured me the taste of tuna cut by a master is entirely different from that of an amateur. "It tastes more complex," he declared.

The Japanese are discreet on the subject of North American sushi, although privately, Miki-san told me, they deplore it. Japanese visitors do not actually laugh aloud at the sight of a Korean chef making sushi, or at brown rice sushi, or at California rolls, avocado, and cooked crab; they are too polite for that. Instead, they laugh behind their hands; but Miki-san winces for them. On the other hand, he has been reassured that the Japanese do not believe their sushi culture will be annihilated by the American apostasy.

This made me feel better. Once again I had been trapped by my own greed into abandoning what I thought were my cherished beliefs—that natural, organic, "real" food was better. It ain't so. Behind Miki-san's back I had been eating spicy salmon rolls, crab rolls, marinated farmed salmon with avocado, and sushi pizza, a deep-fried rice cake topped with raw farmed salmon soaked in soy sauce, or sometimes

smoked salmon. And best of all, crunchy sushi, which is sensational. The first crunchy sushi was tempura chopped up in
a roll, and it caught on. Tempura is itself something of a
fusion food—at least that is how it is sometimes explained.
Tempura, the story goes, is the Japanese translation of European deep-fried food, which was introduced to the East in
the sixteenth century by the Portuguese; the name is said to
have come from the Latin *tempora* meaning meatless Fridays.
The Japanese quickly picked up the idea and made it ever so
much better. Recently, I ate a tempura-coated frozen softshell crab in a roll seasoned with Kewpie, the Japanese industrial mayonnaise. For me, it beat out all the raw fish at a sushi
bar, even the genuine wild and fresh black cod from the
Pacific.

North American children beg their parents to take them to
sushi bars, or McSushis, as they are now becoming. Parents
are apparently happy to pay about four times as much as they
would for Big Macs on the grounds that fish is healthy, without considering that the ever more popular crunchy sushi
isn't really sushi at all—just another addictive industrial
treat in deep-fried batter with mayonnaise. It's the old low-
fat-muffin routine. People eat low-fat muffins on the
grounds that they are avoiding fattening fat. They don't
realize that the muffins are made edible, even tasty, only by
being over-sugared, or that sugar is more fattening than fat
and less good for you than butter. *Sic transit* the consumer.

Cod and Kedgeree

Right beside the tuna at Mike's counter, I see cod. I skip it. I know it's been vanishing ever since the collapse of the cod fisheries in Newfoundland ten years ago.

I don't consider cod a fish at all. It's like eating twenty-dollar bills. The discovery of apparently infinite schools of cod on the Grand Banks off Newfoundland was comparable to the discovery of gold in California. Europeans rushed to colonize the waters, and the land, for themselves, so they would have easy access to this cheap protein, which they sold at fat prices back in Europe. Cod was a commodity second only to the enormously profitable herring. A fish's taste and texture is determined partly by its diet, and a cod is entirely undiscriminating. It is the pig of fishes—a cod eats anything. It swims with its mouth open and everything floats in. This must account for its vapory flavor, as well as for the fact that its muscles break down when it is cooked, so the fish falls apart in shards.

Cod was the fish forced on us children at boarding school in England every Friday, and if it wasn't cod, it was a cod clone. I didn't know a single child who said, "Yippee, it's fish day!" The custom of eating fish on Friday continued long after the church demanded that good Christians do so, probably because fish was cheap, and perhaps to keep the fishing industry buoyant. Never discount the commercial implications of any diet. The church edict, I believe, did more to destroy fish's reputation for taste than anything else. Anything one is forced to eat becomes a tiresome chore.

But if we found our cod on Friday dull, how much worse it must have been for the Christians of the Middle Ages. The church mandated fish eating several days a week. Meat was considered an aphrodisiac and fish anaphrodisiac—I think that proves how superior the taste of meat was. The fish most readily available was pickled and salted. To get an idea of a medieval person's diet, try eating salt cod. (However, if you soak the salt cod and then mash it up into fishcakes, it is very good indeed.)

Haddock is another white fish, but superior in taste and texture to cod. Everyone who lives close to haddock-browsing pools loves the fish. At Shillingford, when finding food became so difficult, my mother itched to make kedgeree, one of the glories of the old English breakfast. After World War II, it was in demand as a stout luncheon dish. Kedgeree or kidgeree is early fusion, a dish from the Raj. It is now as rare as caviar, with less reason.

KEDGEREE

Serves 4

This recipe is adapted from *Wyvern's Indian Cookery Book* by Colonel A. R. Kenney Herbert. He preferred his kedgeree with peppers, green ginger, and fried onions.

1 cup long-grain rice

3 cups water

2 pinches nutmeg

2 Tbs olive oil or butter

1 cup smoked haddock fillet

2 Tbs unsalted butter

2 large, hard-cooked eggs, peeled and chopped

Salt and pepper to taste

½ cup heavy cream

1–2 sprigs fresh parsley, minced

Put rice, water, nutmeg, and oil into a large sauté pan or Dutch oven, bring to boil, stir, then reduce heat to simmer, place cover on, and cook for 10 minutes. Remove the pan from heat and allow rice to continue to stand for at least 15 minutes. Do not stir. When rice is done, fluff it with fork (never with a spoon, which breaks the grains).

Cover the smoked haddock with water and gently poach in a sauté pan, turning once, until the fish begins to flake (5–10 mins). Remove from the poaching liquid and break apart carefully with a fork. Heat 1 Tbs of the butter in a large skillet and add the fish, stirring gently for a few minutes. Mix in the rice and, when the mixture is hot, the hard-cooked eggs. Season with salt and pepper to taste. Remove from the heat and quickly stir in the cream, the minced parsley, and the remaining butter. Turn into a heated serving dish and serve at once.

Ragamuffin Fish

Lying on the ice at Mike's are some delicate little fans of
pinkish fish. They are skate. I can't believe it. A skate in its
full imposing glory, two huge wings flapping ominously
through the sea, used to be ragamuffin fish, those that
looked so ugly they simply couldn't be served at any decent
middle-class table, let alone a noble board. These fish were
caught and tossed right back into the sea to sink to the bottom, where they belonged. One night in London, my mother
appeared with a large triangular piece of black mackintosh
that she flipped over to reveal corrugated pink and white
flesh. We were aghast. "It's wonderful," she said, as she sur-
veyed the wing of webbed cartilage that held the white flesh
together. The pink-streaked cartilage was soft and bent easily. "Skate," she proclaimed. She'd never had skate in New
York, but she remembered how good it was in Paris, where
it was prepared with butter and capers, though she couldn't
recall the recipe. So she opened up her André Simon (*André
Simon's Concise Encyclopaedia of Gastronomy* was the bible
before Elizabeth David) and looked for *Raie au beurre noir*. A
French bistro dish, skate in black butter and capers was never
served in any house I visited, and I wasn't old enough to
have sampled the restaurants in Soho or the new little bistros
inspired by Elizabeth David where the English were being
tempted with squid.

There was, however, another reason for despising skate
that nobody talked about. A skate stinks. Fresh skate smells

of urine. This is entirely natural, if unappealing. To survive, all sea-dwelling fish have a reverse osmosis water system. Because they are less salty than the water they swim in, they lose water by osmosis to the sea. To thwart this, the skate makes urea that permeates its entire body and prevents water loss. The smell goes if the fish is soaked in cold water, or when it is cooked, and it is gone if you buy it a day old. I think that's what Alexandre Dumas means in his *Dictionary of Cuisine* when he says that skate should always be "mortified."

My mother never mentioned the smell. Her skate had been soaked, I assume; but she did worry over the length of time it had to be cooked. Simon recommended fifteen minutes per pound in a court bouillon, and it turned out just right. The flesh fell away from the cartilage in fat ribbons, chewily delicious. Just a couple of boiled potatoes filled out the plate, excellent for mopping up the butter.

Raie au beurre noir is now an endangered dish. When cod declined, skate was forgiven its looks and transformed into fish and chips. The result is that skate is now said to be extinct in the North Sea, and it's even getting rare elsewhere. Thorny skate, the best-tasting variety, flourishes in the Gulf of Maine. Once so cheap, skate's price is rising; what a turnabout if it becomes a luxury.

Monkfish, just next door, is chalky and headless, and looks innocuous. But with its Hannibal Lecter mask of a head left on, the monkfish would be a deterrent to fish eating. Like the skate, the monkfish was too brutish even to consider for the dinner table, so it swam unmolested in the sea. It was so despised that no records were kept of how often it was caught. But I'm pretty sure a monkfish was served to my American grandmother when she first came to Shillingford. The moment she saw the Thames, she felt at home. The upcountry Thames might not be as majestic as the Hudson on which she grew up, but to those who live on the river, almost any river will do because it signifies a journey of some kind, a path to discovery.

As soon as my grandmother stepped out on the balcony of the river room that had been built over the boathouse and saw the river below curling around in a double bend, she not only felt at home but she had to fish. She hadn't fished since she was a small girl. My parents didn't bother to tell her that the river had long been fishless—it was more than a hundred years since a salmon had come out of the Thames. Instead, they concentrated on the story of the great pike, a monster fish, said to gobble up ducks on a moonlit night, that lay fathoms down in the pool, Pike's Pool, outside the house. She let my father organize a rod and cast the line over the balcony to the river below. There it rested. She waited patiently because she was a patient person. Finally, my father took pity on her and drove into Wallingford to the fishmonger, where he chose the oddest fish he could find. He could never remember what it was except that it was grotesque. I don't think it would have been a John Dory—a ringer for a Toby jug—because I don't believe a self-respecting fishmonger would have anything so horrible on display. In those days, fish was very genteel.

My father took the rowboat out, paddling silently, and attached the sea monster to Carrie's line. By this time, she was dozing overhead. Hastening upstairs, he jerked her line, and cried, "Why, you have something!" My grandmother nearly died of delight, then shock, when she saw the ugly mug. "How good the river fish is here," she commented that evening as the family kept mum.

Monkfish is now in some demand—its dense flesh engages with the teeth the way the meat of a lobster tail does, and the monkfish is one of the few white fish that stands up to grilling. In the spring of 2002, an alarm was issued about monks, as they're known in the trade. But then the data was found to be wrong, and now it seems there are plenty of monks. For the moment, anyway.

Invader Fish

"Fresh Nile Perch," says the sign, and below it are streaky pink fillets. "Where on earth?" I ask the manager of Mike's. "They're from the source of the Nile, Lake Victoria," he replies, with an air of insider knowledge. It sounds so romantic. The fish is a bargain. When I get home, I sauté a fillet gently in unsalted butter, and then sample it. Not bad at all, although the flesh loses a little firmness as it cooks. What is the provenance of this good fish? I waste no time e-mailing my nephew Patrick, who spent years working in Zambia, to ask his opinion of Nile perch. His reply is dismaying: "Did not eat any fish from Lake Victoria (not knowingly anyway). Understand Lake Victoria fish got fat on eating bodies from genocide in Central Africa." I throw away the remaining perch.

The Nile perch, in fact, is an invader fish that was put into Lake Victoria to boost the fishing industry and promptly ate up the native cichlids, so there are now few local species left. The non-native cichlid is a tilapia, which Patrick recommends. *Tilapia* in Botswana means simply "fish," but it is being farmed all over the world. You often see them massed in tanks in Chinese groceries—thick, bored fish that cut up into white, firmish flesh with a mild taste. It is a vegetarian fish liked by the environmentally correct eater. As for the Nile perch, pollution is killing it. When the English explorer John Speke discovered Lake Victoria in 1858, the water was pristine. Today, it is filthy.

How to Cook a Fish

As I bought the Nile perch, I overheard a buyer asking how it should be cooked. People agonize over cooking fish because an overcooked fish is an abomination. For years, home cooks stumbled about trying to find a reliable formula for cooking an animal of varying thicknesses.

Cookbooks would advise times and particular methods, but their message was that of the original *Joy of Cooking*: "A good cook knows through experience how to cook fish, but even she will watch the proceedings with a vigilant eye to guard against overdoneness." Thirty years later, Julia Child in *Mastering the Art of French Cooking* recommended poaching fish fillets in simmering liquid for eight to twelve minutes, and added: "Do not overcook; the fish should not be dry and flaky." Thirty-five years after that, the *Café Boulud Cookbook* gives the following advice for six-ounce Arctic char fillets:

> Cook for about three minutes on a side, or until the fish is firm to the touch and still moist and rosy on the inside. If you like your fish more well done, add another one to one-and-a-half minutes on a side for fish that is cooked through to an even degree of doneness—*just take care not to overcook the fish*, because it will dry out. [italics added]

In other words, you're on your own.

A steak can be cooked to the minute, a pork roast to the second, a leg of lamb the same; a boiled egg gets four minutes. But every chef I've read always uses the word "about" when it comes to timing fish. No wonder people often feel frustrated.

The clearest advice comes from the Canadian Department of Fisheries: all fish should have a total cooking time of ten minutes for each inch of thickness at 450 degrees Fahrenheit. The fish is measured at its thickest part.

For example, in grilling a halibut steak that is three quarters of an inch thick, the total cooking time is seven and a half minutes. (Four minutes on one side, three and a half on the other.) If you are sautéing a fillet that is six tenths of an inch thick, it should be cooked for three minutes on each side.

Problem solved, I thought. But then I read in *The Oxford Companion to Food* (a wonderfully entertaining book) that the method doesn't work unless the piece of fish is completely uniform. For wavering widths of fish, physics must be applied. In other words, the time taken for heat to penetrate an object is not in simple proportion to its thickness, but to the square of the thickness.

The thickest width of the piece of fish I am going to cook is four inches. Using the Canadian method, I would cook the fish for forty minutes. Squared, the fish's width is sixteen inches. So I should cook the fish for 160 minutes.

Now I'll reveal that the piece of fish in question was an eighteen-inch-long whole salmon.

I checked with my sister Lynn, who cooks whole salmon blithely. She has never heard of the Canadian method or the physics of cooking salmon. She says she just tells her fishmonger in London how many are coming to dinner, and he produces the salmon. Usually, it weighs between three and four pounds. She poaches it in a bath of white wine or vermouth, and a handful of shallots, perhaps a bouquet garni, for fifteen minutes, keeping a piece of buttered foil over the fish. It is always perfect, her family says.

I asked my friend Hilary, who often cooks a whole salmon for her large family. She, too, had never heard of the Canadian method. The last salmon she cooked, she says, must have been four to five inches thick at its thickest, and so long that she couldn't get it in the oven. "I had to put it on the gas grill. I wrapped it in foil, and I think I cooked it for ten to fifteen minutes—because the grill was so hot, I was so scared of overcooking. Then I took it off and left it in the foil for a while. It was cooked perfectly." Then she adds, "I don't know if I can repeat it."

Many people who enjoy sushi now like their fish to be undercooked. If I cook a chunk of salmon, I prefer the center to be almost raw, so I reduce the cooking time to six or seven minutes an inch. I try to buy the piece that is closest to the tail, and still has the skin on. Then I fry it, using the skin as the oil, and I don't turn the fish, but cook it until only a line of raw flesh remains on top. Once, I watched a chef cooking a fillet of red snapper. He cooked it that way but, at the last moment, he put the whole pan in a hot oven for a minute or two to finish off.

The Confusion of Names: How Many Bass Are There?

Mike's has several fillets of ice-white orange roughy. Orange roughy is a new fish, discovered about thirty years ago in the waters around New Zealand, and it is very fashionable. Its flesh is firm, but the taste doesn't wow me. When it was first hauled from the deep—and the orange roughy comes from fathoms deep—it was called the slime fish. Obviously, that wouldn't sell. So the marketers took a cue from the way the fish changed color when it was caught, metamorphosing into an attractive orange shade. Orange roughy, which weighs three pounds on average, was an immediate success. But now it's overfished or, more correctly, it is being caught when it is too young and before it can reproduce. An orange roughy grows to a great age, averaging around a century. The age can be told from its scales. But of course it's too late to do anything about a fish once it's in the net.

It is fitting that right beside the orange roughy is the Chilean sea bass, which isn't a bass at all. There are a few dozen fish called bass. Anyone can name a fish what they like, and they do. The Chilean sea bass looks like a snow-covered block of iceberg. It was originally the Patagonian toothfish, and in Britain, it is called the Antarctic sea bass. The European Union has come up with a way to clear up confusion over fish names and get rid of any politically incorrect names like the aforementioned jewfish, and the squawfish, now known as the pike minnow.

All fish should be given Latin names that describe the species. Fish and chips would be *Gadus morhus*, haddock would be *Meanogrammus aegefinus*, halibut *Hippoglossus hippoglossus*. Only Dover sole survives with something easily pronounceable at the fish counter, *Solea solea*.

The Chilean sea bass is another new fish that was brought to market as the fishing industry panicked over declining stocks of groundfish. This sea bass is a grossly predatory fish from Antartica that is caught at Captain Nemo depths by long lines with a thousand hooks. Everything else is also caught by these hooks, which understandably upsets environmentalists. Like the orange roughy, the Chilean sea bass has been promoted beyond its ability to deliver much taste or texture, but I don't have to worry about that. I wouldn't want to eat a fish caught by the pirates who are taking so many Chilean sea bass from the deep seas that the fish may soon be extinct.

Snob Fish

What's missing on Mike's counter is the European turbot. Not much demand for it, Bill Gerencer told me, except from European chefs, who should not, he quickly added, be ignored. My mother used to say it was the greatest of fishes, even greater than the Dover sole, and she spoke from the viewpoint of an American from the East Coast. Nothing in North America can compare with turbot. It is a clear example of how the cold water of the North Sea produces superior taste and texture. The European turbot is a large, orotund fish, and there is a special diamond-shaped pan in which to poach it. The turbot was a gift to Escoffier and his school of cooks because it absorbed sauces so splendidly; it was regarded as a grand fish, capable of gracing the most luxurious table. The grand fish—turbot, salmon, Dover sole—were favorites of the Cunard Line, and it was on a Cunarder that my mother sampled Turbot Ali Bab, named for the famous chef: turbot fillets shrouded in a bubbling browned sauce of cream and white wine, and minced whiting or haddock.

My parents had some of their most effulgent meals aboard ocean liners, and they claimed that fish never tasted better than while at sea. The great shipping lines insisted on fresh fish, often stocking up at the ports where their vessels stopped. My parents could still recount the extraordinary meals they had eaten on the *Bremen*, the *Normandie*, or the *Mauretania* between the wars. So much delicious fish: smoked eel, sole quenelles, coulibiac of salmon kiev, deviled seafood pancakes gratinées. Sole Cunard, a recipe from the *Berengaria*, consisted of sole fillets bathed in Béchamel, studded with shrimps and truffle, and a round slice of tongue "previously heated in a little white wine."

The food aboard these ships was stupendously rich. Sea air also apparently promoted sexual licence. Stories of people "coming out" on board abounded, and the same freedom evidently prompted them to eat without inhibition, passengers crunching on the first beurre marie at 6 a.m, swallowing restorative bouillon at eleven, nibbling caviar sandwiches with the first martini at twelve-thirty, then gorging on lobster mayonnaise around one, and so on to Turbot Ali Bab. They rolled down the gangplank several pounds heavier at journey's end.

Naturally, when we were told we were to eat turbot, our mouths watered. My father was still a director of the chain of luxury hotels, which was how we'd got to the South of France, and in London we were occasionally taken to one of the hotel restaurants as a treat. For some reason, I suppose because it was all that was available, we always seemed to eat fish. It was usually turbot. My mother would signal surprise and delight. Invariably, we were disappointed. The turbot came covered in a thick, floury white sauce. It was inedible! There was nothing to do but mourn. "This isn't what a turbot should be," my mother would say sadly.

. . . .

TURBOT BONNE FEMME

Serves 4

1 Tbs unsalted butter to oil dish

4 6-oz fillets of fish (without skin)

3 oz button mushrooms, or sliced mushrooms

2 Tbs minced shallots

2 Tbs unsalted butter

1 cup a Macon or St. Véran or un-oaked California Chardonnay

2 cups water

1 Tbs all-purpose flour

1 Tbs heavy cream (more then 35% butterfat if possible)

Preheat oven to 350°F.

Arrange fish in a well-buttered ovenproof dish.

Sauté mushrooms and shallots in 1 Tbs of the butter for about 2 minutes—until golden. Then add the wine and water and pour the mixture over the fish.

Cover the dish with foil and put into the oven. Baste twice and check for doneness after 10 minutes (it may need 15 minutes). Always be sure to replace the foil.

Remove the fish and drain off the liquid.

Melt the flour with the remaining 1 Tbs of butter to make a roux and beat into the liquid, which should thicken in 5 minutes. If not, make a little more roux and add it slowly. Taste to be sure the flour is cooked. Season to taste, add cream, and pour the sauce over the fish. Scatter a few little stars of puff pastry on top.

. . . .

The Ghost of Monster Pike

Next up in the glass case at Mike's is pickerel—a young pike from the Great Lakes. This takes me back. After World War II, the Thames was as empty of fish as it had been before, but we children yearned to fish. The river invited a rod. There were those tantalizing rings in the water that indicated a jumping fish. Herons were seen dipping their long beaks into the muddy water. So, with a couple of old rods and plenty of earthworms, we set out to catch our supper. All we ever dragged up from the industrial effluent were dace, chub, and roach, all members of the muddy carp family—small, shiny fish with softish and sometimes red fins. Occasionally we hooked a perch, as armored as a tank, and however small, a perch bristling with spikes can do considerable damage to the fingers. We once tried eating our catch, and choked. The fish were packed with fine bones. It was like eating a pincushion; the pins pricked as they went down.

The pike, if we had caught it, would have been no better than the carp. A pike is absolutely full of bones, like all fish who dwell full time in fresh water. River and lake fishes need a web of fine bones to keep them afloat, unlike the sea fish, which are made buoyant by salt water. And the pike was again, like all freshwater fish, extremely aggressive, perhaps because freshwater fish have to compete harder for food than their peers in the sea.

But nobody judged the pike's character when it was needed as food, and even though its texture was dry and coarse along with the bone problem, cooks made the best of it. Izaak Walton has the most elaborate recipe for roasted pike, one that is "too good" for any but anglers, "or very honest men." No food writer could get away with anything so ambiguous today. Walton's pike was stuffed with anchovies, oysters, butter, herbs, even garlic, and held together in a fretwork of laths while it roasted; oranges were added to the sauce. No warning about the bones. Once the more edible sea fish were available, the pike lost much of its allure. Observing serious anglers who stood in a rowboat casting for the pike with spinners, my father laughed and said, "What is the purpose of catching a pike? There's only one way to cook it, and that's as quenelles."

Classic French cuisine solved the bone problem. The pike was pounded into dumplings, like gefilte fish, in which eggs were mixed, then the dumplings were poached and served with a cream sauce and lashings of Montrachet. The process took ages, as Julia Child recounted, and her *Mastering the Art of French Cooking* was published in 1961. Not only must the pike be pounded by hand, but the dense mixture must be hand-rubbed through a sieve, the cook stopping every five minutes to scrape the emerging mousse mixture from the other side of the sieve. This explains why quenelles went out of fashion with the decline of kitchen staff. Of course, it's now much quicker and simpler with an electric food processor.

I discovered the hard way that pike was no prize. I made quenelles from the pickerel and they had the texture of savoury *Oeufs à la neige*, but they didn't taste of much. The lobster sauce did, though. Next time, I'll make the quenelles with salmon.

· ·

SALMON QUENELLES

1 ¼ lbs of salmon fillets make 18 quenelles

Choux pastry
1 cup water
4 Tbs (½ stick) unsalted butter

Salt

1 cup all-purpose flour

2 large eggs

2 large egg whites

Bring the water, butter, and salt to boil in a saucepan. As soon as the butter is melted, remove saucepan from heat, and beat in the flour all at once with a wooden spoon. Continue beating mixture over moderate heat just until it forms a mass. Off the heat, beat in the eggs and egg whites, one by one, and then turn into a large mixing bowl.

Grind up the salmon in a food processor. Beat the purée into the now cool choux pastry.

Roll the mixture into a long tube, cut off 2-inch lengths, and drop them into salted, simmering water in a large skillet or sauté pan. They will rise as they cook and gradually expand. Make sure the water does not come to a boil because that deflates the quenelle. Quenelles will take 15 minutes to become fully puffed up. Remove them to a paper towel, then serve immediately with the sauce of your choice.

Butter sauce

½ cup Chenin Blanc or other dry white wine

3 Tbs fish stock or clam juice

6 minced shallots

1 Tbs heavy cream

6 Tbs (¾ stick) unsalted butter

Put wine, fish stock, and shallots into the top pan of a double boiler, place the boiler over a low heat, and reduce the mixture to a quarter of its original volume.

Boil water in the lower pan of the double boiler and place over it the top pan with the stock reduction. Add the cream, then slowly—in small pieces—the butter, beating continuously with a wire whisk so that the butter froths. Serve immediately.

. . . .

The Neglected Eel

There are no eels on display at the fish counter. The salesman sniffs. They are sometimes available at Christmas time, he tells me, and then I would have to skin them myself. I've never eaten eels in North America, although they must be everywhere because an eel is incredibly hardy, and fierce. They go after any fish, notably salmon, trout, and shad, and this diet may explain why an eel tastes better than a pike. Our Nanny occasionally pined for the jellied eel of her childhood. She would describe going to Eastbourne, the nearest seaside town to her village, and as a real treat, eating cockles and winkles sold at the fish stalls along the front, together with jellied eels, and the tiny crustaceans shrimped from under the lea of Beachy Head, the highest white cliff of Dover.

I first ate an eel in a little hotel that hung over a river in the Dordogne. The eel was chopped into pieces and served in a green garlicky sauce so rich I had to fast the next day to get my liver back in shape. An eel is a really good example of how we in North America ignore good food that is still all around us. Most of the world gladly eats eels. The Japanese, who have the most adventurous fish palates, have several ways of preparing eel, and the Europeans have any number of good eel recipes. Dutch smoked eel is far tastier than the better known smoked trout. Years ago, North Americans didn't overlook the eel, either. I have photographs of New England fishermen fishing for eels from little boats; but now they seem to have lost that earthy feeling about food, and revile the eel as an unpleasant-looking bottom feeder. Europeans on the other hand consider eels rather endearing, particularly the way little eels twist themselves together in an eel ball, and they love the stories of eels as pea eaters. In one account, the eels stole out of the river at night to a vegetable garden, where their presence was revealed by the smacking sound they made with their lips as they munched peapods.

As with so many fish, eel life was unknown until about a hundred years ago, when scientists discovered that eels are salmon in reverse. While the salmon must return to the rivers to breed, the eels spawn in the seaweed-crusted Sargasso Sea near Bermuda and then drift to the rivers, where they fatten up before returning to sea again. Nobody has turned the eel's long journey into the heroic endeavor of the salmon, although the eel was just as likely to be snatched up by a predator. The eel, of course, didn't have to leap up waterfalls to get to its breeding ground, but this may simply indicate that it is intelligent. Moreover, the ocean was a far pleasanter breeding ground, with better food. I may not be able to find fresh eels, but I can find excellent smoked eel from the Netherlands or Japan.

The Paint-Stripped Scallop

At the market in Toronto, there are two kinds of scallops: the small bay scallop and the large sea scallop, which is always the one to buy if you're looking for flavor. Scallops, according to Bill Gerencer, are recovering in New England waters, thanks to strict limitations on the days they may be caught. Neither scallop is on the shell, nor do they have roes. Roes are torn off by scallopers in North American waters and thrown away. When my mother arrived in France, she immediately fell in love with the sight of a scallop with its pink roe intact, and for years she and other scallop lovers complained about the philistine way the scallop was treated in America. Only now do I discover why.

In the warm waters where the dangerous red tides bloom, the scallop's roe may absorb the toxic bacteria that can throw a human into paralytic poison shock. To be on the safe side, fishermen throw the roe away.

Scallops come frozen to the market, but they defrost without much textural damage. A scallop is 80 percent water, and tends to dry out fast, so it is often kept moist by sodium-tri-polyphosphate (STP)—the active ingredient in carpet-cleaning solutions and paint strippers. As Bill Gerencer explains, "Someone found that if you supersaturate water with STP, and let fish soak in it, the fish picks up water weight—in some cases as much as forty percent." The FDA, which is so keen to ban natural cheese, has approved STP as "generally recognized as safe" (GRAS). Its guidelines state that shellfish preserved with STP must be so labeled and that scallops with more than 84 percent water content cannot be marketed. But Bill points out that "the latest trick is to use STP and then run a two-day soak in plain water to just under eighty-two percent moisture content, and label the scallops 'Dry, chemical-free.' Those three words are the tip-off that it has probably been soaked."

So, beware the large, white, shiny scallop and ask to examine it for the giveaway ridges, the stretchmarks on the side.

Whenever my family went to France, we all ate the most popular fish dish in the bistros—*Coquilles St. Jacques*, scallops and mushrooms in a Béchamel sauce ringed with mashed potatoes and served in a scallop shell.

. . . .

COQUILLES ST. JACQUES
(THE GENERIC RECIPE, WHICH CAN BE ALTERED TO THE COOK'S OWN TASTE)

Serves 4

4 Tbs unsalted butter
½ lb smallest white button mushrooms (if
    larger, chop into small pieces)
3 Tbs all-purpose flour
1 lb large scallops
Juice of 1 lemon
Pinch or two of sea salt
1 cup dry white burgundy
⅔ cup water
2 parsley sprigs
4 whole black peppercorns
1 bay leaf
½ cup minced shallots
1½ cups mashed potatoes
A dusting of cayenne pepper

Melt 1 Tbs of the butter in a skillet and gently sauté mushrooms until golden. Set aside.

In same skillet, melt remaining 3 Tbs butter with the flour
and cook together over medium heat 2–3 minutes, stirring
constantly. (This is the roux.)

Cut the scallops into chunks, toss in the lemon juice with
a little sea salt, and place in a soup plate.

Combine the white wine, water, parsley, peppercorns, bay
leaf, and shallots in a 1½-quart saucepan and bring to boil.
Then place the soup plate of scallops over the boiling mixture and turn them once or twice—5 minutes is usually
enough for them to spring back spongily when poked. Be

careful not to overcook; scallops quickly become rubbery, hard—and tasteless. The liquid should boil for a minimum of 10 minutes: it should be reduced to 1 cup.

Pour the hot liquid into the roux and whisk constantly until mixture thickens. Stir in sautéed mushrooms and cooked scallops.

Spoon the mixture either into scallop shells that have been lightly buttered or into a pretty casserole dish; using a pastry tube, pipe a trim of mashed potatoes round the coquilles. Sprinkle with cayenne pepper.

Place under the broiler for 1–2 minutes to freckle the surface.

. . . .

The dish is vanishing in France, where once it was served by the humblest bistro. The recipe fell afoul of Nouvelle Cuisine chefs whose influence remains strong. A gastronomically correct sauce today is just jus—the liquid in which the fish is cooked, mixed with cream or butter. Good of course, but nothing, absolutely nothing beside the Béchamel and Velouté when it comes to a worthy accompaniment for fish.

The Dry-Cleaned Shrimp

Mike's counter is loaded with shrimp, which are among the three most popular fish in North America, even though they are almost always frozen. The best to be had are the wild whites from the Gulf of Mexico and the farmed Ecuadoreans.

I learned this one day while waiting my turn at the counter. Next to me, a large man in whiskers, wearing overalls, was spending a couple of hundred dollars on shrimp. "What kind?" I asked, and he replied, "Louisiana shrimp," as if I should have known. He used to work on an oil rig in the Gulf of Mexico, he explained, as he picked up his packages. "They're by far the best shrimp. Don't go near the Tiger shrimps; they taste of nothing." He then gave me a terse briefing.

The ones to buy in North America are the wild, white shrimp from the Gulf; brown and pink are inferior. The seafood restaurants usually serve the brown shrimp because they're cheaper. At all costs avoid the green Tiger shrimp, the humongous shrimp that are the size of lobster tails, and the black Tiger shrimp. They are farmed, my oil rig friend lectured, in rice paddies in the Far East, and they are often carelessly frozen and may even be sold soggy. At first I couldn't believe it. So I experimented with black Tigers and pineapple salsa, and only then did I realize how right he was. The greens truly taste of nothing, like eating plywood.

Now for the really bad news. According to Bill Gerencer, the shrimp industry is also soaking shrimp in STP to plump them up with water, and then freezing them just like scallops.

If that wasn't enough, buying shrimp poses a dilemma within the overall shrimp dilemma. The white shrimp from the Gulf of Mexico are indeed tasty, but shrimp fishing is one of the most destructive kinds of fishing: a great deal of the bycatch (anything that isn't a shrimp) is thrown away. In addition, the Gulf of Mexico, the nest of great shrimp, is full of dead zones caused by pollution and other industrial ills.

But if I go for farmed shrimp, there's trouble there as well. The Ecuadoreans are the crème de la crème of farmed shrimp; they are modest white shrimp with black tails, taste almost as good as a frozen wild white, and are half the price. But the supply is limited, in part because farmed shrimp has been struck by a plague. Furthermore, environmental groups claim that the shrimp farms hurt the environment and that they are destroying the trees in the mangrove swamps that are home to countless sealife. The environmentalists ask why the shrimp can't be farmed inland. There speak people who don't care about taste. The reason the Ecuador shrimp taste good is that they are farmed in the sea; inland, they would taste of nothing. I don't see the point of farming tasteless shrimp. Sometimes I wonder whether environmentalists are more interested in industrializing guilt than being practical about why people eat good food.

Why can't the scientists work on ways to save the mangrove swamps *and* the farmed shrimp? Isn't that why we have scientists? I buy the Ecuador shrimp without any guilt: I reason that unless consumers stick up for taste, there won't be any.

The Perfect Fish

Sole is certainly the most useful of all the fish that visit us
in London—not only being delicate of flavour and easily
digested, but being also of convenient size—large or small,
as one could wish; being found in plenty; cheap enough; in
season all the year; and keeping sweet longer than any of
the finny tribe—E. S. Dallas, *Kettner's Book of the Table*

What a damning adjective: "useful." The Dover sole to
which Dallas was referring is sublime. For some reason, the
sole went straight from useful to overeaten without anyone
pausing to proclaim it from the rooftops. I can't work out
why. Now the sole is going the way of all fish: it has become
a museum piece. People go to Europe, particularly London,
where the Dover sole is most at home, inhale a sole along
with the British Museum, and take for granted that it's the
best. Few chefs have ever wasted their breath describing how
wonderful the sole is. They, too, take it for granted. I think I
know why. The sole transcends the chef. A sole is the beef-
steak of the fish world. It can't be improved upon. It is wonderful just in itself.

But to start at the beginning. The Dover sole is not from
Dover. It was simply that the catches were landed at Dover
on their way to London. The Dover sole is not British alone.
The Dutch, Belgians, Spanish, and French catch the Dover
sole; they are always careful to call it by its proper name, and
the concerned eater should be sure to specify that name when

ordering sole. As there is no honor among fish promoters, it seems only natural that there is now a Dover sole in the Pacific. It's an imposter.

If I didn't know the ineffable taste and consistency of the Dover sole, I would turn away from the little drab fish with its eyes crammed together. I tested my reactions as I entered a fish chain restaurant in Boulogne on the French coast. Boulogne is a charming old port that in the past was often the home of criminal or impoverished English exiles, whose lives must have been improved by the splendid food.

On the ice at the fish counter in the front of the restaurant were a few Dover sole, on the small side, but definitely Dover, looking modest as usual. A salmon, now, there's a great fish to see. But a sole could be just any old fish.

Then I stepped inside the tiled dining room, which, like any agreeable fish restaurant, smelled of the sea and gave me the feeling I was sitting in the fish locker itself. Sure enough, the special was Dover sole—the French call it *Douvre*. When the sole arrive, there are two of them, each about six inches long. This confirmed what I was sure was true, that the Dover sole is on its way out. Not that anyone will say this out loud. When I ask a London fishmonger about the size of sole these days, he shrugs and says, it's the weather, or the time of year, or whatever.

The soles were grilled, excellent, but they were not presented properly, no doubt because they were too small. A properly grilled sole should be boned for the customer in situ. At the top-tier fish restaurants, you will be served grilled sole correctly. I was served such a sole in a Paris brasserie at a memorable birthday lunch with my family. We started with splendid three-tiered platters of *fruits de mer*, Belon and Marenne oysters, little *amandes de mer* clams, tiny crunchy crabs, split lobsters, scarlet prawns, whelks, mussels, langoustines. After that came the sole. The fish arrived hot from the grill—a fine fish that filled the plate, for my inspection. Next, the waiter whisked away the plate and boned the fish. He cut all around it, then pulled the spine out in a single movement without disturbing the fish at all. The sole came back to me looking just the same but boneless, with a thick pat of maître d' butter melting on top, and accompanied by two waxy boiled potatoes which, for some reason, are only good in France. It must be the type of potato.

The sole tasted good. And so did my two little sole in Boulogne. Another sign of the sole's consistent goodness. I realized belatedly that this contradicted the whole idea of natural food being unpredictable, since unpredictability is normally what separates natural food from industrial food. The Dover sole has industrialized itself, apparently.

The sole's taste is delicate but stubborn—milkily sweet, like hazelnuts. The texture is deceptively fragile; in fact, as you eat the sole, its consistency is as firm as silk crochet. The only drawback to a small sole is that it can't be filleted because there wouldn't be enough meat. If the trend to smaller sole continues, then the true fillet of sole may be no more, and with it will vanish a library of the most delicious recipes.

A sole survived any chef's imagination. There used to be a fish chain in London called Wheeler's that prepared fillet of sole a couple of dozen ways. Once you had tried the whole fish grilled, or fried, a bread-crumbed *Sole Colbert* was very fine. So was *Duglère*, with fresh tomatoes and Velouté sauce; or *Dieppoise*, fillets of sole poached and garnished with mussels and shrimps, covered in white wine sauce. *Goujons* are strips of sole, fried and served on a white napkin with fried parsley in the center and the sauce of your choice, perhaps the vinegary tartare. I don't know why people don't make *goujons* of other fish today. I can only suppose frozen fish fingers have taken their place, or that frying fish is now considered unhealthy.

Escoffier loved the adaptable sole, and he had almost 200 recipes for it. I referred to *André Simon's Concise Encyclopaedia of Gastronomy* to find out how the sole did after World War II, and found plenty of recipes. Going through them is like taking a tour through Escoffier's cuisine. *Meunière* means the sole was floured and then fried in butter. I never get a fish *Meunière* any more; too much butter in the recipe, I suspect, for those watching their weights or hearts; but fish floured and fried makes a splendid supper. Any of the anonymous fillets on the fish counter will do as long as they are firm.

. . . .

SOLE MEUNIÈRE

Serves 4

6–8 fillets of sole, or 4 oz firm white fish per person
Salt and pepper
½ cup all-purpose flour
8 Tbs (1 stick) unsalted butter
1–2 lemons, sliced

Season fillets with salt and pepper, dust with flour. When butter is bubbling, put the fillets into a heavy frying pan; turn them after 20–30 seconds. A 6-oz fillet should take less than two minutes, but each fish has its own character and flesh density, which should be taken into account. Garnish with lemon slices.

. . . .

Sole Mornay, of course, has a cheese sauce, and *Florentine* means that the fillets are sautéed in butter and laid on fresh, buttery spinach. *Véronique* is fillets of sole served in a velouté and studded with sour muscat grapes. My mother made a very good *Véronique*. It was my introduction to sole, and she made sure the grapes were sour. *Véronique* is popular today as a sauce for fish, but it is often changed to suit the current fondness for sugar; sweet grapes are used, and the sauce becomes a kind of ice cream.

. . . .

SOLE VÉRONIQUE

Serves 4–6

2 lbs fish fillets, skinned and boned

1 lb medium shrimp

6 parsley stems

2 shallots, minced

4 cups water

3 Tbs unsalted butter

¼ cup a Macon or St. Véran or un-oaked California
    Chardonnay

¾ lb refrigerated skinned/pipped muscat grapes

Preheat oven to 375°F.

Place the fish in a buttered ovenproof skillet.

Bring the shrimp, parsley, shallots, and water to boil in a saucepan, reduce immediately, and simmer for 20 minutes. Remove from heat and let stand a further 20 minutes. When cold, strain through a sieve over the fish. Dot with ½ oz of the butter.

Bring fish to simmer, cover with foil, and place in the middle of the preheated oven. Check in 8 minutes; the fish should be firm but not flaky. If you're worried, cut off a tiny piece to test (do not of course overcook).

Remove fish from oven and drain out fumet, then cover the fish again with foil. Add the wine, reduce the liquid to a syrup, add the remaining butter, and swirl the sauce over the fish before placing the dish under the broiler for 1 minute.

Serve the fish on a warmed plate around a pyramid of very cold, skinned grapes.

. . . .

I was going to say that the state of sole cookery has declined along with the numbers of sole, but then I realized that *all* fish cooking has declined. Now that fish are considered health food, the favored preparation is plain. Grilled fish follows grilled fish in depressing procession. If I'm served mussels, I may be sure they will be in a soup, the ubiquitous *Moules marinière*. What I really want is Fernand Point's *Barquette de moules*, one of those dream dishes that the Austrian food writer Joseph Wechsberg described as "a fine buttery crust shaped in the form of tiny boats, filled with mussels cooked in white wine, served in a pinkish sauce."

In the 1950s, Wechsberg ate this delicacy at Le Pyramide, Point's legendary restaurant in Vienne and a temple of gastronomy to Wechsberg's generation. Symbolically, as truffles and cream were departing the scene, Point himself was dying. I can smell the food. Not only the buttery pastry with the mussels, but the roasted duck with a sauce of duck jus, port wine, truffles, and cream, and Point's inspiration, a few drops of Fine Champagne and a terrine of foie gras.

Occasionally, I taste an echo of Point. In a satiny, expensive Paris restaurant, a little tempura fish was set down before me on a square glass plate. The tempura encased a slice of red mullet, and beside it was a line of curry powder, like a line of coke, along with a dribble of curry jus and a minuscule carved carrot. Presentation like this would have me eating fish every day. It was witty. When I looked around for the chef, a ringer for Jeff Bridges, who had been assiduously working the room, he was gone. Fernand Point, I thought, would have been offering his guests his favorite eau-de-vie; but there's no time for that today. Point, like Escoffier, was a Bon Papa, and Bon Papa restaurants, like fish, are a declining species. The chef's marketing manager told me that Jeff Bridges had to leave to check up on his other restaurant, a baby bistro.

The Dover sole must be ancient. Just look at its prehistoric appearance, those eyes, that mouth. It was preserved by the chilly waters of the North Sea, only to have its life wrecked by the coming of the dragger. When English fishmongers' livelihoods depended on their knowledge of every fish they sold and where the fish came from, the sole's breeding grounds were a sales point. Just as my New England fish mentor, Bill, knows where the best cod and swordfish come from, the old fishmongers in London knew that the Silver Pit in the North Sea was where the sweetest sole could be found, and these fish were identified by the color of their skin and the variety of the camouflage. Nobody knows quite why the Dover sole, and its fellows of the order of

Heterosomata—a species of flat fish that ranges from the halibut and turbot to the humble dab and flounder—evolved the way they have, with wandering eyes. My father used to say that God made the sole just after He'd finished the perfect shark; exhausted by the task, He let up on the sole's details, and allowed the whole face to slip.

All flatfish start off as ordinary fish, poised vertically in the water and swimming straight ahead, their eyes properly situated each side of their head, close to the snout. Then, at puberty, one eye migrates to the camouflaged side, and they start swimming horizontally, eyes looking up. A Dover sole's eyes move to the left side of its head, the usual route for flatfish eyes, with the exception of the flounder, which can't decide which side is best and therefore sometimes has eyes on the right and sometimes on the left. Such indecision may explain why a flounder has an indeterminate flavor. After its metamorphosis into swimming disc, the Dover sole moves sideways, from left to right, relying on body sensors to warn of approaching predators.

Exactly why a Dover sole tastes so special, why its texture too is unique, is a puzzle. The firm flesh and the unvarying taste compared to other flatfish can only be due to the sole's character. Unlike the indecisive flounder, the sole is focused and purposeful. During the day, it buries itself in the sand or mud, its small brown eyes flashing occasionally in alarm at the sound of a predator. Only at night, when it feels safe, does it take off like a slowly flying saucer to feed on tiny shrimp called artemia, the only food it can get into its small, twisted mouth. Sated, it sinks back to the mud, a dull little fish hiding its magic in the murk.

Scientists are working hard to farm sole, and the Europeans report some progress. The drawback is that the Dover sole prefers tiny shrimp, difficult to duplicate in the lab.

I look on the coming of the false Dover sole with a sense of doom. There may be a philosophical reason for the saying that all good things come to an end. I just haven't found one myself.

EPILOGUE

Imagine flying over North America and Europe in, say, the next couple of generations. The first thing you note is how much of the land is domed with transparent plastic. All fruit and vegetables that can be are grown under glass, and those that can't are gone, with the exception of some field crops. As far as the eye can see, wind turbines march across the land, even into the sea, like armies of giant cranes. The coastlines are back to their old shape, though, because the fish farms are no more. All factory farms have been banned since excrement, human and animal, was threatening to overwhelm the earth. Fish and beef are produced in small quantities and the animals are treated kindly. Pigs play football in their spare time and calves swing baseball bats—both sports found popular among the animal brethren.

The foodscape has changed at ground level. The two foods that scientists discovered as healthiest, most likely to extend life, were alcohol and dark chocolate. As a result, people became drunk and got fat. This sent scientists rushing back to the lab. How could it be that the healthiest things were in fact the unhealthiest? This latest crisis of confidence in food science prompted the government finally to step in, and alcohol and chocolate are now strictly rationed. Each consumer is given coupons with which to buy their weekly share, along with their beef and fish rations. This hasn't stopped wave after wave of lawsuits from consumers claiming their lives are being shortened. While they wait for justice, however, they can go to the foodeasy. Foodeasies sell forbidden food after dark.

Once the amount of time the industrial human spends watching something rather than doing it was put at 90 percent, the authorities decided that the human aiming at eternal life, "kick the death habit," must change diets, concentrate on lighter food, mainline liquids constantly. So the state authorized hydration stations, run privately, which look like old-time Coke machines and dispense organic, plasticlike packs of liquid nutrients, flavored and sweetened artificially. At first, there was fear that water might run out; but then a cheap way to desalinate the oceans was discovered, and global warming did the rest.

Food often looks different. Eggs now come shelled in transparent packs of some kind of organic material. Milk no longer exists; it has been replaced by genetically modified soy, once it was found there was no way to wipe out pathogens in industrial cattle. There is no butter because of the cow problem; it has been replaced by a genetically modified canola oil spread, which tastes of nothing. There is no honey because bees were redundant once we had genetically modified plants, and only bumblebees were needed, with the occasional vibrator. There are no more apples because they were too much trouble to grow, and we are now in a trade war with China and can't import them.

The most popular fruit is the GM Viagraberry, a huge strawberrylike fruit, strawberries and raspberries crossed and spiked with Viagra. After much polling and many in-depth focus groups, consensus was reached on the favorite fruit: strawberries, of course. Raspberries scored high, but they are no longer grown as they are too labor-intensive a crop, and no machine seemed able to pick them as capably as humans, so the search was on to find some way to keep the flavor. Viagra was a no-brainer as the increasingly aging population has no end of sexual problems.

It is now common for transgenic fruits and vegetables to be spiked with vaccines, vitamins, and mood-changing drugs, excellent add-ons when it comes to sales. The AIDS-vaccine pear is hugely successful and has revived pears as a fruit. Onions are banned because they rotted too fast in the markets. They have been replaced by transgenic scalery, a mix of celery and scallion. Another successful transgenic cross is the pinemelon, a smooth orange melon tasting like pineapple, pineapples themselves proving too unreliable a commercial crop.

Only one supermarket chain is left. Only one is necessary because most people don't cook, they eat takeaways as in

"Come on over for a takeaway," and the takeaway cooks buy wholesale. Takeaway is almost all ethnic-industrial—sushi, fajitas, lasagna, chicken tikka, fish and chips.

There are still a few restaurants serving Grandads, as meals are now called, and they are patronized by old and older people, those who still remember what an *omelette fines herbes* used to taste like. The chefs are French almost without exception as they were the only cooks to hide their cookbooks when the Food Police decided to eliminate all gastronomically incorrect cookbooks, the kind that featured verboten foods like butter and wine, beef and fish. Some restaurants are licensed to serve the small amount of meat that has been organically raised and closely supervised, and a Porterhouse steak is what Beluga caviar once was—expensive and hard to get. You need at least five people's rations to buy it. On nights that steak is advertised, the restaurant is invariably sold out, although some pesky perfectionists grumble that the meat is obviously wet-aged, not dry-aged.

It is generally agreed that the best place to eat a Grandad is at home, but then the problem arises how to find a home that still makes Grandads. After the supreme technological kitchen of the nineties was declared environmentally unfriendly, those who had them felt so guilty that they tore them out and replaced them with the sole essentials for modern eating: the microwave and the refrigerator. People who kept their old kitchens are frowned upon as insensitive. "Have you thought at all about how the non-aligned nations have to eat?" Owners of old kitchens are careful not to boast, but their kitchens are regarded the way a fine Boulle cabinet was once, as a priceless antique. See the great six-burner stove and the copper hood, the bar sink and dish sink, the silent Rolls-Royce of a dishwasher where the only sound is the *click* when the cycle changes, the glistening freezer-fridge, the home coffee-roaster, the blender, electric beater, food processor, the maple chopping blocks, the battery of knives, so many wooden spoons and metal whisks, the gleaming cookware . . .

Guests who attend a Grandad are invited by self-destructing e-mail, which means the invitation is destroyed the moment the recipient reads it, so no one else gets wind of it and tries to crash. To get invited to a Grandad, you have to join a Health Club, the cover for Grandads, and you receive a password with which you can log on to an encrypted Grandad newsletter that gives you the addresses of new foodeasies, and accounts of recent Grandads that featured leg of lamb with *flageolets verts*, osso bucco, pork roast with crackling, and of course Montrachet and Haut-Brion, and Scharffen-Berger chocolate from the foodeasy. Sometimes a Grandad veteran gets carried away—usually after too many glasses of contraband Dom Pérignon—and cries when he talks about the bad old days, when people ate so well and enjoyed their food. But he is quickly shushed because it is all too painful. Food is dead, continuity is dead, as the new Ice Age finally closes over our heads.

BIBLIOGRAPHY

Apicius. *The Roman Cookery of Apicius: A Treasury of Gourmet Recipes and Herbal Cookery*. Oakland, CA: Hartley & Marks, 1984.

Aron, Jean-Paul. *The Art of Eating in France. Manners and Menus in the Nineteenth Century*. London: Peter Owen, 1975.

Auden, W. H. *A Certain World: A Commonplace Book*. New York: Viking Press, 1970.

Beck, Simone, Louisette Bertholle, and Julia Child. *Mastering the Art of French Cooking*. New York: Alfred A. Knopf, 1961.

Beeton, Isabella. *Mrs. Beeton's Book of Household Management*. Oxford: Oxford University Press, 2000.

Bode, W. H. K. *European Gastronomy: The Story of Man's Food and Eating Customs*. London: Hodder & Stoughton, 1994.

Boulud, Daniel, and Dorie Greenspan. *Café Boulud Cookbook*. New York: Scribner, 1999.

Brillat-Savarin, Jean-Anthèlme, trans. Ann Drayton. *The Physiology of Taste*. New York: Penguin Classics, 1970.

Browning, Frank. *Apples*. New York: North Point Press, 1998.

Burgess, G. H. O. *The Eccentric Ark: The Curious World of Frank Buckland*. New York: Horizon Press, 1967.

Carson, Rachel. *The Silent Spring*. Boston: Houghton Mifflin, 1962.

Chaney, Lisa. *Elizabeth David*. London: Pan Books, 1999.

Child, Julia. *From Julia Child's Kitchen*. New York: Alfred A. Knopf, 1970.

Claiborne, Craig. *The New York Times Cookbook*. New York: Times Books, 1975.

———, and Pierre Franey. *Classic French Cooking*. New York: Time-Life Books, 1970.

Dallas, E. S. *Kettner's Book of the Table*. London: Centaur Press, 1968.

David, Elizabeth. *A Book of Mediterranean Food*. London: John Lehmann, 1950.

———. *French Country Cooking*. London: Penguin, 1958.

———. *Italian Food*. London: Penguin, 1963.

Davidson, Alan. *North Atlantic Seafood*. New York: Viking Press, 1979.

———, ed. *The Oxford Companion to Food*. Oxford: Oxford University Press, 1999.

Davies, Jennifer. *The Victorian Kitchen Garden*. London: BBC Books, 1987.

————.*The Wartime Kitchen Garden*. London: BBC Books, 1993.

Dixon, Edmund. *The Treatise of the History and Management of the Ornamental and Domestic Fowl*. London, 1849.

Donaldson, Frances. *Edward VIII*. London: Weidenfeld & Nicolson, 1974.

Drexler, Madeline. *Secret Agents*. Washington, DC: Joseph Henry Press, 2002.

Dumas, Alexandre. *Dictionary of Cuisine*, adapted, abridged, and trans. Louis Colman. London: W. H. Allen, 1959.

Ellacott, S. E. *The Story of the Kitchen*. London: Methuen & Co., 1964.

Escoffier, Auguste. *The Complete Guide to the Art of Modern Cookery*, trans. H. L. Cracknell and R. J. Kaufmann. New York: John Wiley & Sons, 1979.

Fisher, M. F. K. *The Gastronomical Me*. New York: Duell, Sloan & Pearce, 1943.

Flandrin, Jean-Louis, and Massimo Montanari. *Food: A Culinary History from Antiquity to the Present*. New York: Columbia University Press, 1996.

"Francine." *Vogue's French Cookery*. London: Condé Nast Publications, 1961.

Freeman, Sarah. *Mutton and Oysters: The Victorians and Their Food*. London: Victor Gollancz, 1989.

Frere, Catherine Frances. *The Cookery Book of Lady Clark of Tillypronie*. London: Constable & Co., 1909.

Graham, Peter. *Mourjou. The Life and Food of an Auvergne Village*. New York: Viking Press, 1998.

Grigson, Jane. *English Food*. London: Ebury Press, 1992.

Halsey, Margaret. *With Malice Toward Some*. New York: Simon & Schuster, 1938.

Hartley, Dorothy. *Food in England*. London: Little, Brown, 1999.

Hess, John L. and Karen. *The Taste of America*. Champaign, IL: University of Illinois Press, 2000.

Hillman, Howard. *Kitchen Science*. Boston: Houghton Mifflin, 1989.

Hoggart, Richard. *The Uses of Literacy*. London: Chatto & Windus, 1957.

Home Institute of the New York Herald Tribune. *America's Cook Book*. New York: Charles Scribner's Sons, 1942.

Howard, Sir Albert. *An Agricultural Testament*. Oxford: Oxford University Press, 1972.

Hume, Rosemary, and Constance Spry. *The Constance Spry Cookery Book*. London: J. M. Dent, 1956.

Hunt, Peter. *Eating and Drinking. An Anthology for Epicures*. London: Ebury Press, 1961.

Huxley, Aldous. *After Many a Summer Dies the Swan*. New York: Avon Books, 1965.

Jekyll, Agnes. *Kitchen Essays*. London: Persephone Press, 2001.

Jenkins, Steven. *Steven Jenkins' Cheese Primer*. New York: Workman Publishing, 1996.

Johnston, James P. *A Hundred Years of Eating*. London: Gill & Macmillan, 1997.

Jones, Evan. *American Food: The Gastronomic Story*. New York: Random House, 1974.

Junior League of Charleston. *Charleston Recipes*. Charleston, SC, 1950.

Kluger, Richard. *The Paper. The Life and Death of the New York Herald Tribune*. New York. Vintage Books, 1989.

Lacey, Richard. *Poison on the Plate*. London: Metro Books, 1998.

MacDonald, Betty. *The Egg and I*. Philadelphia: J. B. Lippincott, 1945.

Mallet, Victor, ed. *Life with Queen Victoria. Marie Mallet's Letters from Court, 1887–1901*. London: John Murray, 1968.

Mariani, John. *America Eats Out*. New York: William Morrow, 1991.

Masterton, Elsie. *Blueberry Hill Menu Cookbook*. New York: Thomas Y. Crowell, 1963.

Masui, Kazuko, and Tomoko Yamada. *French Cheeses*. London: Dorling Kindersley, 1996.

McGee, Harold. *On Food and Cooking*. New York: Simon & Schuster, 1984.

Mitford, Nancy. *The Sun King: Louis XIV at Versailles*. New York: Harper & Row, 1966.

Montagné, Prosper. *Larousse Gastronomique*, trans. Nina Froud, Patience Gray, Maud Murdoch, and Barbara Macrae Taylor. New York: Crown Publishers, 1961.

Moriarty, Christopher. *Eels*. Newton Abbot, Devon: David and Charles, 1978.

Orwell, George. *The Road to Wigan Pier*. New York: Harcourt Brace, 1958.

Paddleford, Clementine., *The Best of American Cooking*. New York: Scribner's, 1970.

Plutarch. *Plutarch's Moralia*, trans. W. C. Hembold. London: William Heinmann, 1939.

Pomiane, Edouard de. *French Cooking in Ten Minutes*, trans. Philip and Mary Hyman. New York: North Point Press, 1998.

Porter, Roy. *The Greatest Benefit of Mankind: A Medical History of Humanity*. New York: W. W. Norton, 1999.

Porter, Valerie. *Cattle—A Handbook to the Breeds of the World*. London: Christopher Helm, 1991.

Pullar, Phillippa. *Consuming Passions*. London: Sphere Books, 1970.

Rance, Patrick. *The Great British Cheese Book*. London: Macmillan, 1982.

———. *The French Cheese Book*. London: Macmillan, 1989.

Ritz, Marie L. B. *César Ritz, Host to the World*. Philadelphia: J. B. Lippincott, c. 1938.

Rogers, Ben. *Beef and Liberty*. London: Chatto & Windus, 2003.

Rombauer, Irma S., and Marion Rombauer Becker. *The Joy of Cooking*. Indianapolis: Bobbs-Merrill, 1931.

Schlosser, Eric. *Fast Food Nation*. Boston: Houghton Mifflin, 2001.

Shaw, Timothy. *The World of Escoffier*. New York and London: Vendome Press, 1995.

Simon, André. *A Concise Encyclopaedia of Gastronomy*. London: Bramhall House, 1947.

Smith, Page, and Charles Daniels. *The Chicken Book*. Boston: Little, Brown, 1975.

Steiner, Rudolf, ed. Adalbert Graf von Keyserlingk. *Birth of a New Agriculture, Koberwitz 1924*. Forest Row, East Sussex: Temple Lodge, 1999.

Tannahill, Reay. *Food in History*. New York: Three Rivers Press, 1988.

Thompson, Flora. *Lark Rise to Candleford*. London: Penguin Classics, 2000.

Toklas, Alice B. *The Alice B. Toklas Cook Book*. London: Michael Joseph, 1954; New York: Harper, 1954.

Toussaint-Samat, Maguelonne. *History of Food*. Oxford: Blackwell Publishers, 1992.

Trager, James. *The Food Chronology*. New York: Henry Holt & Co., 1995.

Walden, Howard T. *Familiar Freshwater Fishes of America*. New York: Harper & Row, 1964.

Waters, Alice. *Chez Panisse Menu Cookbook*. New York: Random House, 1982.

Weaver, William Woys. *Heirloom Vegetable Gardening*. New York: Henry Holt & Co., 1997.

Weber, Eugen. *France, Fin de Siècle*. Cambridge, MA: The Belknap Press of the Harvard University Press, 1986.

Wechsberg, Joseph. *Blue Trout and Black Truffles, the Peregrinations of an Epicure*. New York: Alfred A. Knopf, 1953.

Wells, Patricia, and Joel Rebuchon. *Simply French*. New York: William Morrow, 1991.

Wright, Carol. *Cunard Cook Book*. London: J. M. Dent & Sons, 1969.

ACKNOWLEDGMENTS

When I started to search for taste in food today, I imagined I would talk to organic growers, fishermen, and farmhouse cheesemakers. Instead, I ended up talking mostly to scientists, who more and more are determining what we eat. Thanks therefore to all the patient scientists who answered the often ignorant questions of a non-scientist—especially Bill Gerencer, the biochemist who buys fish for Foley's of Boston; Dr. Donald J. McNamara of the Egg Nutrition Center; Tim Smith, a cooperative extension agent at Washington State University; Dr. Brian Glebe of the Atlantic Salmon Broodstocks Program in the province of New Brunswick, and at the University of Guelph in Ontario: Dr. David Noakes of the Axelrod Centre for Ichthyology, Dr. Ian Duncan, professor of ethnology, and Dr. Barry Micaleff of the Greenhouse Vegetable Project.

As well, I want to thank the following people for providing me with information about specific foods: the chef Claude Bouillet; Denis Cottin, who distributes Quebec cheeses; Fried De Schouwer of Eurofresh; Allison Hooper of Vermont Butter and Cheese; my cousin Philip Mallet on apple growing; Brian McCulloh of the Certified Angus Beef program; Margaret Morris of Glengarry Cheesemaking and Dairy Supply, Alexandria, Ontario; Jodie Storch at the Peter Luger Steak House in Brooklyn; John Taylor of Stolt Sea Farm, Toronto; and Robb Walsh, who wrote a series of articles about the decline of beef that appeared in the *Houston Press* in August 2001.

The Toronto Reference Library was an excellent resource, notably researcher Heather Wilson.

Lines from *Don't Let's Be Beastly to the Germans* are quoted from *The Lyrics of Noel Coward*, copyright © by Noel Coward, and reprinted with the permission of Overlook Press.

The book's context was immeasurably enriched by my sister Lynn and her marvelous memory. Special thanks to my old friends Charlotte Gere and Hilary Simpson for information and support, and I'm grateful to all those who helped me, including Stephen Adler, Phillip Brooke, Simeon Bull, Jerome Couelle, Charles Danzker, Gay and Peter Darwent, the late John Gere, Marty Gross, Katharine Holmes, Mary Jolliffe, Mary McIver, Ann Storm, M. Z. Thomas, Bill Toye, and Michael Vaughan, who suggested the title.

The idea for the book came to me after Cecily Ross of the *Globe and Mail* asked me to review restaurants in Toronto. It took shape in the late nineties, when Harriet O'Brien and Jaimie Hubbard of the *National Post* gave me the opportunity to explore what was happening to food.

It was Pat Kennedy's steadfast support at McClelland &

Stewart that made the book a reality. Finally, my thanks to all those at W. W. Norton who took such trouble over the book: Erik Johnson, Ann Adelman, Stephen King, Nancy Palmquist, and of course Maria Guarnaschelli—a wonderful editor.

INDEX